# THE FAR EAST
*A Social Geography*

1. A street in Udaipur City (Rajasthan). The bullock-cart and the dress of the well-to-do Indian walking away have not changed for hundreds of years. The ornamented balcony in the background is the police station.

# THE FAR EAST

*A Social Geography*

by

A. D. C. PETERSON, O.B.E., M.A.

GERALD DUCKWORTH & CO. LTD.
3 HENRIETTA STREET, LONDON, W.C.2

First published in 1949
Second Edition, revised, 1951
Reprinted 1951
Third Edition, revised, 1957

REPRINTED BY LITHOGRAPHY IN GREAT BRITAIN
BY JARROLD AND SONS LIMITED, NORWICH

## CONTENTS

# LIST OF ILLUSTRATIONS

Acknowledgements are due to the following for permission to reproduce illustrations:

Black Star Pictures, 23.

B.O.A.C., 27.

Central Office of Information, 2, 11, 12, 29, 30, 32.

Exclusive News Agency, 16, 20, 24, 41.

French Ministry of Information, 25.

High Commissioner for India, 7.

Lord Horder, 1, 3, 4, 5, 6, 8, 9, 14, 15.

Keystone Press Agency, 42.

Netherlands and Netherlands Indies Information Bureau, 28, 31.

Paul Popper, 10, 13, 18, 21, 22, 26, 33, 38.

Topical Press Agency Ltd., 17, 43.

The Philippine Embassy in London, 34.

The Chinese Legation in London, 19, 20.

The Imperial War Museum, 39.

# LIST OF SKETCH MAPS

# PREFACE

THIS book is intended as an introduction to the countries of the Far East. It does not pretend to add anything to the world's sum of knowledge, and the last chapter is almost the only one to contain any personal judgments. It is not meant for those who know the Far East already.

For the greater number who do not know the Far East, or know only one corner of it, I have tried to write an account, however sketchy, of the peoples and nations which lie between India and Japan. The book is not a reference book and is meant to be read, not used to look up facts or pass examinations. It contains, therefore, little physical geography or statistical information. A very brief section on structure and climate heads each chapter, brief not because these are unimportant subjects, but because the life of the people and their modern problems are of more immediate importance; in any case, climate and structure do not change and can therefore be perfectly easily looked up by those who require more detail in such books as Professor Dudley Stamp's *Asia*.

Some statistics are included, but again not much detail, since no reader, as opposed to student, expects to memorise detail, and because statistics do change. I have used mainly *The Statesman's Year Book*, and it is much better for the student to go back to the original source; moreover, many figures given here will be out of date in a year or two, if not before the book is published, and the student would be much better off consulting a later edition of the *Year Book* himself. For these reasons and from a personal distrust of figures, I have usually preferred to say that the population of an area is 'about ten million' rather than 9,876,543.

The place of 'Principal Towns and Rivers' has been taken by fairly long historical sections under the general heading, 'History and People'; principal towns and rivers can be found on the map.

It may be objected that what happened to the Japanese people 2,000 years ago is almost as remote from modern problems as what happened to the Japanese rock formations two million years ago; one of the main contentions of this book is that this is not so. A people is the sum of its past. This is even more true of the Far East than of the West, and it is impossible to understand what is happening there to-day without some knowledge of what happened hundreds of years ago.

The size of the area presents another problem. Certain subjects, such as Rice-cultivation, Mahayana Buddhism, Overseas Chinese, Census Statistics, etc., concern many or even all the countries in the book, yet the advantage of arranging it by countries rather than topics seemed to me overwhelming. I have tried to meet this difficulty by dealing with each general subject of this kind in one place only, e.g. Census Statistics in Chapter IV, and trusting to the reader's memory. If a subject appears, therefore, to be passed over too briefly, it may well be that a reference to the Index will show that it is treated at greater length elsewhere.

Short bibliographies are attached to each chapter and the reader, as opposed to the student, will see that these include a number of novels. Those who have never visited these countries will often get a much better idea of them by reading *Kim* or *Lord Jim* than from any geography textbook ever written.

The bibliographies contain most of the works that I have used, and also one or two others that the serious student of special areas would find useful. My thanks are also due, and most gratefully offered, to H.M. Colonial Office, the Royal Institute of International Affairs, the editor of *The Statesman's Year Book*, Dr. Victor Purcell and many others for help in regard to particular areas, to Mr. Walter Harding for the maps and much other advice, and to my wife for typing.

Finally, it is impossible for anyone interested in this area to escape a deep obligation to the Institute of Pacific Relations, under whose auspices so much of our limited information on the subject has been printed.

Adams' Grammar School. 1949

# CHAPTER ONE

## INTRODUCTORY

A TERM like the 'Far East' is apt to be misleading. It is not merely that few people are quite sure which Easts are 'Far' as opposed to 'Middle' and 'Near,' but also we most of us have an unconscious conviction that the East is hot. It is easy to see why. Our English grandfathers, if they went out East, probably went to India and found it very hot indeed; but a Russian grandfather would have gone to Siberia, which is about the coldest and most unpleasant area of the inhabited globe.

The difference between 'Near East,' 'Middle East' and 'Far East' is confusing too, but the names are such an old tradition that it is impossible to get away from them. Even the Japanese, who proudly maintained that Japan was the centre of the world, referred officially to their conquests as 'Greater East Asia,' though all of them lay well to the west of Japan. It is just as well to state, therefore, which are the countries which this book includes in the Far East. They are the Russian territories east of Lake Baikal, Japan, China (including Manchuria), Korea, the Philippines, Indo-China, Siam,* Malaya, Indonesia, Burma, Ceylon and India.

This part of the world has every right to be considered separately. For hundreds of years it was cut off from Europe and Asia Minor by the vast deserts and mountains stretching eastwards from Syria, and by the endless steppes of Eastern Russia. Real contact with America was not established till Magellan opened the Pacific to European ships in the sixteenth century. There was no serious contact with Australia in historical times until the eighteenth century, though the prehistoric Polynesians who colonised the Australasian islands probably came from the area known as Malaysia; that is, not only Malaya itself, but the nearby islands of Sumatra, Java, Borneo, the Celebes and Philippines.

* This country presents a problem in title. Until the nationalist regime of Pibul Songgram just before the war it was known in English as 'Siam' and its people as 'Siamese'. Pibul changed this to Thailand and Thai, but this leads to confusion between those who are racially Thais and those who are politically citizens of Thailand. During the war the Allied powers reverted to 'Siam' and this name was accepted by the post-war Siamese government. While this book was in progress Pibul, having returned to power, changed the name officially back again to Thailand. I have compromised by keeping 'Siam', which is much more familiar to English readers, in the text, but going back to 'Thailand' which is, I suppose, now geograph-ically correct, in the maps and diagrams.

Of course, occasional traders did make the journey. The Roman Empire was accustomed to trade overland with China for silk; and in 1274 the famous Venetian explorer, Marco Polo, made a journey to China, and even heard of, but did not see, Japan. By and large, however, the Far East until the fifteenth century was almost as completely isolated from Europe and the Mediterranean basin as America was. It is a strange fact of history that when we in Europe finally made contact with America and the Far East, we found in the Far East a number of flourishing civilisations more eminent than our own, and a population of over two hundred million comprising at that time more than half the total population of the globe; while in all the vast and fertile continent of North America there were probably less than a million Red Indians, living in tents and subsisting mainly on hunting.

There is one exception to this general fact of the isolation of the Far East. India has always been, if remote, reasonably accessible. Alexander the Great, for instance, who spread Greek civilisation over all Asia Minor, succeeded in crossing Afghanistan and adding most of that part of north-west India which is known as the Punjab to his empire. There are still legends in those parts of a great conqueror called Iskander Khan and his two magicians, Aflatun and Aristu, whom we know better as Plato and Aristotle. The same path was followed by all Moslem conquerors. India, however, has played and must in future play so great a part in the life of the Far East that it could not be left out of this book. It is after all quite possible that its future role will again be to form the link between Europe and the Far East.

This vast area with which we are dealing is itself divided into two halves, sharply separated from each other. The first is the seaboard of the Indian Ocean, India itself, Burma, Ceylon and the north-west coast of the Malay Peninsula. The second is the seaboard of the Pacific and South China Sea, Siberia, China, Korea, Japan, the Philippines, Indo-China and Siam. These two seas are divided by the Malay Peninsula and the islands of Indonesia, an area at times densely populated and highly civilised itself, but a barrier to sea traffic, since there are only two navigable straits in all the thousands of miles of land barrier, and both these were until late in the nineteenth century infested by pirates. Between the two land masses stretches the greatest mountain chain in the world, the Pamirs, Himalayas and mountains of Yunnan. It was only with the building of the Burma Road in 1938 and the development of air traffic over 'the Hump' that any larger scale movement over this barrier became possible.

North of the second or China area and covering almost the whole of Far Eastern Russia, bitterly cold and uninhabited plateaus stretch in seemingly endless progression to the Arctic Ocean.

The most difficult thing for the European to grasp at first acquaintance with the Far East is the immensely larger scale of geographical features. With an effort of imagination, we can remember that Mount Everest is nearly twice the height of the highest mountains in Europe—as if an average Indian were eleven feet high—but even then we do not grasp that, having crossed this range from India, you have only reached Tibet, where tens of thousands of square miles of plateau are all higher than the highest mountain in Europe.

Similarly, we realise from our own experience that the river valleys are the best land, and their estuaries the most suitable places for ports. It is harder to remember that the Yangtse River is navigable for boats for the first 2,000 miles from the sea, and that more people live in the Delta of the Ganges than in the whole of England.

## STRUCTURE AND CLIMATE

Granted this enormous difference in scale, it is possible to describe very simply the main geographical shape of the area. Its core is formed by the largest mountain mass in the world, the centre of which is the plateau of Tibet, rising on its southern edges to the towering wall of the Himalayas, which include Mount Everest, the world's highest mountain. This wall is prolonged on the western side by the Pamirs and mountains of Afghanistan and Baluchistan, so that it forms a boundary, cutting off India from the West. To the westward, on our side of the boundary, lie Samarcand and the wild romantic territory, now Russian, that drains to the Caspian Sea, the land through which flows the River Oxus, of which Mathew Arnold writes at the end of *Sohrab and Rustum*:

> But the majestic River floated on,
> Out of the mist and hum of that low land,
> Into the frosty starlight, and there mov'd,
> Rejoicing, through the hush'd Chorasmian waste,
> Under the solitary moon: he flow'd
> Right for the Polar Star, past Orgunje,
> Brimming, and bright, and large: then sands begin

> *To hem his watery march, and dam his streams,*
> *And split his currents; that for many a league*
> *The shorn and parcell'd Oxus strains along*
> *Through beds of sand and matted rushy isles—*
> *Oxus, forgetting the bright speed he had*
> *In his high mountain cradle in Pamere,*
> *A foil'd circuitous wanderer: till at last*
> *The long'd-for dash of waves is heard, and wide*
> *His luminous home of waters opens, bright*
> *And tranquil, from whose floor the new-bath'd stars*
> *Emerge, and shine upon the Aral Sea.*

At the eastern end another spur, represented by the Patkai and Lushai Hills and the Arakan Yoma, separates India from Burma; this and other ridges running down from the Yunnan plateau are prolonged in the long mountain chain of Malaya, Indonesia and New Guinea to form that chain of islands which separates the Indian Ocean from the China Sea and joins Asia to Australia.

The solid mountain mass itself stretches from Tibet in the south right up to Siberia in the north, and forms a wide block between China and Central Russia, so formidable that only one road crosses it, and there is no railway south of the Trans-Siberian. Incidentally, you will get some idea of the scale of these countries if you remember that the journey from Vladivostok to Moscow on the Trans-Siberian takes ten days' and nights' solid travelling in the train and is the most boring journey in the world. Each day you wake up to find the scenery exactly the same, until you forget-whether it is Friday or Tuesday of next week.

The populous areas of the Far East consist mainly of the valleys and deltas of the great rivers which flow down from this mountain mass to the sea. Of course, there are minor spurs, foothills and plateaus also, but these are generally feared as the haunts of barbarous tribes, evil spirits and malaria; the centres of population and the cradles of culture and civilisation are the great river valleys and deltas. On the western side of the dividing line formed by the Malay Peninsula and Indonesia lie India, Burma and Ceylon. India has two of these great river systems: the Indus with its five great tributaries forms the river system of north-western India (Punjab means five rivers), and was one of the earliest homes of human civilisation. The Ganges and Brahmaputra similarly drain the north and north-east. The centre and south of India consist of a plateau sloping from west to east, the rims of which look like mountain ranges from the plain and are called the Eastern and Western Ghats. This plateau tapers off to a point which is extended across the Palk Straits in Ceylon.

Burma, on the western side of the dividing mountains which run down from Yunnan, and Siam on the eastern side, are countries built around single river valleys; in Burma the Irrawaddy and in Siam the Menam. In each case the great bulk of the population live in the delta areas.

Malaya has no great river, and therefore by Far Eastern standards no great population. Southern Viet Nam and Cambodia owe their life to one of the greatest of Far Eastern rivers, the Mekong, 2,800 miles long. The Mekong rises in Tibet, flows first through China, then for 1,200 miles forms the boundary of Siam with Laos and Cambodia, and at last reaches the South China Sea, after flowing through Southern Viet Nam. Saigon, its main port, is as usual on a minor channel of the delta. In the same way, Tonkin (northern Viet Nam) is dependent on the Red River.

China itself, for all its vast size, has always been divided into the valleys of the three great rivers, the Yangtse (fourth river of the world in length and approximately 3,000 miles) the Yellow River (approximately 2,500 miles) and the West River.

It is these plains, river valleys and deltas sloping away from the central mountain mass, along with the island chains of Japan, the Philippines and Indonesia, that form the 'Far East' with which this book deals. Only in the far and barren north do the rivers flow sluggishly north to the Arctic, and provide neither fertility nor means of communication.

After the actual shape of the country, the next most important thing in any place is the weather, for on this depends not only the vegetation, but the life of man. There are parts of the world so dry or cold that life becomes intolerably difficult either for plants or men, so that they give up the struggle and die or move away: there are other parts so warm and moist that life is too easy, and plants and men grow up so thick together that each one lives an indolent, crowded, hopeless sort of life, swamped by its, or his, fellows. There is a sort of parallel between the lush, parasitic vegetation that is found in the semi-darkness of tropical rain forests and the teeming, ever-increasing population of, let us say, the Ganges delta, pressed down by poverty and ignorance and constantly threatened with famine by the least failure in the weather. The Far

B

East as a whole includes all kinds of climates, but it has a smaller area of temperate changeable weather such as we enjoy in England than the West has.

The greater part of India, and all Burma, Ceylon, Malaya, Indonesia, Siam and Viet Nam lie within the tropics, and except for the dry country of central and north-west India, have a climate that is both hot and wet. The outstanding feature of their weather is the monsoon—a protracted season of wind and usually rain, quite different again in scale from anything we know in Europe. The special causes of the Indian monsoon will be dealt with in the next chapter. The general effects are much the same in all monsoon countries, though the following description refers specifically to India.

There is usually little rain in the winter months, but each summer, as the sun climbs higher and the heat grows more intolerable day by day, so a low pressure system is built up and the rainy winds from the sea are summoned in; clouds begin to appear in what was before a hard sky of burning blue, but at first their moisture is absorbed by the dry, hot atmosphere; there is a growing tenseness in the air, and old-stagers, who know the country well, say that this, the month before the monsoon breaks, is the danger time for riots. People's tempers are on edge. On the actual sea-coast you can see each day the rollers begin to swell and thunder on the beaches; and the clouds, instead of drifting in puffs across the sky, bank up and drive towards the shore, until at last, in a tempest of storm and rain, the monsoon breaks. When it does break, it rains hour after hour, day after day, in a way Europeans can scarcely imagine. The temperature drops, and everyone comes out laughing and splashing in the rain, like frogs in a dry pool that is suddenly flooded.

Of course, there are moments when it stops raining, even in the monsoon, but a monsoon climate means that almost all the rain for the year falls within the monsoon months. Calicut, on the south-west coast of India, gets three-quarters of its total rainfall for the year in the three summer months of June, July and August, and there are freak spots on the arid coast of Arabia that get their total rainfall for the year in the form of a two days' downpour. Monsoon rainfalls, apart from being predictable, as English rainfalls are not (you can be *sure* that it will rain heavily on July 15th in Calcutta and not rain at all on February 15th), are much heavier than ours. Akyab, which during the war was the main Japanese base in the

Arakan, has a mean annual rainfall of about 300 inches, of which about 170 inches fall between June and September. Compare this with Liverpool in England, where the approximate rainfall is between 30 and 40 inches a year. The average amount of rain that falls on a rainy day in Bengal is seven times as much as falls on a rainy day in England.

From the point of view of weather, and therefore of vegetation, the Far East may be divided into three zones: the first or equatorial zone stretches from 10° S. of the Equator to 10° N. and therefore includes Indonesia, Malaya, Ceylon, the southernmost tip of India, the south coast of Viet Nam and of south-east China and the Philippines.

This gets a heavy but more or less evenly distributed rainfall, since both the summer monsoon, blowing from the south-west, brings it rain from the South Indian Ocean, and the winter monsoon, blowing from the north-east out of Asia, has picked up a little rain in crossing the Bay of Bengal or South China Sea. This area, in addition to the monsoon, also gets the typical equatorial rain showers. North of it stretches a purely monsoon zone from 10° N. to 40° N. covering India, Burma, Siam, Viet Nam and Southern China. This area depends for its rain on the summer monsoon alone, and has dry winters. Mean annual rainfall tails off as you go north. (Figures for China and Japan are: Hongkong 85 inches, Shanghai 45 inches, Tokyo 58 inches and Pekin 25 inches.) Yet again north of this zone stretches a temperate zone with a climate not unlike that of Europe, followed by the sparsely inhabited forest and tundra area of Eastern Siberia—very dry, cold and uninviting. Only along the Pacific coast is there any appreciable rain here, and that coast is a land of clinging fog not unlike Labrador. The sea freezes over for four months in the year round Vladivostok, although it is on the same latitude as Marseilles, and the Aleutian Islands were one of the worst air bases in the world, because there was practically always ten-tenths cloud.

## VEGETATION AND FOOD CROPS

In the tropical zone the vegetation is intensely thick. Flying over Sumatra is like flying over a green furry rug, and for hundreds of miles the only break in the solid pile of tree-tops is the occasional course of a stream. What goes on beneath those tree-tops no white man has ever seen. It is a country which is quite impenetrable except by air.

The food crop for human beings in this zone, where a river delta
or broken mountain country allows clearing of the ground, is rice.
Most of the inhabitants have lived for hundreds of years almost
entirely on rice—this is true of Indonesia, Ceylon, southern Burma,
southern India and Bengal, Malaya, Siam, Viet Nam and Southern
China—and when there is not enough rice, the poorest among
them starve. One of the tragic absurdities of the Bengal famine
of 1943 was that British people—in trains, for instance—who tried
to give the starving Bengalis other foods, like bread, found that they
literally could not eat it. Their stomachs could take only rice.

Rice as a food crop has many advantages. Fertile land will always
bear two and sometimes three crops a year, year in and year out,
without any rotation. It is a crop of the monsoon countries, for it
demands that the fields should be several inches under water for
part of its growing time. It is also a crop of the small peasant cultivator, for it grows best in small plots, banked in to prevent the water
running away, and has to be transplanted and thinned by hand, the
peasants, both men and women, working all day in standing water
to do this. This need of rice for standing water means that lands
which depend on rice for their food crop depend on rain for their
life, and the periodic famines in the Far East are all produced by
variation in the fall of rain—either too much falls, so that the rivers
burst their banks and wash away the fields and crops, or else too
little, so that the rice harvest is spoilt. The danger in Bengal was
only too obvious for years before the famine; the population continued
to increase, until it was all the province could do to feed the people
in a good average year. Yet the normal variation in rainfall from one
year to another was 16 per cent., and agriculturalists reckon that a
25 per cent. deficiency of rain will injure the crop, and a 40 per cent.
deficiency ruin it. It only needed the combination of a cyclone
when the crops were growing, with local floods later, and the cutting
off of supplies from Burma to cause a shortage resulting in two or
three million deaths.

In pre-war days of peace, transport was so well developed in
the Far East and throughout the world that such local famines
could be met by importing rice from elsewhere, and therefore there
grew up not only a confidence about famines, but a tendency in
these areas to grow more valuable but less edible crops, which were
used for trade with the rest of the world. Such 'cash' crops, as they
were called, because they were grown for sale and not to eat,
included tea, rubber, jute, coconuts and kapok. Thus the vegetation

of this tropical zone of the Far East could be divided into untouched forests, rice-fields and cash crop plantations. Travelling through Ceylon from the coast to the central hills, for instance, you would pass through dense jungle of huge trees, whose tops shut out the sky and were lost to sight themselves, to come suddenly on little villages, around which were clearings of terraced rice-fields, each a tiny patch of the vividest green—for rice is the greenest of all crops—and finally reach the tea plantations, set out in orderly rows, interspersed by 'shade' trees and looking as civilised and monotonous as anything well could. In one journey of three hours you would have seen all the main types of vegetation in this tropical zone.

The importance of rice as a locally grown food crop can be judged from the fact that before the war nearly 97 per cent. of the world's total rice crop was produced in the Far East, and of all these countries only Burma, Siam and Viet Nam could afford to spare any at all for export. India and China, which between them produced about 70 per cent. of the world's rice, needed all their crops to feed themselves.

As you go north from the tropical zone or up into the hills, the tropical jungle gives way first to more open forest, then to scrub or open woodland and vegetation more like that of Europe. Deserts are found where the rainfall fades away virtually to nothing (the hot Sind Desert in north-west India and the cold Gobi Desert in China). The food crops in these temperate and drier zones are wheat and millet, while in China large quantities of fruit and vegetables are grown. New cash crops such as cotton, sugar-cane, oil-seeds and soya beans are found, the last mainly in Korea and Manchuria. We are inclined to regard Canada as the one great wheat-producing area of the Commonwealth, and it is surprising to find that between 1935 and 1939 India's wheat crop was, on average, greater than that of Canada. The people of the Punjab and north-western India generally are, like the northern Chinese, just as inveterate eaters of wheat as the Bengalis, southern Indians and southern Chinese are of rice. And they too run the risk that failure in the monsoon rains, or more important still, in the light winter rains, may bring crop failures in areas where the water supply is not entirely drawn from irrigation.

In the northern sub-Arctic zone (and in the interior of the temperate zone) there is a certain amount of steppe grass, on which live wandering or nomadic people, whose larders are filled not from their crops, but from their flocks and herds. Most of the northern

(a) Harrowing: only a water buffalo could do it.

(b) Ploughing: Note the ridges dividing the paddy fields.

2. FOUR STAGES IN RICE CULTIVATION:

(*c*) This woman is collecting seedlings from the nursery for planting out

(*d*) Planting out: Everyone helps, men and women alike.

NOTE THE HEAVY RAINFALL NEEDED.

zone, however, is sparsely inhabited pine forest, until the bare
Arctic tundras are reached; only along the foggy Pacific coast near
Vladivostok is an additional source of food for this area found in
the fishing grounds, similar to those off Labrador, which have been
a bone of contention between the Russians and the Japanese for
many years.

### RACES OF THE FAR EAST

There seems to be very little doubt that the great races of mankind
were first differentiated in Asia and from there spread outwards.
Over most of the Far East there is a general racial pattern, consisting
of a predominant race, who were originally immigrants from Central
Asia, and pockets of more primitive survivals. The great racial
groups may be roughly divided as follows:

### (a) Aborigines

Who were the original inhabitants of most parts of the globe is
still almost as much a mystery to us as the 'autochthonoi' were to
the Greeks. Like the Greeks, we know for certain only that the
present inhabitants came from somewhere else. It seems reasonably
probable, however, that the original inhabitants of India and south-
east Asia were an unspecialised, small, dark-skinned race, with
wavy or sometimes even woolly hair and primitive features, rather
like the present-day negritoes or Australian bushmen, or races
mixed with them. They survive in pockets all over south-east Asia,
wild Dravidian-speaking tribes in India, Veddas in Ceylon, Semang
and Sakai in Malaya, Moi in Indo-China, negritoes in the Philippines
and Andaman Islands.

### (b) Caucasians

The name 'Caucasian' will serve as well as any other for the
great race which spread from south-west Asia round Bokhara and
Samarcand, westward over all Europe, eastward into Central Asia
and south-eastward to India. In origin they are a long-headed, fair-
skinned, hairy people with markedly rugged skull structure. In the
Far East to-day they appear twice, in India and Japan. India seems
to have been populated by successive waves of this race, of whom
the famous Aryans were by no means the first, coming in from the
north-west and supplanting or mingling with the original inhabitants.
To this day the gradual diminution of Caucasian features among
the Indians can be traced as you go from the north-west, where

the Punjabis and Kashmiris are as Caucasian as any Europeans, to the south-east, where the effect of other strains is much more marked.

While the main bodies of the Caucasian race spread westward or south-eastward, a branch seems to have rounded the great Tibetan mountain block to the north and wandered right round north-eastern Asia to end up as the Ainu in the northern island of Japan (see photograph on p. 253).

### (c) Mongoloids

The Mongoloids are the second great racial group of the world; in numbers, distribution and achievement at least the equal of the Caucasians. They are markedly different from the Caucasians in almost every feature: they have smooth, hairless skins, yellow or light brown in colour; the hair of their heads is straight without curls and very rarely even wavy; their faces are flatter and rounder than the Caucasian, with small noses and high cheek bones; they are shorter in stature, the difference being largely in the legs, and they have less waist. One feature which is very common, and which seems to persist in people of mixed Mongoloid and Caucasian blood, is the Mongoloid eye fold, which produces the 'slanting' eyes, apparently flat in the face, of the Chinese.

It seems likely that the cradle of the Mongoloid race was Central Asia and that they moved south-eastwards, as the Aryans did, in entering India. The Chinese, for instance, are a purely Mongoloid race, and the earliest records of Chinese history are of expansion from the north-west, and mention 'black dwarfs' among the tribes then inhabiting the coasts of southern China. Apart from the Chinese themselves, other pure branches of the Mongoloid race are: the Mongols themselves and central Asiatic nomads, the Burmese, the Gurkhas of Nepal and Assamese hill tribes (the nearest the Mongoloids got to India), the Annamites and the Thais. Mongoloid stock predominates in the Indonesians—that is, the inhabitants of Malaya, Indonesia and the Philippines—the Cambodians and the Japanese. In the Indonesian stock there are traces not only of the earlier aborigines, such as negritoes, but of the former inhabitants of Indonesia, the modern Polynesians, who are possibly a Caucasian race in origin. There are also clear indications that their Mongoloid ancestors arrived in two fairly widely separated waves. The Japanese are one of the problem races of the world, predominantly Mongoloid, but probably uniting several different Mongoloid strains with northern Caucasian and probably also Polynesian.

There are no really reliable estimates of the numbers of people living in the Far East, for no accurate census has ever been taken of China, the most populous area of all. They certainly outnumber the other continents put together.

At first sight, this population seems to be very irregularly distributed. India, China, Java, Japan, Korea, Tonkin and Ceylon are thickly populated, the rest of Malaysia and the Indo-Chinese peninsula moderately, and the great plains of Siberia hardly at all. A principle of explanation can be found, however, which is that any area capable of growing rice is thickly populated unless it suffers from either malaria or civil disorder. A secondary principle might be suggested as worth consideration, that even in such circumstances rice yields are low and population at least manageable where the economy of the country is based on the export of some other cash crop. Examples of countries with unusually low rice yields per acre of this kind are Ceylon and the Philippines.

## Religion and Culture

Grouping them all as a single body it would seem impossible to describe what they are like, and yet there is a sufficiently striking difference between Westerners and Easterners as a whole to make it quite reasonable sometimes to speak of 'Orientals' as a different type of person. What exactly this difference is may be hard to see at first; anyone whose knowledge of the Far East only extended to India and the other countries of the tropical zone might well say that it lay in a way of life based on a vastly greater regard for religion than for science; but such a judgement does not allow for the Chinese, who are a strongly traditional but not what we should call a religious people, nor for the Koreans, most of whom have no religion at all. A truer explanation would be that the Far Easterner does not regard himself, as we do, as an individual living his one life here and now on earth. He thinks of himself rather as part of a family, and it is the fate of the family, not of the individual, that matters. This means that the unit for the purposes of lawsuits, quarrels and all the activities of this actual life such as marriages is the family. They all live together, and if anyone is unfortunate or 'down and out,' he finds it quite natural to do what we should call 'sponging on his relations' for the rest of his life. And the relations find it natural, too, and raise no objections. It is a question which deserves some thought whether our system or theirs is the better.

In many ways in different countries this attitude towards the family stretches out in time as well as in space. Regard for ancestors is the deepest psychological attitude behind all Chinese and Japanese religion and philosophy, so that again the individual does not think of himself as one person living out his single life here and now on earth, but as a member of an enduring family, whose roots go back to the beginning of the world and will, he hopes, go on for ever. It is the fortunes and honour of this family, clan or country, not his private fortunes and honour, that matter in the long run. The doctrine of reincarnation—the belief, that is, that after death we are born again on this earth in new shape—also helps to underline the unimportance of the individual life. Everything has lived before and will live again, and one of the greatest reasons why you should not take the life even of the meanest animal is that it may be your great-grandfather born again as a lizard, in order to pay for the sins he committed as a man.

This attitude of regard for the group rather than the individual is supported by the immensely powerful forces of Hinduism and Buddhism, the two most widely practised religions in the world, and in China by the equally powerful force of Confucian tradition. It must be remembered that in talking of Orientals we are dealing with a people four-fifths of whom, at least, still live in remote villages, carrying on a mode of life that has hardly altered for hundreds of years. Among such people religion and tradition count for far more than they do in the West.

## (a) Hinduism

Hinduism is probably the oldest surviving religion. In its purest form to-day it is a lofty if rather vague philosophy, which welcomes as good all attempts to find and know God, who in the end is unknowable and indescribable. In a great many ways it is not at all unlike what Christianity would be without the miracle of the Incarnation and revelation through Jesus of the nature and love of God. Mr. Gandhi, whose power in India was based on the belief that he was a saint, once said in discussion with Christian leaders: 'I do not know what you mean by "the living Christ." If you mean the historic Jesus, then I do not feel His presence. But if you mean a spirit guiding me, a presence nearer to me than hands and feet, than the very breath in me, then I do feel such a presence. If it were not for the sense of that presence, the waters of the Ganges would long ere this have been my destination. Call it Christ or

Krishna—that does not matter to me.' It is the last sentence which
indicates most clearly the exceptional factor of Hindu religious
philosophy, its acceptance of all approaches to God as being right
in their way; and it is this which accounts for another saying of
Gandhi's which has shocked many Christians: 'I yield to no man
in my worship of the cow.' The philosophic Hindu would explain
this by saying that the cow, with her mild acceptance of suffering
and life of service, is a symbol of those qualities, and that the
remark is therefore no more idolatrous than it would be for a
Christian to say: 'I yield to no man in my reverence for the
Cross.'

Unfortunately, Hinduism as practised by the vast, illiterate
masses is a very different thing from the philosophical faith of the
great teachers. To the Indian masses Hinduism can mean the
worship of hundreds of gods and a deep reverence for a certain
tree outside the village, on the branches of which numbers of magic-
fearing peasants have tied scraps of rag; or it can mean awed attendance at a temple where the blood of sacrifices is poured out in
honour of Kali, the goddess of destruction; or where girls are kept
as temple prostitutes in a magical attempt to increase the fertility
of the fields. Again, to the more spiritual it can mean a deeply
personal religion founded on love for Krishna, the human incarnation
of God, who said: 'Abandoning every duty, come to me alone for
refuge; I will release thee from all sins. Sorrow not.'

It is one of the weaknesses of Hinduism that its acceptance and
approval of all ways of approach to God render it often open to
reproach, and make the Hindu religion difficult to describe and
tolerant of abuses. Among its saints are men whose lives would be
counted saintly by any standards, but there are whole sects of Hindus
whose practices, if they claimed to be Christians, would be condemned out of hand by the Christian Church, as such orgiastic or
antinomian heresies have always been condemned.

Very briefly, the peculiar features of the type of social and religious
life which Hinduism would expect from the ordinary man, and
which most Hindus would preserve from change on religious
grounds, are, in addition to the general features of the oriental
way of life already described:

(1) A prohibition of the taking of animal life, particularly that of
the cow, but often of other animals. Good Hindus are usually
vegetarians.

(2) An emphasis on the importance of the sexual side of life.

Hinduism is the only great religion which for the ordinary man rather encourages sexual indulgence than the reverse.

3. The Hindu 'Jagdish' Temple at Udaipur (Rajasthan).

(3) The caste system, by which all Hindus belong from birth to one or other grade of a static social system and may not mix with other grades.

(4) A belief in reincarnation and fate.

At the top, of course, there may be modifications in the way these attitudes are expressed—the actual practice of *suttee*, for instance, has almost vanished—but as attitudes they are still fundamental to the vast mass of Hindus, and if you think of them carefully it becomes obvious how very different life must be to someone for whom these and the unimportance of the individual are the great truths of existence; and therefore how foolish it would be to expect him to react to any situation in the same way that we would.

### (b) Buddhism

Buddhism, which arose out of Hinduism in about 450 B.C. and is now the most widely acknowledged religion in the world, is in some ways more like Christianity than Hinduism is, and in some ways less; it is even more of a philosophy and less of a religion than Hinduism, but, like Christianity, it springs from a single founder, whose teaching has been spread all over the world.

The Buddha himself must have been one of the noblest of all mankind. He was an Indian prince, born in the middle of the fifth century B.C., a great warrior, hunter and games-player. When he was twenty-nine years old, horrified by the misery which he had just recognised round him, he abandoned all his riches and his position and went out as a beggar to try to find a cure for human misery, for want, disease, old age and death. The comparison with St. Francis of Assisi is obvious, except that St. Francis felt that he already knew what the cure was. Buddha sought it first in the mortifying of that flesh which seemed to him the source of all these ills; but after going through all the practices which we now associate with Yogis, he found that this was not the answer, that the body and the flesh did not really matter and should neither be indulged nor mortified. He discovered that the cure for misery and want was not that everyone should get the things they wanted, but that they should cease to want the things of this world at all. His philosophy seems a pessimistic one, for it is based on the conviction that all individual human existence is inevitably misery—note again the insistence on the wrongness of individual existence—and that the misery can only be escaped by plunging so far in contemplation of divine things that you cease to exist as an individual or to have individual wants.

The connection with Hinduism is clear, and the 'wheel of life' from which Buddhism preaches escape is often represented as constant reincarnation. Westerners sometimes feel, when they have got so far, that Buddhism is purely a religion of escape and denial, and that therefore the people who practise it will be fatalistic and uninterested in human affairs. Instead they find them surprisingly happy, gay, enlightened and interested in everything. The explanation of this is partly, of course, that the Buddhist races happen to be that kind of people, and even if they followed a gloomy religion of despair, cheerfulness would keep breaking in; but much more important is the fact that Buddha taught from the first that this contemplation of divine things could only be achieved by people who had for a long time previously lived a good life of ordinary practical morality; and this is as far as the ordinary Buddhist, like so many ordinary Christians, ever gets or is expected to get.

Because Buddhism is a way of life rather than a religious approach to God, Buddhists have always been great teachers, and their educational system in countries like Burma has long been far ahead of other parts of the Far East. Whereas in India, in spite of all our westernisation, only 12 per cent. of the population can read and write, the figures for male Burmans in 1931 were over 70 per cent. And it is not only reading and writing in which they excel. John L. Christian, an American teacher who lived for many years in Burma, says: 'In the schools of the West you learned how to make money: in the Burmese monastery schools a youth learns to be happy and contented.'

These schools are conducted by the Buddhist monks, whose bright yellow robes are conspicuous all over the Far East. They live according to a strict rule on the alms which people put into their begging bowls, and are not supposed even to look into the face of a woman. But unlike Christian monks they may renounce their vows and go out into the world or return to the monastery as often as they please.

Of course, Buddhism, like Hinduism, has its degenerate and corrupt followers, but it does not, like Hinduism, suffer from having to accept any strange sect that chooses to describe its practices as the worship of Vishnu.

Buddhism, like Christianity, has also its weaker brethren, who if asked whether they were Buddhists, would say, 'Yes,' but who have in fact either no religion at all or none but the worship of demons or their ancestors. Like Christianity, too, Buddhism is divided into great territorial schools of thought, Southern Buddhism

(Hinayana or Lesser Vehicle), which is practised in south-east
Asia (Ceylon, Burma, Siam and Annam), and Northern Buddhism
(Mahayana or Greater Vehicle), which is practised in Tibet,
Mongolia, Manchuria, Korea and Japan. There are Buddhists all
over the world, of course, and I was once called upon in Bangkok
by a Latvian who claimed to be the Buddhist Archbishop of Lenin-
grad. Hinayana Buddhism is described in greater detail in Chapter V
(Ceylon), and Mahayana Buddhism in Chapters III and X (China
and Japan).

## (c) Islam

The third great religion of the Far East, Islam (Mohammedanism)
is, like Christianity, an importation from the West. Like the
Buddhists, the Mohammedans· follow the teaching of a great
founder, who is not believed to have been an incarnation of God
Himself, but rather the great prophet who revealed the will of God
or the laws of the universe to mankind. The faith of Islam is more
like Christianity than either Hinduism or Buddhism, and for that
reason perhaps there have been more bitter conflicts between the
two. Islam insists, unlike Hinduism, on the worship of one God,
and even regards the Christian doctrine of the Trinity with suspicion
as implying the worship of three Gods. It regards both Moses
and Jesus with veneration as forerunners of the final revelation
of God to Mohammed, who lived in the first half of the seventh
century A.D.

Again like Christianity, Islam is based on sacred writings (the
Qu'ran or Koran), which they claim to be divinely inspired and to
embody the teaching of Mohammed. The Mohammedans as a whole
regard religions which are based on such sacred writings as the
Koran or the Bible as being of a higher order than traditional
religions, and respect their followers as 'people of the Book.' Islam
is a religion of conquest: its followers in early days believed that it
was their duty to convert the rest of the world—if necessary by
force; and it reached the Far East in the wake of conquerors, either
by sea across the Indian Ocean or through Afghanistan.

Thus it has formed in the past and may form again a link between
the Far and Middle East. The most significant example of this,
perhaps, is that when Vasco da Gama, the first European to reach
India by sea, arrived at Calicut with an Arab pilot from East Africa,
the messenger whom he sent ashore, and who, of course, had
never heard any of the languages of the Far East, was greeted in

Spanish by a Moslem merchant from Tangier. Long before Christian Europe had established regular contact with India, Islam spread unbroken from Southern Spain to Java.

The parts of the Far East which were converted to Islam by land or sea conquerors from the Middle East were north-western and parts of north-eastern India, Malaya and Indonesia, except Bali, parts of inner China and the southern parts of the Philippines.

4. The Moslem mosque at Ajmer (Central India).

There are, of course, Moslem tribes elsewhere, mainly on the sea coasts, but these are the main areas.

Islam in the Far East has for a long time been in a period of decline, which dates from the days when the Moslems as the conquering race were supplanted by the Western Christians. For some time as a result of this they were particularly inclined to hold themselves aloof from Western ideas. There are signs now, however, of an Islamic revival on somewhat nationalistic lines not perhaps

c

entirely unconnected with the revival of the Arab states of the Middle East.

These three faiths are the great official religions of the Far East. There are in addition millions who worship stones, trees and idols. There is an increasing body scattered all over the Far East of converts to Christianity, and, in the Philippines, one predominantly Christian community. In China there are millions who are really ancestor worshippers, and whose code of conduct is that of Confucius, a moral philosopher rather than a religious leader.

## ECONOMIC ORGANISATION

The normal form of economic organisation in the Far East before the arrival of the Westerners was that of an agricultural peasantry paying rent to the landlord or taxes to the king in the form of produce. Traders and merchants there were, of course, but rights over the produce of the land formed the usual basis of wealth from the earliest days. No traveller in the Far East to-day can have failed to notice that immensely greater differences in wealth exist than in the West. The rich are richer even than our most fantastic millionaires. The poor are degraded by poverty to a life whose material conditions are very much worse than those of many domestic animals. This vast discrepancy in wealth is not new—it is rather the levelling up of incomes in the West that is new—and has existed for centuries in the Far East along with a tendency for the rich to immobilise more and more of their excessive riches in the form of treasure. The two fundamental problems which face the Far East to-day are how sufficient wealth can be produced to feed an ever-growing population and how the distribution of that wealth can be made more even and just without the chaos and starvation which would inevitably follow on a violent revolution.

## IMPACT OF THE WEST

### (a) Historical

Such was the isolated area of the world, agricultural, strongly traditional, religious at all levels from magic to mysticism, and anti-individualistic, which Vasco da Gama, the great Portuguese navigator, found when he reached India in 1498. Although the Europeans soon established their military superiority throughout most of the Far East, it was not until very recently that they began to alter the way of life and the outlook of the Oriental.

The great majority of Westerners reached the Far East in the first place by sailing round Africa and Indonesia. First, for the whole of the sixteenth century, it was the Portuguese who brought Europe to Asia: then at the beginning of the seventeenth century they gave way, exhausted by their immense effort of exploration and empire, before the newer imperial powers of Britain and Holland. For a brief moment in the eighteenth century France appeared as a rival to Britain in India, but by its last quarter it was clear that Britain was to be the dominating power in India, Burma and Ceylon, with Holland confined to Indonesia. In the nineteenth century Britain added Malaya to her sphere of influence, and France capitalised her long-established influence there by acquiring political control of Indo-China.

The Philippines, on the other hand, were occupied by Spaniards, who crossed the Pacific from South America, and were named after Philip II, who dispatched the Armada against England. As in South America the Spaniards really contrived to Latinise and to convert the inhabitants to Christianity, for they came as imperialists and apostles of the Faith, not like the British and Dutch, as merchants. Apart from this one area, there was little contact across the Pacific, where the power of Spain was waning, and the empires of China and Japan went on undisturbed by the West until the middle of the nineteenth century.

One of the most momentous dates in world history is 1853, when, partly under American compulsion and more as a result of internal developments, Japan, which for 200 years had excluded all foreigners from its shores, opened its ports to trade. At that period the European powers were hurrying to establish themselves in the eastern half of the Far Eastern area, as for three centuries before they had established themselves in the western half: Britain, France and Russia all sought special privileges in China; France annexed part of Indo-China in 1862 and established protectorates over other parts in 1863 and 1865; Siam only preserved her independence by playing off Britain against France, and even then lost some border provinces; the U.S.A. acquired the Philippines from Spain.

Yet it was also from this moment onwards that Japan began to build herself up as a modern power, determined to play as imperialistic a part in the Far East herself as any of the Western powers on whom she was now modelling herself.

The turn in the tide of Western domination in the Far East was the Russo-Japanese War of 1905. Those who have not lived in or concerned themselves with the Far East often fail to realise what a profound effect this victory of an Asiatic over a European power had. For nearly three centuries it had been assumed by those Far Eastern peoples who were subject to them that the Westerners were invincible, and here was this new, young, Asiatic nation of Japanese defeating one of Europe's greatest powers in open war. The myth that was exploded was not, of course, one of Western superiority in culture, for that had never existed; it was the legend of Western invincibility in arms.

Before we go on to consider the individual countries of the Far East, it remains to be seen what effect this 'impact of the West' has had. In the first place, it should be remembered that, except in the Philippines, the Westerners came to the Far East originally to trade under any conditions, and then to maintain law and order with a view to expanding that trade. They were not, in spite of the many Christian missions, primarily interested in spreading either their religion or their culture, and they were interested in ruling only where oriental anarchy made trade impossible, or organised oriental resentment attempted to drive them out. Consequently, we should expect to find, and we do find, that the first effect of the Western impact has been economic, the second social and the third political.

## (b) Economic

In China, where vast tracts of country were inhabited by a settled agricultural peasantry, even the economic effect has been very slight, and millions of peasants continue to live as they lived before: but countries like India, which was rescued from famine and civil war, or Malaya and Java, which have been developed for their exports of cash crops and minerals, now support a vastly larger population than before, and maintain great world ports like Singapore and Batavia, which were hamlets before the Westerners came.

Apart from the cash crop, which has its dangers in time of war or slump—for if you grow *nothing* but rubber, and rubber is unsaleable, you starve—the greatest difference that the Western economic impact has brought has been law and order. This has not proved the unmixed blessing that the British at least assumed it would be. European law is a complicated procedure, and in the hands of the oriental lawyer it becomes too often an utterly unintelligible series of magic formulæ by which the clever lawyer enslaves the peasant to the money-lender and calls in the whole mechanism of the State to rivet on the chains. Order too has profited the moneylender. That there must be moneylenders in an agricultural society is obvious, for the peasant often has to wait six months for his crop to ripen, and meanwhile cannot always feed himself from his savings. Before law and order reigned, the moneylenders lived in the village, and if they became too rapacious the peasants either did not pay, or even knocked them on the head. Their rates of interest were therefore very high, since the loans were risky ones in more senses than one. Unfortunately, when law and order were gradually established and loans became less risky, it was the moneylenders who profited, for the high rates of interest were traditional, and the peasants simply went on paying them without their traditional last resort if things got too bad. Of course, in the suppression of piracy or banditry and petty wars 'law and order' on the Western model has immensely benefited the people of the Far East, but it is as well to remember that for the simple peasant who forms the vast majority it has had its disadvantages.

Western economic development, with its cash crops and irrigation, and now the beginnings of industrialism, has also greatly increased the productivity of the whole area: but this has *not* in many cases raised the standard of living, as anyone who has seen the slums of Bombay and Calcutta or the poorer villages of Java will have noticed. The reason is that all the religion and tradition of the Far East, Hinduism, reincarnation, ancestor-worship (which means that you must have sons to worship you), coupled with the ordinary economic motive of a peasant family where children help with the work, have urged men to breed larger and larger families. Consequently, every irrigation project, every industrial development has led, not to a rise in the standard of living, but to a rise in the population. The population of Java alone is now about as great as that of Britain, and if any part of the world is overcrowded, it is the Far East. It is not surprising, therefore, that many Indians, like Mr. Gandhi, see no advantage in Western economic methods, and have led crusades for a return to the old economy, which supported the people on just as high, if not a higher, standard of living without putting them into the power of politicians or foreign employers.

### (c) Social

The social life of the average Westerner who visits or lives in the Far East is, of course, very different from that of the Orientals themselves. Nevertheless, in purely social habits, quite apart from economic and political influence, the Western example has considerably affected Eastern practice. And although the Westerners are a tiny minority of the population, their way of living cannot help being of interest to the Western reader. If, for instance, you are thinking of taking a job in the Far East, what you want to know first is how you, as a Westerner, are likely to live.

5. Waiting for the train at Rawalpindi (Pakistan). Note women in purdah in foreground.

The very earliest Western travellers may have accommodated themselves to oriental customs, but as early as the eighteenth century in the British and Dutch Indies the life of the European was an attempt to reproduce European customs in an oriental setting. There were the balls, the dinner parties, the innumerable bottles of port and claret, the race meetings and all the life of upper-class eighteenth-century Europe. This has been the pattern ever since. As the European hold on these countries was more firmly established, European quarters spread in the cities and the

crumbling Italianate palaces of the Calcutta merchants set in their
own gardens still give some idea of the society for which they were
built. To-day if you like night clubs and super-cinemas you will
find plenty in Bangkok or Bombay, and if you like horses and
fishing and shooting you may easily find that the Far East is the
only place where you can still afford to indulge your tastes. But in

6. Excise officials at the roadside near Murree (Pakistan).

the eighteenth century there was always the climate, and Rose
Aylmer was not by any means the only one buried in her youth
beneath an eighteenth-century monument in the Park Street
cemetery of Calcutta.

To-day even the climate has been largely circumvented by the
development of hill stations, where by going anything from 3,000
to 6,000 feet up into the mountains the Europeans are able to
reproduce not only the climate, but the natural scenery of their
homes. Simla, in the midst of the Himalayas, is a tin-roofed Godal-
ming, the vale of Kashmir is like France, Ootacamund like the
Downs, and the battlefields around Imphal strangely reminiscent

of Western Ireland. Even for those who cannot get away to the hill
stations there is always air-conditioning.

The attractions of life in the Far East have always been very
great for the Westerner. Above all, it meant a far higher social
position, more servants, better food and drink, and, if you could
afford to move about, actually a better climate. Its disadvantages
were at first the climate and the very serious danger of disease, and,
as they improved, a growing sense of isolation and frustration.
The Westerner undoubtedly lived on a higher standard of comfort
than he could command at home—and he can still command this
commercially—but he felt cut off from the life of his day. He was
an exile from his own country and either would not or could not
enter into the life of the country he lived in. Almost the only exception to this judgment was the Dutch in Indonesia.

The growing nationalism of the Orientals increased the isolation
of the Westerners, and in the last years before the war there was
something peculiarly arid about British society in India or French
in Indo-China. The feeling that their presence was resented by the
very class among Orientals with whom, because of their Western
education, they might most easily have mixed perhaps made the
Westerners more unsure of themselves and more apt to indulge in
those occasional petty gestures of individual arrogance which did
more than anything else to arouse Oriental resentment. Of course,
there were innumerable Westerners whose social behaviour was
entirely free from this weakness, but one has only to read the life
stories of some of the most violently anti-Western leaders to realise
what an effect these small personal affronts had. One silly woman
often undid the work of years of patient understanding and
education.

A young man going to work in the Far East now would still find,
I think, that he could command a far higher standard of living
than he could at home. It is quite just that he should do so, for
most of the commercial openings in the Far East involve operating
essentially Western types of economic organisation, and in these
the Westerner is to some extent a natural expert. It still pays a large
Westernised oriental firm to employ Westerners at higher salaries
to do certain jobs that they are better at doing.

Because most Far Eastern countries are now politically independent, he will probably find that the isolation and frustration are not
nearly so bad; it will be easier to make friends and to get inside
the life of the country, as it always was in independent Siam. On

the other hand, political security will be less; the whole area is obviously threatened by continual outbreaks of violence. To a young man who does not mind risks, it still seems a very attractive prospect.

The influence of this self-contained Western society on the social life of the Far East has been obvious though mostly superficial. It is the pressure of economic contact with the West which has really done most to break down the traditional social system, but there is no doubt that in the small wealthy class at the top sheer imitation of the Western society has had a considerable effect. Certain inventions, the motor bus and the radio have had a great effect even on village life. In India at least it is much rarer than it used to be to find a village where no one has ever even visited the neighbouring town; and in many villages there is one family that owns a radio and passes on the news to everyone else.

## (c) Political

Politically it is important to remember that the dominant powers in the Far East during the imperial nineteenth century were Britain and later on to a lesser extent the U.S.A. Both these powers, whatever their failings in practice, have been in theory liberal, and have in fact tried to teach the colonial peoples of the Far East self-government; self-government on their own democratic lines, that is, for the Far Eastern peoples have always been perfectly capable of self-government on Asiatic lines, as Siam has shown. When people say that 'they doubt whether Malaya is ready for self-government,' what they mean to say is that they doubt whether it is ready for *both* self-government *and* Western democracy.

The avowed British and American aim of developing their Far Eastern territories as free and self-governing states was formally stated at the very beginning of the process by Macaulay in his famous pronouncement of British objectives in India:

'It may be that the public mind of India may expand under our system until it has outgrown that system; that by good government we may educate our subjects into a capacity for better government; that, having become instructed in European knowledge, they may in some future age demand European institutions. Whether such a day will ever come I know not. But never will I attempt to avert it or to retard it. Whenever it comes, it will be the proudest day in English history.'

The effect of this policy and of the Western education which
became increasingly popular throughout the Far East was to develop
an increasingly violent nationalism, as a result of which, and of the
tactlessness of certain Europeans mentioned above, relations between
Westerner and Oriental became during the twentieth century less
and less cordial. The European has tended to regret 'the old days'
of easy friendship and respect between the races, based on a certainty
and acceptance of each one's political station in life, not unlike the
easy friendship which existed between the squire and the village.
The Oriental has felt that the Europeans, while continuing to put
off the day of thei political abdication, are not even the men their
grandfathers were.

But in truth, having once started on the path towards oriental
self-government, it was not possible, even if it were desirable, for
either side to turn back, and there was much to be said for what
appears to have been the British and American policy of finishing
the process as quickly as possible; for until it *was* finished, the youth,.
enthusiasm and self-sacrifice that were available among the politically
educated Orientals were wasted in sterile attacks on the Europeans,
instead of being used to set their own houses in order. As long as
it was possible to blame the French or the British or the Dutch for
everything, it was never possible to develop a genuine public enthusiasm to carry out the social reforms that were so badly needed.
This has been clearly recognised by the younger people of the Far
East; and a number of parties, often calling themselves 'Bolshevik,'
'Trotskyist' or 'Communist,' but having either no connections or
very sketchy ones with Moscow and 'Leninist-Stalinist' doctrine,
grew up between the wars.

Allowing for the elements of corruption and gangsterism in all
Far Eastern politics, it is fair to say that these parties were essentially
'have-not' parties, concerned with the social problems of a new
industrial slum-dwelling proletariat or an old peasantry enslaved
to the landlord or moneylender. They were anti-European, because
as long as the Europeans retained political power no political party
in the colonial territories of the Far East could hope to gain support
unless it was anti-European. Moreover, as long as they retained
power, the Europeans were held responsible for social conditions.
But these parties no longer made political freedom their main interest.
They regard that battle as won, and their split with the older
nationalist parties became clear during the war against Japan, when
such parties as the Malayan, Burmese and Indian Communists

eagerly co-operated with the Allied forces. And that part of the battle really does seem to be over. India, Pakistan, Ceylon, Burma, the Philippines, Indonesia, Viet Nam, Laos and Cambodia have achieved self-government. The declaration of Independence in the Federation of Malaya is scheduled for August 1957. This will leave under Western control only the trading cities of Singapore and Hong Kong, which are obviously not viable as independent states and whose future is still uncertain; the historical anomaly of Goa; and the three small British controlled territories in North Borneo.

In some respects this transition seems to have been accomplished at less cost in human suffering than was at first feared. Notably in India, Ceylon and the Philippines, stable, effective and democratic governments have been established, while within southern and south-east Asia as a whole there is a growing experience in the arts of national co-operation. After the first ten years there seem to be two main political dangers which are an immediate threat to this stability and progress. The first is political disintegration. In many cases the unity of large areas was established only by the acceptance (rather than imposition) of alien government. The withdrawal of that alien government has already split the Indian sub-continent and there is danger that it may split further. There are now four Asian administrations in Indo-China, where formerly the French exercised a unifying control. It is clearly uncertain how long Indonesia can remain a unitary state embracing the former territories of the Netherlands East Indies. Both in Burma and Malaya there are problems of integration. This fragmentation of the whole ex-Colonial area may be an inevitable result of the end of Colonialism and may indeed repeat itself in Africa, but it carries economic as well as political risks which should not be overlooked.

The second danger, in spite of the enunciation of the 'five principles of co-existence,' is Chinese communist expansionism. And the first could, of course, so easily contribute to the second.

BIBLIOGRAPHY

*Asia*. Dudley Stamp.
*Mankind So Far*. William Howells.
*A Short History of the Far East*. E. K. Latourette.
*Peoples of South-east Asia*. Bruno Lasker.
*A History of South-east Asia*. D. G. E. Hall.
*South-east Asia between Two Worlds*. Tibor Mende.

# CHAPTER TWO

## INDIA AND PAKISTAN: THE BACKGROUND

THE politicians have done the geographers a great disservice in choosing for one of the two Dominions the name which has previously served for both; and as there is not yet any other name for the whole subcontinent I shall continue to call it India.

### STRUCTURE

It consists of a single vast triangular peninsula projecting southwards from the Himalayas. The core of this peninsula is the plateau of the Deccan, which slopes downwards from west to east; the high escarpment which forms the plateau's western edge is known as the Western Ghats, the lower escarpment at the eastern edge as the Eastern Ghats: at the foot of each is a narrow coastal plain, wider on the east, where the plateau is fading away and the clear line of the hills is more broken.

Between the Himalayas and this plateau lie two huge plains, each containing a river over 1,000 miles long, the Indus and the Ganges. Both rivers rise fairly close together in the north-western Himalayas, but the Indus runs south-westwards through the desert country of Sind to the Arabian Sea near Karachi; the Ganges eastward, through the incredibly fertile plain of Hindustan, to the Bay of Bengal near Calcutta. It is worth noting that neither of these ports actually lie on the mouths of the rivers: the great rivers of the Far East form deltas so wide, swampy and shifting that the ports are almost always on small streams or cuts at one edge or other of the main river delta. Calcutta is not on the Ganges, nor Karachi on the Indus, nor Rangoon on the Irrawaddy, nor Shanghai on the Yangtse. Yet it is their connection with the great river valleys which has, of course, made the ports prosperous.

Between these great plains and the Deccan plateau a series of parallel mountain ranges, of which the Satpura is the most important, runs east to west. They are not very high in themselves, but they are very difficult to cross and have been of the greatest importance historically; there are, for instance, two great indigenous languages of India, and it would be roughly true to say that north of this mountain line Hindustani is spoken, south of it Tamil. North of this line the history and civilisation of India have been profoundly influenced by the Moslem world of Central Asia, particularly during the years of the Moghul Empire; south of it is a different India, affected by Moslem and Christian influences, it is true, but closer in all probability to the old India than any part of the north.

This great subcontinent is closed in on the north by the highest and most impassable of all mountain ranges, and open on the south to the world's greatest expanse of sea. For India lies all in the Northern Hemisphere, the southernmost tip of Ceylon lying in Lat. 6° o N.: and south of Ceylon there is nothing but sea stretching over a whole hemisphere to the South Pole.

This strange position in the world has had two notable effects: first, that India enjoys a climate unlike that of any other country in the world; second, that she has for long periods been isolated from the rest of the world, and to this day virtually the whole of her contact with the outside world is sea or airborne.

## CLIMATE

Asia is the largest land mass in the world and, as land grows hot or cold much quicker than sea, the uplands of central Asia are, apart from the poles, the coldest places in the world in winter. Verkhoyansk in Asiatic Russia has an average January temperature of 90° of frost. Now, cold air is heavier and drier than warm air and presses down upon the earth; hence the phrase 'high pressure belts,' where there is little moisture in the air. In winter, therefore, there is an extreme high-pressure belt in Central Asia, which is felt in the form of exceedingly cold winds flowing out to the comparatively low-pressure areas around the sea coast and the warm regions of the south. These winds howl over China and affect even the Red River area of French Indo-China, but they do not cross the Himalayas: the mountain barrier therefore gives India a winter climate of its own, cool but not excessively cold, dry but not actually rainless. Indeed, the south-east coast gets quite a good rainfall in November and December, because the winds which strike it from the north-east have absorbed a good deal of moisture in crossing the Bay of Bengal. As the summer comes on the land mass of Asia begins to hot up; the 'cold weather' is really only pleasant for two months in Calcutta and four in Northern India. As the plains of north-west India become hotter—and they are ultimately one of the hottest places on earth—the warmed-up

air creates a low-pressure system which spreads slowly southwards
from the centre of the heated land mass. It cannot be filled up
from the north, for again the Himalayas interpose themselves: it
is hotter and therefore at lower pressure than the great equatorial
low-pressure belt to the south of it into which the rain-laden south-
east trade winds are blowing full across a hemisphere of sea; but it
cannot yet be filled up from these either, for the remains of the
Indian high-pressure belt remain between them, as a dwindling
barrier between the two lows. This barrier slowly melts away, like
a snowman before the sun, until one day it is gone, the winds from
the ocean sweep over India and the monsoon breaks. These monsoon
winds, when they do strike the coast of India, are so warm and
so laden with moisture that the slightest rise above sea-level, with
its drop in temperature, causes them to precipitate heavy bursts of
rain. The latent heat released in this condensation of vapour into
water warms the air again and causes it to rise still further, into still
colder layers of atmosphere, where the condensation and rain are
repeated: thus the monsoon when it breaks in Bombay comes, not
in regular, driving rain from the sea, but in a series of torrential,
pulsating storms. In Bengal the same thing happens; the ocean
winds are, as it were, sucked into the heart of the Indian furnace,
and, unable to cross the Himalayas, sweep up the Ganges valley,
depositing their rain as they go: for the effect of the mountains is
felt long before the warm wet winds reach them, the air currents
piling up against them and being forced continually up into layers
of atmosphere which, further removed from the radiation of the
earth, are many degrees colder.

It is clear from this theory of the behaviour of the monsoon—
by no means certain, but the most likely advanced yet—that it
cannot be predicted with exact certainty when the high-pressure
barrier will vanish and the monsoon break. Late monsoons and
even complete failures of the monsoon are in fact possible and when
they come they spell crop failure and famine to the country. It will
be seen, therefore, that the date at which the Indian monsoon breaks
is of capital importance, not only to Indians but to all those, all
over the world, who deal in Indian produce. This accounts for the
fact that it is the one news item which occurs inevitably and annually
in the London *Times*, unchanged in form but on differing dates:
'From our correspondent in Trivandrum: The monsoon broke
here to-day.'

## GEOGRAPHICAL DIVISIONS

India's isolation from the rest of the world is not so marked as that of the Far East as a whole, but the only practicable routes, those through Afghanistan and Baluchistan, the Gilgit Pass and the Manipur Road, are very difficult. Within India itself there are geographical divisions almost equally marked.

### (a) Indus Valley

Of the two great river valleys of northern India, the territory drained by the Ganges is considerably the richer in natural resources. Yet it was in the Indus valley, as far as archæological research has so far established, that civilisation in India began. The excavations at Mohendjo-Daro have uncovered traces of civilisation well developed as early as three or four thousand B.C. and possibly antedating those of Mesopotamia or Egypt. From the lack of swords and spears among the implements discovered, some people have deduced that one of its peculiarities was that it had not progressed sufficiently far to invent war.

In historic times, however, the lower course of the Indus, like the lower course of the Tigris and Euphrates, had become desert or delta marsh and the area with which we are first concerned in this chapter is the valley of the Upper Indus and its five tributaries. This territory, known as the Punjab, or five rivers, occupies the north-west corner of India and is marked off by clearly defined frontiers, in the north-east by Kashmir and the Himalayas; in the north-west by Afghanistan and the Pamirs (a frontier that in British times became the North-West Frontier Province); in the south-west and south by the mountains and deserts of Baluchistan and Sind; and in the south-east and east by the Thar Desert and Aravalli Mountains, leading down to the narrow gap between them and the Himalayas which is guarded by Delhi. The history of the Punjab has reflected this geographical position; it has often been a country on its own, whether Greco-Indian, Sikh or Moslem, but it has also been the route by which all invaders of India, before the Portuguese arrived, and often enough their stopping place. The decisive spot for the control of all Northern India has always been Delhi.

This area is now, and in historic times has always been, a wheat-growing and flour-eating district. Canal irrigation in modern times has, of course, enormously increased its productivity, but the five rivers, and the fact that over large parts of the south-western plains the spring level is high enough to permit of the primitive type of well irrigation, in which the water is raised in a hide bucket by oxen driven down a ramp, means that even from the earliest times relatively good crops must have been possible. The rainfall is mostly concentrated in the monsoon season and averages 18·1 inches per year at Lahore; equally important rains for the wheat-growing areas, however, are the light rains in January and February which averages 1 inch or rather less per month, but whose failure may seriously endanger the crops. In the time of Alexander the Great and Asoka the chief city of the Punjab was Taxila, between the Jhelum and the upper Indus, but at least from the time of the first Moslem invaders in the tenth century A.D. it has been Lahore on the Ravi.

### (b) Ganges Valley

The River Ganges is not joined by the Jumna until it reaches Allahabad, 500 miles from the source of the Ganges and 600 from the source of the Jumna; but the two rivers run so close to each other and so nearly parallel that their joint valley may be taken as a single feature, running from the Delhi gap to the twin deltas of the Ganges and Brahmaputra in the Bay of Bengal. The valley is bordered on the north by the Himalayas and on the south by the Vindhyas or Satpura range. Most of the important tributaries came from the north, and, as these are snow-fed, the river, though much shrunken in the hot weather and flooded in the rains, is never dry or anything approaching dry. From the junction at Allahabad, the combined river runs almost due east for 350 miles, until, turning the corner, as it were, of the southern mountain block, it flows south-east into the Bay of Bengal. From the point of view of vegetation, the upper Ganges valley is very like the Punjab, with the rainfall, and therefore the spring level and prevalence of wells, increasing as one goes east towards the sea and the source of monsoon rains. In the middle valley it is possible, by delicately adjusted husbandry, to get three crops a year, but such farming is, of course, peculiarly exposed to danger from irregularities in rainfall. As one moves down from this area to the delta region, the mouths of the Ganges get inextricably tangled up with those of the Brahmaputra, a river of even greater length (1,800 miles) which has run parallel to the Ganges for all its course, but *north* of the first Himalayan range; having done this, the Brahmaputra flows first south through a gap between the

D

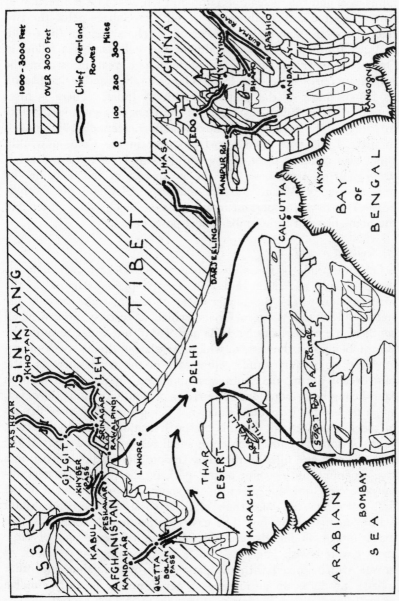

II. Land routes entering Northern India are all difficult and there is no railway. Internal routes converge on Delhi.

Himalayas and the plateau of Yunnan, then west in the direction of its own source and finally south to join the Ganges delta, the two rivers between them making the greatest delta system in the world.

Apart from the fabulous wealth of the soil—land lies fallow in Dacca one year in 147 compared with one year in two in the American north-west—the lower Ganges valley and delta has on its fringes most of the mineral wealth of India. There is first-class iron ore in Bihar, just south of the Ganges, conveniently close to India's only sizeable coalfield—a field, incidentally, big enough to make India now second coal-producer in the Commonwealth. Bihar also contains most of the world's supply of mica and a fair proportion of manganese. To the north-east of the delta lie the hilly district of Assam, the Brahmaputra valley and the foothills of the Himalayas, important nowadays as a major source of tea and the home of what little timber India possesses.

### (c) Coastal Plains

On either side of the high plateau of the Deccan, which forms the peninsula of South India, are coastal plains, narrow on the western side where the higher edge of the plateau presents the steep wall of the Western Ghats, which is scarcely broken at all south of the twin rivers Narbada and Tapti, but wider towards the Bay of Bengal on the east, to which the plateau drains. Both plains, however, enjoy very similar climates : in the north there is little rain except during the south-west monsoon; in the south there is rain during both monsoons. The rivers of Southern India, however, are little use for irrigation, since, not being snow-fed, they dry up in the rainless season; for this reason irrigation is mostly effected, as in Ceylon, by tanks. These are small reservoirs hewn out of the rock or earth and filled in the rainy season. Both plains subsist on a rice economy, but coconut palms, perhaps the world's greatest all-purpose crop, are also grown in the south. From the advent of the first Europeans the spice trade of these coasts has been a constant feature in their economy. The east coast, although wider, has the disadvantage of slightly less rainfall than the west and of large areas covered with laterite. This is an unproductive red rock or gravel, which, mixed with the dark green of the palms and other foliage, produces an entrancing scenery familiar in early English water-colours of the Madras countryside, but which cannot support a large population. Both coastal plains are singularly lacking in natural harbours, Bombay and Goa being the only natural harbours in the west, while in the east the main port, Madras, is, like Karachi in the north-west, entirely artificial.

## HISTORY AND PEOPLES

Apart from the aboriginal savages, traces of whom remain in the forest tribes, the prehistoric peoples of India came from the west in two great waves, generally known on account of their language as the Dravidians and the Aryans. Of the Dravidians little is known except that they were in possession when the Aryans began to arrive about 2000 B.C. It is even possible that the advanced urban civilisation of the Indus valley was Dravidian, for the Aryan habit of referring to them as black savages may well have been only the intolerance of an alien and a conquering race. Their descendants form the bulk of the population of South India (hence the separatist movement for setting up 'Dravidistan' in the South), and Tamil, the main Dravidian language, is as much a *lingua franca* in the south as Hindustani in the north.

About the Aryans we know a great deal more. It is important to remember that both names are properly applied to a language group and not to a race, and that the peoples speaking Aryan languages include such different types as the Bengali and the Swede, so that Hitler's search for a pure Aryan master race was an unusually romantic bit of nonsense. In the course of the wanderings which spread this group of languages all over Europe and Asia, tribes speaking Aryan languages, white-skinned, cattle-rearing and organised in monogamous families, began to enter India from the north-west about 2000 B.C. Gradually, over hundreds of years, they must have been assimilated with those of the Dravidians who were not driven down into southern India, and sometime between 1000 and 500 B.C. the centre of their civilisation passed from the Punjab and the Indus-Ganges watershed to Kampila and the upper Ganges valley. At some time during this period the religion or way of life known as Hinduism emerged; and this accounts for the great sanctity of the holy places on the upper Ganges in all subsequent Hindu history. Exact dates are impossible to fix, but it is certain that India has been Hindu at least 1,000 years longer than the west has been Christian or the Middle East Moslem. As in geography, so in history, it is the scale which Europeans find most difficult to keep in mind when dealing with the Far East. Two examples are worth remembering: the Moslem moves to dominate north-west

India, which we tend to think of as a comparatively recent invasion, started before William the Conqueror; and a fairly well developed Hindu civilisation had existed for another 1,000 years before the Moslems appeared on the scene.

In this long period of pre-Moslem Hindu civilisation in north India there are three irruptions of historical importance. The first of these was spiritual, the second cultural, and the third racial. The first, between 560 and 480 B.C. (the year of Marathon), was brought about by the teaching of the Buddha, and was immensely more important for the Far East and for the world as a whole than for India, where even Buddhism has been ultimately re-absorbed in Hinduism; for several hundred years, however, Buddhism did flourish in India, notably in the lower Ganges valley, and it has left in the record of the Maurya Emperor, Asoka, one of the finest examples in the world of the genuinely moral and enlightened despot.

The second disturbance of Hindu society followed 150 years later, when Alexander the Great entered India and tried to add much of the Punjab to his vast Asiatic Empire. The Persian King Darius had already spread his power over some of this part of India as early as 518 B.C., and although Alexander's immediate successor, Seleucus, ceded it in 305 to the great Indian conqueror, Chandragupta, it reverted to Hellenistic rule by 200 B.C. and remained in their hands until the third of the great irruptions about 150 years later. It is worth noting, therefore, that for 400 out of the last 500 years of the pre-Christian era this corner of north-west India formed part of the Greco-Persian world. Indeed, throughout most of recorded history the north-west has normally been either independent or incorporated in an empire whose centre lay further to the west. The occasions when it has been governed from a centre further east, such as the capitals of British India, have been the exception rather than the rule; and the creation of Pakistan, which has been described as a geographer's nightmare, is historically a reversion to normal as far as western Pakistan is concerned.

The third irruption just mentioned was that of nomadic tribes from Central Asia, the Saka, who may possibly have been what the Greeks called Scythians, just before the Christian era, and the White Huns about A.D. 500. These people seem to have settled down among the Indians—as I suppose we may now call the Aryans—and, adopting Hinduism, have left no trace behind except perhaps an additional caste or two in the already elaborate system.

It was the next arrivals after these who brought a social system which even Hinduism was unable to absorb. By A.D. 650 the first Moslems had overthrown a Brahman dynasty in Baluchistan, and from the eighth century onwards Sind and a part of the Punjab were brought under Moslem rule. By A.D. 1030 Mahmud of Ghazni had established a Moslem power in the western Punjab which, apart from the brief empire of the Sikh, Ranjit Singh, at the end of the eighteenth century, passed out of Hindu hands for ever. By 1200 the Moslems had occupied Delhi, the key to Northern India, and the first of a series of Turkish dynasties, which ruled until they were overthrown by the Moghuls in 1526, was set up. These Turkish kings maintained a constant war with the Hindu kingdoms of southern India, but never brought them under their control or converted the people, though small Moslem communities did spread along the sea-coasts.

It was the Moghuls, another Moslem dynasty, entering India from Persia in the sixteenth century, who brought the country nearer to unity than anyone, except possibly Asoka, before the British. To the east, they added Bengal to the Moslem Empire, converting a large number of its inhabitants, whose devotion to Hinduism may have been weakened by the fact that Bengal was the area where Buddhism had been strongest. These east Bengal Moslems, utterly cut off from their fellows in the north-west, are the greatest problem in the foundation of modern Pakistan. To the south they brought most of the Deccan under their control, but did not effect many conversions. When the Moghul Empire began to break up after the death of Aurangzeb in 1705, the Moslem Viceroy in this area made himself an independent king with the title of Nizam. His descendants became the rulers of the great inland State of Hyderabad (population 16 million) which had always a Moslem ruling minority and a predominantly Hindu population. Its incorporation in Hindu India in 1948 was only brought about by a display of force.

The age of the Moghuls was one of great splendour, fairly good administration, delightful gardens and exquisite art. The greatest of the Moghul emperors was undoubtedly Akbar, almost an exact contemporary of Queen Elizabeth, who, in his determination to secure religious tolerance (which was the policy of the more enlightened Moghuls), went so far as to invent a religion of his own, combining Islam with Hinduism. In Fatehpur Sikri, Akbar's abandoned capital and above all in the Taj Mahal, one of the few buildings in the world so exquisitely proportioned and sited that it seems almost to float off the ground, the Moghuls have left India and the world treasures beyond price.

It was in their time that regular European settlements were first established (Goa, the first, was founded by the Portuguese in 1510), and before going on in the next chapter to consider the problems of India under the impact of Western influence, this will be a good moment to stop and review the permanent elements in India's social and economic life which have been produced by the inter-action of Hindu and Moslem cultures.

## HINDU INDIA

### (a) The Family

We have seen in the previous chapter that the social unit in the Far East is the family and not the individual. This was so with the Aryans and has remained so in India up to the present day; but whereas among the Aryans the wife probably held a position of some authority, as she does in many Far Eastern countries to-day, she gradually lost this in India. It is true that most Indians have a great reverence for their mothers and will tell you that for this reason the position of the wife in the family is and always has been high in Hindu India; but whether reverenced or not, she has had no practical say in the ordering of family affairs, and until the Westerners forbade it, her devotion to her husband was expected to be so great that, in high society at least, she willingly committed suicide on his funeral pyre. No husband was ever supposed to commit this act of devotion (*suttee*) for his wife; and the position of the unmarried woman or widow in Hindu India was for long almost that of an outcast.

### (b) The Village

Most Indians for the last 2,000 years have lived in villages. The usual village organisation has consisted of a number of families, probably originally related to each other, who tilled the village fields and managed their own affairs. Whether the village land belonged to them or to the king is one of the disputed facts of Indian history. It seems clear that in practice each family behaved as if it owned its share of the land. It passed down from father to son and in most cases at least could be sold or mortgaged. On the other hand, a certain amount of the produce had to be paid over to the king, and the debated question is whether this was rent or

7. The Taj Mahal at Agra. The most exquisite building in India and possibly in the world, built as a tomb for Shah Jehan's wife in the middle of the seventeenth century.

taxes. The most probable solution seems to be that nobody at the time knew the difference, and it seems fairly certain that the idea of a landlord who was neither the king nor the cultivator but simply an imitation squire was an introduction of the British.

Even if each family did treat their share of the village land as if it were their private property, there were certain limits imposed on their freedom as owners by tradition and by the nature of Indian agriculture. Most of India lives on rice, and rice-growing is in its very nature a co-operative form of agriculture. You have got to have some body which controls the distribution of water through the irrigation channels, and in all rice-growing lands there has always been some sort of village committee for this, and for the arrangement of mutual help in the fields. In the Indian village this committee was called the *panchayat* and consisted of the heads of families, probably the five senior ones. Of course, in time this village committee came to settle many other things besides the watering of the rice-fields, and grew into a genuine local self-government such as villages have had all over the world. This self-government, however, was a purely local thing and, apart from forming an intermediary for the collection of rent and taxes, it played no part in the administration of the state.

## (c) Religion

We have seen in the last chapter that Hinduism is not simply a religion, but a whole social system; and this social system developed very early in Indian history, for the essentials were certainly established before 500 B.C. Essentially Hinduism is a pantheistic religion, as one might guess from the way that it accepts all varieties of creed and approach to the deity. Its chief effects on Indian society have been the sense of brotherhood which it has spread (even the much maligned word *sahib* means brother) and the comparative carelessness of human or animal suffering or well-being which is produced by seeing all life only as a part of some age-long process. The sense of brotherhood is very strong among Indians. With many of them it extends to animals also, so that they actually feel more comfortable if the house is reasonably full of snakes and the garden of monkeys; one gets the feeling that they would find a city with no animal life in it and no Brahmini bulls wandering the streets bleak and uncosy. When it comes to fellow men, Europeans often find the warm, rather sentimental tenderness of the Indian almost overpowering. Hindus love crowds and the contact of each other's

8. A Kashmir farm-cart.

9. Bullocks harnessed to a country water-wheel for irrigation, Central India.

bodies; they will jam together in trains and buses in a way that Westerners could not endure, yet obviously enjoying it; and there is nothing odd in the sight of a couple of Indian soldiers walking hand in hand. All this is age-old and part of the Hindu way of life; so is the passion for travelling and going on pilgrimages, which seems partly due to the pleasure derived from being one of a large company, partly to the historical feeling for certain spots on the earth's surface.

That comparative carelessness for human and animal suffering should be a Hindu characteristic seems strange at first, when we remember that extreme Hindu sects like the Jains have carried the refusal to take life so far that they will not even squash bed-bugs, and that the one emotion which Buddhism, after all a development of Hinduism, allows is compassion. No one can live long in India, however, without realising that, though the life may be sacred, there is no limit to the suffering which may be permitted or even imposed during that life; and in spite of Mr. Gandhi's protests, this suffering is endured by cows as much as by human beings. The reason seems to lie in the attitude towards acceptance of evil. To the Hindu, and even more to the Buddhist, earthly life is mostly evil, perhaps deserved suffering for the sins of a previous existence, and must be accepted as such. This is the classic Hindu defence of untouchability.

### (d) Caste

The nature of Hinduism makes it easier to understand the system of caste, though it would be a mistake to suppose that it produced it; both seem to have existed together from the first, and it is hard to say whether Hinduism is responsible for the nature of caste or caste for the nature of Hinduism. The principle of caste is a simple one; it is that men are born of different kinds and that they cannot change themselves from one kind to another. These kinds, or castes, must keep to themselves. The early Hindu texts refer to four great castes, priests, warriors, commoners, and servants, very much as in Plato's ideal republic. It seems not improbable that historically the system developed from a 'colour bar' imposed by the conquering Aryans against the darker skinned Dravidians. In the course of time two things happened; the number of castes and the complication of sub-castes increased and the rules against caste-mixing became stricter; for instance, in early Hindu times mixed marriages between castes were not exactly common, but certainly possible: in the fully developed Hindu society, until it began to break up under the impact of the West, they were banned altogether.

The connection between caste and the basic ideas of Hinduism is obvious; in thinking of the exclusiveness of caste and the way it puts barriers between man and man, we tend to forget its equal importance in binding men together in a brotherhood. Within the caste, where all keep to the same ceremonial and all are separated off from the world outside, a degree of brotherhood is possible which Westerners, accustomed to an individual world, can scarcely contemplate. Finally, from the economic viewpoint, caste has certain features of great interest. However the system started, the great majority of castes are occupational in origin and remain occupational to-day. Now, certain jobs are repugnant to devout Hindus, and if there were not special castes which performed them, it is difficult to say how they would be done at all. What appears to us the injustice of such a system vanishes before the Hindu conception of the wheel of existence. If you are born a scavenger, a scavenger you must remain; but there is no injustice: you are born thus in order that you may learn humility and purge your soul of the pride with which, perhaps, it became encrusted in your last existence as an emperor. Whatever the philosophic justification of this system, its economic nature is clearly not at all unlike the desperate straits to which the late Roman Empire was reduced, when a baker's son was compelled by law to be a baker in order that baking might be done and life go on. If no one likes going down the mines, and no one is to be forced by economic pressure to do what he does not like, then one way out is clearly to establish a caste of coal-miners who are compelled to go down the mines. If the world is really moving from an era of contract back to one of status, a totalitarian India might yet find caste a very useful device.

## (e) The Government

We do not know very much about the organisation of the Hindu states which existed before the Moslems arrived, or which, mainly in the south, carried on the struggle against the Moslems until absorbed by the British. From what we do know, however, it is possible to give an outline picture of the typical Hindu state which is accurate in essentials and which seems to hold good for most periods and areas. Most of the information comes from a Greek Ambassador of the third century B.C.

The state was a monarchy and the tradition of the king's personal

rule was strong. There was no Constitution, and the king governed
as he personally saw fit; on the other hand, he was a religious leader
also and was supposed to be governed himself by the 'sacred law'
of Hinduism. According to this law, he was expected to take advice
from elder statesmen and to limit the share of the crops which he
collected (as rent and taxes) to one-sixth. The king maintained an
army to fight foreign wars; but it is not very clear whether this
existed as a regular force or was merely a levy called out to meet
emergencies. If it was a regular force, it is remarkable that it played
no part in political intrigue, as the Roman imperial legions did;
and it would be tempting to see in this a parallel with the splendidly
non-political attitude of the Indian Army during all the difficult
years leading up to Indian independence.

There was no form of democratic expression (the *panchayats*
were purely local bodies), and no way in which the people could
make their feelings known to the king. In order to offset this, the
kings, who well knew the dangers of going too far, always maintained
a spy system whose job it was to report on public opinion. The
police informer of modern days who so regularly betrayed terrorist
plots was not, as some American writers believed, an indication of
how British tyranny had corrupted the Indian soul, but one of the
oldest and most accepted figures of the Indian political scene.

Hindu government therefore had most of the virtues and vices
of absolute rule. Under a good king it could be excellent and the
system of raising revenue well in advance of European practice at
the time; but a bad king could always find priests to say that where
the 'sacred law' said a sixth it really meant a quarter or even a third,
and revenue could therefore become little more than plunder. There
was no class of feudal barons to lead the way in a gradual broadening
of the government, for the king was absolute from the first, and
'barons,' where they arose, did so because the king was temporarily
too weak to suppress them. Their fate was always the same: either
they were strong enough to set themselves up as separate kings or
they were not and were suppressed.

The worst fault of the Hindu kings seems to have been economic;
they had no idea of using their vast revenues to build productive
irrigation works, as the rulers of China, Ceylon and Iraq did.
Whatever came into their treasury was sterilised in the form of
gold and jewels, and the fabulous wealth of some of the remaining
maharajahs is even now one of the greatest masses of unproductive
capital in the world.

## THE IMPACT OF ISLAM

In theory it might have been expected that Islam and Hinduism would have been unmixable. No two religions more different could have been found and both were social systems as well as religions. To the invading Moslems the Hindus were, in the first place, not 'people of the book' and therefore required either to be slaughtered or to accept Islam; secondly, they were, above all other people, idolaters, and their temples, covered with representations of men and animals, must have seemed to pass all bounds of profanity; thirdly, they worshipped the cow, which the Moslem was accustomed to slaughter for food; and, finally, their doctrine of caste was as far removed as anything could have been from the theoretical world brotherhood of Islam.

All these apparent incompatibilities were resolved by political necessity and the usual difference, existing in all established religions, between theory and practice. Moslem jurists decided that the Hindus, who were clearly too numerous to massacre, and whose support was in fact necessary to their new rulers, might be accorded the same treatment as 'people of the book' and allowed to live their lives and practice their faith in peace, provided that they paid due tribute; Moslems themselves were not, by this time, quite the equalitarian brothers that they ought in theory to have been, and were able to take wives from among the Hindu aristocracy from the very start. So a common society, not fused, but interlocked, grew up, with the Moslems as ruling minority, but exercising their power often through Hindu vassals. When Moslem rule was at its wisest they consciously tried to minimise the difference between their subjects; when, as under Aurangzeb, they returned to a policy of ruthless anti-Hinduism, it brought about the collapse of their power.

In two important respects, the culture of Islam affected the Hindu social system, the introduction of a common language for northern India, and a further worsening in the position of women. Southern India had its own Dravidian *lingua franca*, Tamil; but until the advent of the Moslems northern India was as broken up linguistically as Europe. To this day the inhabitant of Calcutta is usually happier in Bengali and the inhabitant of Bombay in Gujerati; either may very probably speak English; but it is thanks to the Moslems that there exists, in Hindi, one vernacular tongue which is fairly well understood throughout the north. Hindi is in fact only the dialect which was commonly spoken round Delhi, the Moslem

capital, with the addition of some Persian words. It was beginning
to develop as a spoken *lingua franca* as early as the sixteenth century.
By 1600 Moslem authors in Hyderabad were using its more polished
literary form, Urdu, which contains more Persian words and is
still the favourite vernacular tongue of north-west Indian writers.

The effect of Moslem influence on the structure of the family
was not so beneficial. They brought with them the institution of
*purdah*, or the complete segregation of women. Under the rule of
*purdah*, a woman—or girl, rather—should not be *seen* by any male
eye except those of her own family after the age of eight to ten.
One of the strangest sights of northern India—for it does not hold
in the south—is the *purdah* lady on the rare moments when she has
to emerge from her house, looking like a walking tent under the
huge, stiff garment that covers her from head to toe, with a tiny
slit for the eyes (see illustration, opposite page). Unfortunately,
Hindu society had already adopted a moderate degree of seclusion
of women before the Moslem arrived, and now welcomed, or perhaps
tried to keep up with, the more extreme custom. Not only did it
make normal health and hygiene impossible, but it deprived women
still further of the chance to take any part whatever in life outside the
family and the house.

## First Impact of the West

Such was the civilisation which the first European traders found
in India at the beginning of the sixteenth century. During the
sixteenth and seventeenth centuries the influence of the Europeans
was small; but by the middle of the eighteenth, the Portuguese,
the first-comers, had given way to the British and French, and what
is perhaps the strangest episode in European history had begun.
For it is only familiarity which can blind us to the unique character
of British rule in India, an empire exercised for 150 years by a
handful of Europeans over 300 to 400 million Indians; the union
under a single system of law and administration of a whole sub-
continent which at no period in history had ever been united before;
and the use of this sub-continent as a base for the spread of European
control over the whole of the Far East, so that by the end of the
nineteenth century it was the exception rather than the rule to find
an Asiatic people which was not governed by Europeans. It was a
vast movement in world history and it came about by accident.

The British did not at any time intend to conquer India, nor in
fact did they do so. The British were merchants who had come to

10. *Purdah* ladies looking like walking tents.

trade and were anxious to maintain, with the minimum expense,
conditions that made trade possible; to do this, in an era of civil
war, they began to back one Indian faction against another, and
when those Indians whom the British backed invariably conquered
those whom they did not, it became in fact, and without the merchants
wanting it or intending it, a British conquest. What happened was
that the extending influence of the British East India Company,
whose aim continued to be trade and not the acquisition of political
or military power, coincided with two things: the collapse of the
Moghul Empire and an attempt on the part of the French to strike
at the roots of Britain's commercial wealth in India.

As a result, small forces of British-trained Indian troops came
into conflict with armies either of French-trained Indian troops or
of the troops of the various successor states, many of them 'robber
barons,' who were struggling for the inheritance of the dying
Moghul Empire. It is worth remembering that in all their victories
from Plassey onwards the Indians far outnumbered the British in
the British Indian forces. Plassey itself was won by a force of 3,000
men, mostly Madrasis, and resulted merely in the establishment
of an Indian ruler who was prepared to accept British 'advice' as
opposed to one who very definitely was not. Had the successor
states to the Moghul Empire been either competent or united,
nothing would have been easier than to drive the British out; had
great parts of the Empire not broken up into lawless and disinte-
grating fragments, it is more than possible that the British might
have inherited only the exercise of paramount power, and the
whole of India been governed, in the traditional monarchical
fashion, by Indian princes under British protection.

Thus the principle of indirect rule might have been established a hundred years earlier in the British Empire and the fatal confusion between
self-government and parliamentary democracy excluded from Asia.

Unfortunately, once the Moghul Empire had collapsed, stable
government in India, outside the sphere of British influence, simply
did not persist, and it was not till the middle of the nineteenth
century that the position was stabilised: the British Company then
exercised paramount power over the whole sub-continent: by
direct and autocratic administration over three-fifths of its area,
by treaties with the rulers of Indian states in the remaining two-fifths.
No other paramount power had ever succeeded in uniting the whole
country, yet the number of actual British involved remained
throughout infinitesimal. The unification of India had been carried

out not by the British alone, but by those Indians who had accepted British leadership and who had therefore secured for themselves the benefits of a continued and unified policy, a Western administrative and military organisation, and command of the sea. The clue to this extraordinary event lies in the chaos into which India had fallen on the collapse of the Moghul Empire. It was not the almost united India of Akbar which accepted with relief any regular administration, even that of another foreigner; it was the famine-stricken, bandit-harried remnant whom the destruction of Akbar's Empire had deprived of all protection from the rule of naked and arbitrary force. One or two contemporary judgments quoted from O'Malley's *Modern India and the West* will serve to illustrate how far things had gone: 'This year a mutinous unpaid [Moghul] army was turned loose in the sowing season to collect their pay from the villages. They drove off and sold cattle, extorted money by torture from every man who fell into their hands, and plundered the houses and shops of those who fled' (G. R. Glieg, 1830). 'It is no uncommon thing for large cities in the time of famine to lose three-fourths of their inhabitants, and the country suffers in the same degree; frequently whole districts are swept away and for years remain a jungle. I believe it may safely be asserted that through the whole country (Bengal and Bihar excepted) one acre in fifty is not cultivated' (*Asiatic Annual Register*, 1798-9). Finally, Sir William Sleeman's description of Oudh, the last Moghul kingdom, in the 1850's—a picture, incidentally, of the form of society which the Indian Mutiny was designed to restore to the rest of the country: 'The Talookdars keep the country in a perpetual state of disturbance and render life, property and industry everywhere insecure. Whenever they quarrel with each other . . . they take to indiscriminate plunder and murder over all lands not held by men of the same class; no road, town, village, or hamlet is secure from their merciless attacks; robbery and murder become their diversion—their sport; and they think no more of taking the lives of men, women and children who have offended them than those of deer and wild hog. They not only rob and murder but seize, confine, and torture all those whom they seize and suppose to have money or credit, till they ransom themselves with all that they have or can beg or borrow.' It is only with this picture in mind that one can understand the ready acceptance of British leadership by a population to whom the necessity of re-establishing order appeared for the moment to outweigh all other considerations.

E

The vivid memory of this misery and chaos, from which the acceptance of British rule had saved the country, persisted, though gradually growing fainter, throughout the nineteenth century. The Indian 'Mutiny' failed because it was a revolt, not of the progressive elements in India seeking freedom, but of the ultra-conservative who feared Western interference with their religious life, or of the robber barons who saw a last chance of recovering their arbitrary power. It failed because the last thing that the ordinary Indian wanted was a return to the conditions of pre-British India.

The political impact of the West may therefore be described as the gradual establishment, following the collapse of the Moghul Empire, of a British régime, covering not only all the original Moghul territories, but southern India as well.

Culturally the British had at first little more effect than the Moghuls had had. They were content to leave Indian institutions alone, provided the peace was not broken and the revenue came in. The outlawing of *suttee* is almost the only example of conscious social influence before the Mutiny.

Economically, the good they did by restoring the possibility of trade and industry to wide areas of ravaged countryside far outweighed the ill effect of some of the early mistakes. The most serious of these was probably the permanent land settlement in Bengal, which was a well-intentioned attempt to put an end to agricultural chaos by creating a class of landed proprietors, in order that these might, without too much delay, form an Indian 'landed gentry' who would be capable of taking over the reins of government; for the Company for many years regarded its own 'imperial' position as a temporary expedient, forced on them by the necessities of trade in troubled times and to be got rid of as soon as possible. Unfortunately, their Bengali 'landed gentry' developed into absentee landlords of the worst type and their permanent control of the revenues of the land destroyed the power of the village councils and rendered any improvement in the lot of the peasantry difficult, if not impossible.

### BIBLIOGRAPHY

*A Short History of India.* H. W. Morland and A. Chatterjee.
*British Social Life in India.* D. Kincaid.
*India and Democracy.* Sir George Schuster and G. Wint.
*Modern India and the West.* L. S. O'Malley.
*Strangers in India.* E. P. Moon.

# CHAPTER THREE

INDIA AND PAKISTAN: MODERN PROBLEMS

A DESCRIPTION of modern India and its problems centres round two topics, population and partition: of these the first is far the more important, unless one holds that partition, by re-introducing the danger of civil war, massacre and famine, may put an end to the continual increase in population.

At the beginning of the nineteenth century India was under-populated. Accurate figures are not known, but it is probable that it did not contain above 150 million people. Nowadays the first impression of the traveller, as he picks his way over a railway platform, thickly covered with sleeping forms, or tries to fight off the horde of twenty porters who are squabbling for the few annas they will earn by carrying his bag, is that there are far too many people everywhere; and for once first impressions are right. At the beginning of the nineteenth century there was more land than peasants, and landlords competed to get tenants; consequently, the peasant got decent terms. Now he cannot get land at any price, and the proportion of landless labourers to tenants or owners is rapidly rising.

The period of greatest proportional growth in population was probably the first generation after the Mutiny, when for the first time law and order reigned throughout the whole country and famine was checked. At any rate we know that in 1840 the country was still considered if anything underpopulated; by 1881 it held 248 million and was definitely beginning to be over-populated. To this overpopulation of 248 million another 90 million had been added by 1931, and between then and now, although wages had been driven so low that a landless labourer could just earn himself one meal of gruel a day and one loin-cloth a year, another 122 million were added, making the population in 1954 460 million. When one considers that this is more than three times the population of the U.S.A. crowded into an area less than half the size and with some-thing like twenty times less productivity per head, one can get some idea of the scale of Indian poverty.

According to Rousseau's simple method of judging governments, no government in history has ever been so successful as the British in India, for none has ever produced so staggering a rise in population;[1] the abolition of war and famine, together with even the most elementary control of disease, brought the death-rate down, if not to reasonable proportions, at least far below what it had been, and the nature of Indian society has always maintained the birth-rate at a figure which anywhere else would have seemed unreasonable.

11. A Bengal village market; heat, damp and crowds; not very cheerful.

This huge population, still increasing, is full of danger for India; already Bengal in 1943 has shown that the slightest breakdown in the elaborate famine-control precautions can bring back to India her traditional scourge, and there were plenty who had prophesied, even before the Bengal famine, that the population was now reaching

[1] Rousseau, *Social Contract*, Book III, Ch. 9: 'Other things being equal the government under which . . . the citizens do most increase and multiply is infallibly the best.'

a level where famine control would present a problem beyond the power of even the most competent government to tackle. Famine is not the greatest evil produced by this pressure of population. The traveller in India is sometimes surprised and horrified to see, not the light rickshaw, but heavy ox-wagons being drawn by teams of men instead of animals; or the raw materials in some factory being moved by the endless chain, not of a conveyor belt, but of women carrying baskets. The answer he will be given is that manpower is cheaper than oxen or machinery. The sheer pressure of population has depressed man to an economic position below that of his own domestic animals. Many Europeans in the East at first disliked intensely travelling in rickshaws; watching the sweating back of your fellow man, often a wizened old man old enough to be your father, as he pulls you along in your imperial chair, is a most unpleasant experience, and there can be few who have not got out and walked—at least up the hills. But the rickshaw coolie did not bless you if you had conscientious scruples against employing him. He was selling his labour in a glutted market and if you did not employ him as a 'trap-pony' he might be compelled to accept a position as a dray horse.

All students of India, whether Indians or Europeans, now realise that some answer must be found to this problem of a huge and growing population and there could be no better way of describing all the main features of modern India than in considering the answers they have suggested.

## Agriculture

### (a) General

It should never be forgotten that 90 per cent. of India's population are engaged in agriculture. Like all Far Eastern countries, India is, by numbers at least, overwhelmingly a peasant society, with a very small industrial community and an even smaller leisured class. Moreover, the pressure of increasing population is such, that, although there has been a steady increase in industrialisation, it has been swamped by the vast total increase in population, so that the *proportion* of the population dependent for their living on agriculture has actually grown in recent years. Hence one school of thought maintains that no solution to India's problems is worth considering which is not concerned primarily with the improvement of agriculture and the lot of the peasant. It is a very true statement that poverty in India is 'largely a matter of man land ratio.' Even now a direct correspondence exists between the harvest returns and the birth- and death-rates.[1] This dependence on agriculture is recognised in the fact that 90 per cent of aid under the Colombo plan so far has been devoted to agriculture, communications and rural improvement.

## (b) Rice

Of the basic foods rice accounts for one-third of the total planted area and up to 1942 one and a half million tons a year were imported from Burma. The total exports from Burma today do not reach this figure and though Indian production has increased it is scarcely keeping up with the population increase.

Rice is undoubtedly the crop best suited to Far Eastern social conditions. As a diet, it suffers from excess of starch and lack of protein, but the latter is made up with peas, beans and fish—which accounts for the importance of fisheries to, for instance, the Japanese, the Bengali and the Cambodian. Its great advantages, however, are the very high food yield per acre and the intensive cultivation it requires. It has been calculated that in ideal conditions '50 lb. of rice yields seeds for an acre and this will yield 2,500 lb. (50-fold), which with the addition of small quantities of protein will support a population of 2,000 to the square mile.' India's average yield is well below this, 784 lb. to the acre, but in good conditions, with well-irrigated land, yields of 1,500 lb. are not uncommon, and exceptionally fertile rice lands in Travancore do in fact support a population of over 2,000 to the square mile. The fact that rice cultivation is naturally co-operative and lays great demands on manpower for transplanting, we have already noticed. It is also admirably suited to cultivation in very small plots. This, from the point of view of India, is an advantage. Those who claim that the methods of production determine the social system might well consider India, where a social system utterly at variance with agricultural efficiency has long determined methods of production that have been among the chief causes of poverty. The Indian laws of inheritance, by which five sons will each inherit one-fifth of each of their father's fields, has in many departments of agriculture resulted in the continual splitting up of holdings until they are far too small to be worked economically or to support a reasonable standard of life. It is therefore an advantage of rice lands that they can be economically worked in very small plots.

[1] Radhakamal Mookherjee, *Economic Problems of Modern India.*

## (c) Cattle

Not only the Hindu social system but the Hindu religion has crippled agriculture. The sanctity of the cow—a sanctity, it should be remembered, that extends only to its life, not its condition—has meant that the over-population of cattle in India is even more marked than the human over-population. This area, half the size of the U.S.A., supports, mainly in a state of abject misery, more than one-third of the world's total population of cattle. But these cattle are virtually useless: they may not be slaughtered except by Moslems, and the preservation of the weak and diseased has meant that the average quality is very low. In fact, although India maintains 67 head of cattle per 100 acres of sown area (as compared with 15 in China and 6 in Japan) so many of these are useless crocks with their ribs sticking through their sides that the country is actually short of working bullocks. The large quantity of leather provided by their hides does not compensate for the fodder consumed.

## (d) Wheat

Wheat, which is the staple food of western Pakistan, is almost exactly the reverse of rice. It makes little demand on manpower, gives a considerably smaller yield per acre, and is most unsuitable for cultivation in small plots. It is grown mostly in newly irrigated lands in Sind and the Punjab, and consequently the wheat-growing areas had at first no over-population question to deal with. In spite of strenuous efforts, the size of the plot has tended to decrease as the population increased. The development of fresh irrigated lands has more than kept pace with this, however, and in a good year there is usually an export surplus of wheat from the north-west. Thus western Pakistan, short, as we shall see, of all other resources, is at least a food-surplus area.

## (e) Other Consumption and Export Crops

The most important remaining food crops are millets, which have always been the food of the masses in areas where rainfall was not enough for rice, sugar and oil-seeds. Production of the latter has greatly increased during this century, and we shall see that the Indian market for Indonesian sugar practically vanished in the early twentieth century. India is now herself the largest cane-sugar producing country in the world, and both in oil-seeds and tobacco supplies virtually all her own requirements with a small export surplus. In clothing also India is almost self-supporting, being the second largest raw cotton producer in the world.

The main export crops are cotton, tea, oil-seeds and jute, the fibre of a tall marsh plant which grows in very rich soils, and of which East Bengal (Pakistan) has virtually a world monopoly.

## (f) Conclusion

It will be seen therefore that on her own extremely low standard of living India can be agriculturally self-supporting. Her people can eat, wear, and fill their lamps with the products of their own soil. If the peasant's standard of living is to be raised, however, or even to be maintained with a growing population, the first question is whether the output of agriculture can be increased. This could be done either by increasing the yield per acre or by increasing the number of acres under cultivation. Let us take the second method first. Except for parts of Assam, there is no undeveloped virgin soil in India and any increase in acreage must be brought about by increased irrigation; this has undoubtedly raised standards of living in the north-west in the past, but if the irrigated land is acquired by peasant proprietors it is, within a few generations, subdivided into small plots and supporting the maximum population it can bear. The relief has therefore been temporary and standards are depressed again to subsistence level. The greatest improvement has perhaps been in Mysore, where the irrigated area was increased by 25 per cent. between 1921–31 and the greater part of the new land sown with cash, not consumption, crops. This may point to one partial solution—namely, that new lands should by law be devoted to cash or export crops, thereby increasing the wealth of the community, but not directly increasing the home-grown food supply of the cultivators, and therefore not providing so direct an incentive to increase in population.

Most of those who are prepared to be optimistic at all about this problem, however, are so in the hope, not of increased acreage, but of increased yields. This seems a very doubtful possibility. The soil of India is not as a whole fertile, and where it is fertile the yield per acre is already high. One cause of sterility is the extreme shortage of timber, which has not only had the usual effects of deforestation, but has led to a habit of burning all animal dung as a substitute for firewood, and thus starving the land of manure—a process which has now gone on for hundreds of years. In any case, Indian yields of wheat are not much below those of other great wheat-growing areas, and if it were possible to increase substantially the yield of rice by the use of improved strains, the only results, under the present social and economic system, would be that the density of population of the less fertile rice areas would grow to that which now prevails in the more fertile areas. It is not difficult to see, therefore, why, in spite of the vast preponderance of peasants among the Indian population, few experts feel that improvements in agriculture alone can save the country. They turn either to industrialisation or to drastic changes in the social system.

## INDUSTRY

### (a) Resources

India's natural resources in mineral wealth and timber are neither very great nor very well distributed. We have seen that there are considerable iron and coal deposits in Bihar, but little of the coal is of good coking quality, and apart from Bihar the whole sub-continent is very ill supplied with ascertained or developed mineral resources. In particular, Pakistan has virtually no mineral wealth at all. The shortage of timber, outside the Himalayan foothills, and its effect on soil fertility has already been noted. Hydro-electric power potential is, on the other hand, very high, and most schemes for Indian industrialisation are based on the development of this source of power, often in conjunction with irrigation.

In existing capital equipment India is not so badly off; her railway system, with 41,000 miles of track, is the fourth largest in the world and the greater part of all rolling stock and equipment is produced in Indian workshops. There is also a reserve of liquid capital whose importance is hard to estimate, owing to the economic vice of hoarding which, as we noticed in the last chapter, has been traditional among the wealthy classes of India for centuries, there is now a huge stock of gold and precious stones buried in private vaults throughout the country whose value it is almost impossible to estimate; if this hoard could be brought out and rendered productive it would be some assistance in what is likely to prove the most difficult problem facing those who put their faith in industrialisation, the shortage of capital. India's great hydro-electric resources have been developed to some extent, mainly by the Tata Company round Bombay, but still only provide approximately half a million horse-power annually out of an estimated potential of 27 million horse-power. These capital goods are by now almost entirely Indian owned. The main industries were developed in the nineteenth century by British capital, and the public debt, mainly of the most productive kind, since it arose from the purchase of the railways or the construction of irrigation works, was largely British held. From 1914 onwards, however, Indian capitalists had been buying out the British, and by 1939, to take an example, 70 per cent. of the once Scottish jute industry was Indian owned. The position with regard to the public debt was radically altered by the decision of the British Government in 1939, that Britain, rather than India, should bear the whole cost of India's participation in the war. As an unexpected result, India was defended against the Japanese at British expense, and at the end of the war had a huge credit balance instead of a debt in London. Almost the only industries left in British control are the tea-gardens of Assam, and these, like those of Ceylon, are rapidly changing hands. Let us see to what extent industry is using these resources to increase the wealth of the population.

## (b) Centralised Industry

India's two great traditional mill industries are the weaving of cotton and jute, and to these was added in the twentieth century the production of iron and steel. Jute was originally a crop grown for export, and many finished cotton articles were imported from Europe. In the middle of the nineteenth century the Scottish jute merchants set up the first mill, on the Hooghly above Calcutta, for the weaving of jute in India. The banks of the river are now lined with mills for many miles and Calcutta itself is the second largest industrial city of the Commonwealth; most of the control has, as we have seen, passed to Indian hands. The cotton industry is centred on the opposite coast around Bombay and Ahmedabad, the most favourable cotton-growing area (in the 'rain-shadow' of the Western Ghats) and the only part of India where electric power is reasonably plentiful. Cotton has been an Indian industry from the first, and the capitalists who have stood behind the Indian National Congress have mostly come from the cotton trade.

The iron and steel industry India owes to the vision of the Parsee Tata family and their British advisers. The existence of iron and coal deposits close together in Bihar and within reach of the port of Calcutta made this, India's only modern heavy industry, possible, and the lessons of war had shown the necessity of a country which aimed at independence producing its own steel. The works which

were erected at Jamshedpur, or Tatanagar, as it is more commonly
called, are the largest single iron and steel works in the Commonwealth.

Apart from these main industries, the Tata Company have also

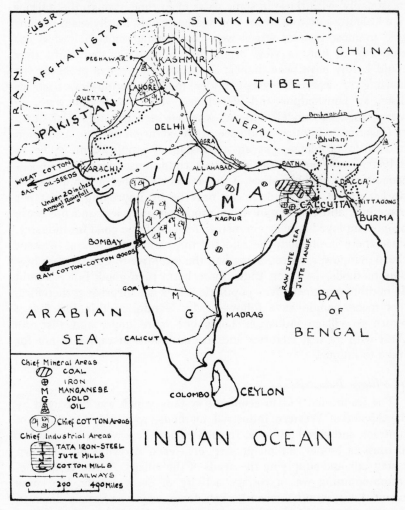

III. India and Pakistan. Distribution of Industries and Exports.

developed the manufacture of soap and oil from India's oil-seeds,
and paper and cement manufacture are sufficiently developed to
supply most indigenous needs.

Such industries do not, however, absorb in employment more

than a fraction of the population. The labour force employed in centralised industry is now about 1¾ million—not very many out of 388 million; conditions in the large mills were said to compare 'reasonably' with those in some parts of Europe, though the interior of a Calcutta jute mill in the hot weather would hardly seem reasonable to most people; wages were low (though not so low as the cultivator's), but, in view of the low output per man-shift, they could hardly have been higher; the worst feature was probably the housing of workers, except under modern employers, such as Tata, at Jamshedpur and elsewhere, where conditions were, in many respects, 'model.' No one who has seen the industrial slums of Calcutta or Bombay could see in an extension of them a solution to India's problems; yet an expansion of employment in heavy industry, *combined* with improved conditions, does not appear economically possible, since, if the standards of the Indian industrial worker are to be raised, it can only be by improving output per man-shift, and this would mean proportionately less and not more people employed in heavy industry. This might be good for industry, since there is much to be said for the view that even at present cheap manpower, by removing half the incentive to improve production methods, is doing India more harm than good: but it would do nothing to remedy over-population. It is not surprising, therefore, that many people have followed Mr. Gandhi in thinking that a return to village industries holds out more hope, and that the West with its vast factories and accumulations of capital is not for India to imitate.

## (c) Village Industries

The traditional Indian economic system, which was destroyed by the advent of Western industrial methods, was one of status, not contract, and based on caste. In each village there would be a worker in brass, a tanner, an oil-presser, etc., each carrying on his own caste trade and supplying the needs of the village. At the same time, cotton-spinning was a cottage activity of every family. To some extent this system has been broken down, as it was broken down in Europe during the Industrial Revolution, by the competition of factory-made articles. The process has not, however, gone nearly so far, and the numbers employed in village industries still far outnumber those employed in centralised industries. It is the contention of many of Gandhi's followers that, quite apart from moral considerations, India cannot afford the Westernised type of centralised industry and the elaborate communications system that it involves. They maintain, therefore, that the recovery both of light industries and of the agricultural community depends on the restoration of these industries to their proper place in the village. Such a plan seems both more feasible and more attractive than the expansion of heavy centralised industry for which India is temperamentally and climatically unsuited; but it must be remembered that it would produce goods for local consumption only and can only raise the real standard of living and meet the threat of increasing population, if it is joined with a real increase in food production or a limitation of population. We have seen that for the first as well as the second of these we are driven back on the possibility of bringing about drastic changes in the social system. The methods by which India, in the ten years since the war, has sought to bring about the necessary social and economic revolution are discussed in the last chapter.

## SOCIAL SYSTEM

To understand this we must first see what changes have taken place already under the impact of the West. Thus we shall not only get an idea of what the social system is like, but also of whether it is intrinsically likely to change with any speed.

In general, religious societies tend to be static—the truth, once revealed, does not change—and this applies to both the Moslem society of Pakistan and the Hindu society of India. On general principles there is no more likelihood of radical social change in Pakistan than there is in the states of the Arab League, and rather less in India. This view seems to be borne out by the history of social change over the last hundred years. No country could have been subjected to more revolutionary influences than were the British régime and the expansion of Western trade and industry to India, and yet the social changes, which appear at first sight very great, have been in fact comparatively superficial and limited to a very small section of society.

The casual Western visitor to India tends to think of the social changes as being very great, because he visits the larger towns or industrial centres and mixes with Westernised Indians. In reviewing the changes which have occurred in these areas, it is absolutely essential to remember what an infinitesimally small part of the population they represent; moreover, the European would be surprised if he knew how much of his Indian friend's Westernism was a polite fiction, maintained for courtesy's sake, but dropped with relief as soon as he returns to his traditional Hindu home and family. The real social dissolvent that the West has brought to India has been the fatal growth of population that it has permitted.

## (a) Effects of Western Industrialism

With these warning provisos, we may proceed to consider the effects on Indian social life of the introduction of Western economy and of the Indian Army—for the influence of Christianity, the other great Western force, has not been to modify social structure, any more than the revival of one of the purer sects of Hinduism would have been. The movement for the redemption of the untouchable, though probably started by missionaries, has become partly Hindu, partly economic, partly political. In the modern towns, then, Western methods have considerably affected both caste and the joint family. This was particularly to be expected in an era of free enterprise; the young man who got to the top of the industrial tree by his own ability, in a society governed by money economy, felt less inclined to allow caste distinctions to stand in his way. Nevertheless, caste has remained an important factor, though with a curious new dynamism injected into it, as the following quotation from Professor Mukherjee's *Economic Problems of Modern India* will show: 'Thus we find in Bombay the upper section of the Nadars looked down upon because they commenced making salt. On the other hand come the shining examples of the Chandbagar, Chaitara and Raisania, sub-castes of the Mochis, who gave up leather work and took to making spangles, paintings and electro-plating. As a result, they are treated like reputable artisans and do not touch their fellow Mochis.' One further quotation from the same work, indicating the effect of enlightened ideas on the more primitive classes, is perhaps worth quoting for its own sake: 'Many primitive peoples and castes in India still regard liquor as a necessity in marriages and other tribal ceremonies. The prohibition policy of Government has operated very harshly on them with the result that many are driven to illicit distillation, or to offer their gods a mixture of sugar and water. This indirectly promotes the decay of rites and ceremonies and adds to the general depression.'

The joint family is another institution unsuited to Western factory towns, since the community of economic interest on which it was based no longer exists; nevertheless, joint families have tended to rent whole tenement houses communally, each married son using one or two rooms within the main building. Among the professional classes its decay was witnessed by the passing in 1930 of the Gains of Learning Act, which laid down that, if anyone as a result of his education secured a lucrative post, his family were not actually legally entitled to live on his earnings, on the grounds that they had provided the education. But the necessity of passing such an Act, particularly since it never was much more than a dead letter, shows the strength of the social tradition.

## (b) The Indian Army

The Western institution which has most affected the peasantry of India has been the Indian Army. This, we have seen, has always been more Indian than British, and when the British Government took over from the East India Company in 1858 there were only 15,000 British troops in the Company's pay. During the nineteenth and twentieth centuries the normal establishment of the Indian Army was about 150,000, of which only one-third were British (roughly one British soldier to every 5,000 inhabitants); it is interesting to compare this with the Philippine Army, which was also divided between American and Philippine troops, but in equal proportions, and never numbered less than one American soldier to every 3,000 inhabitants. During the 1914–18 War, however, the strength of the Indian Army was raised to $1\frac{1}{4}$ millions and during the Second World War to over 2 millions. All these troops were, of course, raised by voluntary enlistment, not a particularly difficult thing in an over-populated and underpaid community.

It will be seen therefore that for ten years of the twentieth century the Indian Army absorbed a larger proportion of the population than the whole of centralised industry; moreover, these men came from the villages and returned to the villages; since no social changes will have any effect unless they affect village life, it is clear that the Army has been a force much more important than is generally recognised. Its value, especially during the last war, when many men were taught a trade, has been very considerable; in particular, it has done much towards breaking down the isolation of the peasant from new ideas, and, whatever its record before 1939, was undoubtedly a great influence for communal harmony from then on. Practically every young officer of the Indian Army to whom you talk will confirm that under active service conditions the elaborate distinctions of Hindu and Moslem melted away, and in the tragic outbursts that followed on partition, the record of the Army was on the whole good; since the partition both in India and Pakistan it has remained one of the great factors of stability and efficiency, and the efforts of Indian troops after the Korean truce greatly enhanced their reputation.

It appears, therefore, that the influence of the West has not been as great as might be expected and is likely to be considerably less than in the past; its main implement, the anglicised Army, has been abolished and the economic trend is away from free enterprise and more in the direction of a régime of status, which would fit in better with India's traditional social system. The outlook for radical change in the social system does not therefore look particularly hopeful. Before going on to consider briefly other remedies, however, let us take note of those changes which have been brought about by the disease itself, by a population already too big for the villages and still growing.

### (c) Effects of Over-Population

Throughout Asiatic peasant societies, as the population of the village grows beyond a certain size, plots are subdivided to a stage where they cannot support a family, and the proportion of landless labourers grows; both these things are happening alarmingly in India. Even between 1921 and 1931, the most prosperous era, the proportion of landless labourers to tenants or owners rose from 291 per 1,000 to 407 per 1,000. With the decay of village industries, there is no outlet for these unfortunates; they are reduced either to the starvation wage and status of beasts of burden, or they make their way to the towns. Once arrived in the towns there is no work for them, but, like the pitiful columns of Bengalis in 1943, they think they are less likely to starve in Calcutta than in the village. The overcrowding of the cities with people for whom there is no economic work produces a degree of squalor that looks, at least, far worse than village poverty; men sleep on the pavement or, during the monsoon, on the steps of tenements; three quarters of all families in Bombay (and that means counted families) live in one room (comparable figures for London are 6 per cent.); the wives and children, if there are wives and children, are left perforce in the village.

### FURTHER SUGGESTED SOLUTIONS

Two other suggested solutions require to be considered, emigration and the voluntary limitation of families.

The main objection to emigration is that it would provide no more than an infinitesimal temporary relief and even so could only be effected by force, by the establishment of a ruthless Indian Empire in south-east Asia; no country will willingly absorb any quantity of Indians, whose presence only serves either to exploit their own people or to depress their standard of living. There was

12. Chowringhee, the main street of Calcutta.

some apprehension among India's neighbours that some such Indian Empire might in fact be contemplated, but this has abated.

The objection to the voluntary limitation of families is that it involves a social change more radical than any that have yet been considered; moreover, even among Western nations it is only among the more highly educated classes that such practices have taken root, and to imagine them extended to 350 million villagers, whose

F

yearly income barely allows for the purchase of food and clothing, seems about as visionary as another proposal of the Indian planners: that every bullock cart in the country should be equipped with rubber tyres.

## PARTITION

Such is the social legacy of 150 years of British rule, admirable on Rousseau's principles, horribly dangerous on any others. The

13. India stakes everything on the Five Year Plans: working round the clock on the Bhakra Dam.

political legacy of Britain was a united nation where neither unity nor nationhood had existed before. Whether this legacy will be squandered depends on the outcome of the present partition of the subcontinent into India and Pakistan. This book is not primarily a political work, but it would be hopelessly unrealistic to write of social life in the Far East without attempting to describe the development of Asiatic nationalism, and in this development India has played the leading part. It is a subject that it is almost impossible to treat without incurring the accusation of prejudice, yet one which cannot be left out.

## (a) The Development of British Imperialism and Indian Nationalism

Although the great majority of Indians are illiterate and too deeply engaged in day-to-day life and in religion to form any view about politics, their whole life has been affected by the gradual resolution of the world's most intricate political problem. This problem has been how the British control of India was to be resigned to the Indians without sacrificing the unity of the country and the rule of law which had been established only under British protection.

Indian opposition to British rule as a national movement looking to the future rather than to the past did not really develop until the end of the nineteenth century, and by then it found that the British attitude to India's future had undergone a slow change. As early as 1818 Lord Hastings, the Governor-General, had written: 'A time not very remote will arrive when England will, on sound principles of policy, wish to relinquish the domination which she has gradually and unintentionally assumed over this country and from which she cannot at present recede.'

This policy was reiterated in Macaulay's famous minute of 1833, maintaining that the day on which the people of India demanded 'European institutions' would be the proudest in English history.

The agreed assumptions of British policy during the first half of the century were in fact that power must, within reasonable time, be transferred to an Indian government, but that in a country as vast and backward as India that government could not possibly be a Parliamentary democracy. Unfortunately, in all this century of British rule, no British statesman ever worked out any clear idea of what else it could be; and this, combined with their fear of Russian expansion in India, stretched out the 'reasonable time' until it seemed to the new generation of Indian nationalists to be completely unreasonable, and, for all they could see, interminable. It is clear, for instance, that the day for transferring power seemed far further off to Lord Ripon, writing in 1884, than it had to Lord Hastings in 1818.

Another factor which had an increasingly bad effect upon relations between Indians and British throughout the century cannot be passed over. In the days of the Company, the few British officials and soldiers in the country saw themselves rather as strangers and adventurers in a marvellous land. They were usually interested in all things Indian and mixed on terms of equality and respect with the leading Indians. Very few brought their wives. In the second half of the century all that was changed. The Englishman had his

own home and club life and it was natural that he should be less
anxious to share it with Indians whose womenfolk never mixed in

14. Udaipur State, the 'old India.' There are only twelve of these elephants
    left in the State.

society; much more serious was the attitude of arrogance and
superiority which a hundred years of virtually unquestioned rule
produced in not a few cases. The harm that has been done in the

past by the occasional boorish Englishman or Englishwoman who bustled 'natives' out of railway carriages or treated highly cultured Indians as inferior servants has been incalculable.

In spite of all this, the Indian nationalist reaction when it first developed was *not* anti-British, and at the first meetings of the Indian National Congress in 1885 the goodwill between British and Indians was marked. Unfortunately, the British, though prepared to proceed slowly with a transfer of certain functions of law-making, were still determined that the transfer of actual executive power to an Indian government of the parliamentary and responsible type would be madness. The Indian leaders, on the other hand, were 'progressives' who argued that if Britain found parliamentary democracy the most suitable form of government for herself, there was no reason why she should not concede it to India.

The Indian assumption that the ultimate Indian government should be a parliamentary democracy, with its corollary of majority rule, meant that the Congress finally failed to secure the participation of the Moslems. The Moslems are a minority in India, forming between a quarter and a third of the population, and they have seen from the first that the rule of the majority in India meant the rule of the Hindus. At no period in the history of India have the Moslems been subject to the Hindus and for hundreds of years they have been the ruling class: it is not difficult to see why they always opposed any solution which involved the British resigning their power to a government elected by an arithmetical majority.

In 1917 the British Government, partly influenced by the magnificent effort of India during the war, partly no doubt by the liberal democratic ideas of President Wilson, but mainly recognising their own failure to provide any alternative, accepted 'responsible government' as the object of their policy in India. In this they abandoned a policy which they had outwardly maintained for over a hundred years, even to the times of the Morley-Minto reforms of 1909, but which was, as far as Indian freedom was concerned, entirely negative.

From this time on the gradual resignation of British power continued by fits and starts, the whole situation complicated and embittered by the following factors: the British, while resigned to the ultimate change, gravely doubted, as they always had, whether a stable democratic Indian government of all India was a possibility: the Congress, dominated throughout by Mr. Gandhi, and representing predominantly the Hindus, resented the continual delays in establishing that democratic self-government to which they thought India was entitled; they therefore refused to co-operate in any gradual reforms on the grounds that these conceded to India less than the full self-government which had been promised; the Moslems, though equally determined that Indians should govern themselves, refused to accept any settlement which left them dependent on the goodwill of a Hindu majority.

### (b) Increased Moslem Distrust leading to Separatism

Throughout this period two things increased the misgivings of the Moslems: first, the growing certainty that within a comparatively short time the British actually were going, and, second, the increased popularity of totalitarian doctrines of State control, which meant that a predominantly Hindu government could now be expected to exert a far greater influence on the daily life of the ordinary Moslem than had ever been imagined in the liberal nineteenth century.

The final result was that in March, 1940, the Moslem League adopted as their policy the division of India into two states: Pakistan to contain the Moslem majority areas of the north-west and north-east, and Hindu India the rest of the country.

It would be impossible to enter into the rights and wrongs of the settlement that has now been made and whose success still hangs in the balance, but two points often made by propagandists must be eliminated. It is quite untrue to say that the Moslem League did not represent the Moslems: quite apart from the tragic violence which followed on partition, of 61 by-elections for Moslem constituencies between 1937 and 1943 the Moslem League won 47, independent Moslems 10, and Congress Moslems only 4. Secondly, it is a travesty of history to say that the British have, at any time in the last fifty years, intentionally fostered the Hindu-Moslem conflict on the principle of 'divide and rule.' No one who had any direct experience of the heartbreaking effort put by the British officials into reconciliation of the two parties could believe such nonsense for one minute. Nor were these officials being betrayed by a sinister secret service from Delhi, as some foreign commentators seem to have supposed. Even in 1942, when, in the face of what appeared an imminent Japanese invasion, almost any device to stimulate resistance might have seemed justifiable, and when it would have been easy enough to represent the Japanese to the Moslems as allies of 'Hindu traitors like Bose,' the overriding directive was that no propaganda of any sort was permissible which might lead to an increase in communal bitterness. The accusation is about as ludicrous as it would be to suggest that the British stirred up Jews against Arabs in Palestine—presumably with the object of endangering the lives of their own police. In modern administration 'Divide and Rule' is a maxim which has been replaced by 'Divide and Withdraw.'

### (c) The Final Act of Partition

Finally, at the close of the Second World War, Great Britain determined to renounce altogether her control of the Indian subcontinent. As usual, the motives were mixed. Some of those who supported the decision did so because it seemed to them plain justice, some because they feared to involve Britain in a costly and futile war, some because they felt that our commercial relations in the Far East and our friendship with the U.S.A. were being needlessly poisoned by the maintenance of a political anachronism which could at most only be prolonged for a few years. Almost everyone in the end agreed that no other policy was practicable. And so the close of the Far Eastern War saw the curious anomaly that while France and Holland, who disposed of little or no force in the Far East, were determined to recover political control of their colonial empires, Britain and America were equally determined to do the opposite with theirs. India, Burma, Ceylon and the Philippines were all offered independence. Indonesia and Indo-China were expected to come to heel and their refusal to do so led to bitter conflict.

To bring to an end British Imperial control in India was one of the most delicate political operations with which any government can have been faced. There were three main dangers:

(a) A violent outbreak of anti-European reprisals comparable with the Mutiny.

(b) Civil war. This seemed certain if Britain handed over power to a majority government at the centre which was bound to be Hindu, and possible if she herself enforced partition.

(c) A complete breakdown of the primary forces of law and order: 'not a rupee or a virgin safe between Peshawar and Calcutta.'

There was no real likelihood of the first of these once it was clear that the British Government was honest in its intentions, and, fortunately, in Lord Mountbatten they could command the services of the one man in whose integrity the leaders of south-east Asia and India had sufficient trust. The other two dangers were very real.

The first move of the British was to announce, in February, 1947, that they proposed to leave India for good, whether the great Indian parties could agree on an alternative government or not, by June, 1948, at latest, handing over either to a central or to provincial governments. It was clear from this announcement that the Moslems were in a position, if they did not wish to accept a unified central government, to enforce partition. They were determined to do this, and by April both Moslems and Hindus had accepted the partition as inevitable.

The break-up of India was a tragedy—it is to be hoped not an irretrievable one—but with no outside power to hold the country together it was unavoidable. From the British point of view, it was clearly preferable that the decision should be made by Indians themselves. This principle of the responsibility of Indians for their own future was carried right through the negotiations, which ended in the establishment of two new Dominions of the British Commonwealth, India and Pakistan, on August 15th, 1947. The speed with which the transfer was made has been criticised, but it seems more probable in fact that it was the main reason why the partition did not cost even more bloodshed than it did. Once partition was accepted as inevitable, Hindus and Moslems became increasingly incapable of working together, and a long period of waiting might well have resulted in the complete breakdown of administration at the centre, before the actual act of partition.

Unfortunately, the history of the dispute and the passions that had been inflamed meant that partition had to take place on an entirely religious and communal basis. The result fully justified every stricture Lucretius ever made against religion.

First, it meant that two provinces, the Punjab and Bengal, would have to be split up.

Second, it meant that there were bound to be large Moslem and Hindu minorities on the wrong side of the frontier.

Third, it made geographical and economic nonsense. Eastern Pakistan (parts of Assam and eastern Bengal) is separated from western Pakistan (Sind, Baluchistan, North-West Frontier Province and the Moslem half of the Punjab) by nearly 1,200 miles of Indian territory. There is no real historical or cultural connection between them except the accident of east Bengal's conversion to Islam under the Moghuls; and whereas there is every historical justification, as we saw in the last chapter, for the existence of a separate Central Asiatic state in north-west India, there is no such basis for an independent Moslem state in the north-east. Economically, the division is even more absurd: Calcutta (India) is severed from half its hinterland (Pakistan); the jute (Pakistan) is separated from the jute mills (India).

North-west Pakistan is both culturally and economically more

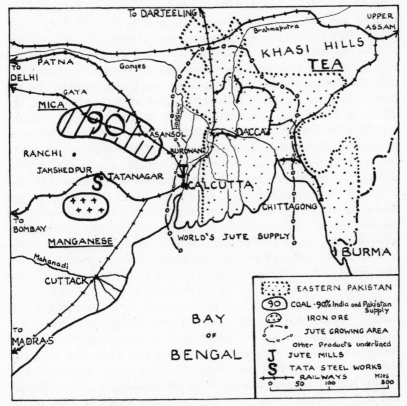

IV. Eastern Pakistan. Note the position of Jute, Iron and Coal and the lack of railways east of Calcutta.

homogeneous; it is a food-surplus area, and though sadly lacking in minerals and entirely without heavy industries, it has almost unlimited hydro-electric potential in the head-waters of the great rivers and in the huge irrigation barrages. Unfortunately, the sources of this power as well as of the vital irrigation water are in many cases commanded from Kashmir—a fact which goes far to explain the bitterness of the present struggle over the fate of that state.

The splitting of the two provinces and the existence of the minorities were not, of course, such serious disadvantages in the long run, but at the actual moment of partition they were responsible for communal riots on an increasingly serious scale. At first these were more violent in Bengal, but, partly owing to the personal influence of Mr. Gandhi, partly to the less bellicose nature of the Bengali and partly, in all probability because of their very spontaneity, they subsided as independence was achieved. August 15th was a day of sudden fraternal rejoicing in Calcutta in which all Bengalis and even Europeans took part, and after that the troubles subsided.

In the Punjab the position was made much more difficult by the existence, almost exactly around the line of demarcation, of the Sikhs—a community distinguished for warlike methods, violent anti-Moslem feelings and a particular taste for plotting and intrigue. It seems probable that the violent series of massacres which broke out at the actual time of partition was initially due to a Sikh plot, and carried out subsequently by both parties as reprisals. The loss of life in these massacres was on a scale parallel with the Bengal famine of 1943 and was due not so much to direct violence as to disease, floods and starvation attacking the columns of refugees, who, like the Arabs in Palestine, abandoned their homes in terror as soon as the news of one or two major atrocities spread abroad. The chaos and strife threatened to spread to Delhi and the United Provinces, but was checked by the firmness of the Indian Government and the arrival of troops from Madras. It is perhaps not well enough known that in the whole of the Madras presidency and India generally except the partitioned provinces the transfer of power was effected without bloodshed—a feat which the critics of Government policy had constantly predicted would be impossible.

The second danger arising from the outbreaks in the Punjab was that it would block the transfer of minorities or even of the Pakistan Government, much of which, with its files, was caught in Delhi. This difficulty was overcome by a very large scale air operation, mainly undertaken by B.O.A.C., in which over 40,000 people were flown from one Dominion to the other.

The final problem of independence, which embittered relations between the two Dominions, was the position of the Indian states which had previously recognised British paramountcy. All but two of these acceded to one or other of the two Dominions, though in one case the Indian Government used the threat of force to compel the ruler's accession.

The two exceptions were the states of Kashmir in north-west India, with a Hindu ruler and a predominantly Moslem population, and Hyderabad in Central India, with a Moslem ruler and a predominantly Hindu population. Hyderabad, with a population of sixteen million (equal to that of Burma or Siam), was a well-ruled state with an excellent record of freedom from communal strife. Economically and strategically, it is completely cut off from Pakistan

15. The bullock cart is still the principal local haulage vehicle throughout India. (An animal with a double horn, such as appears here, is extremely rare.)

and it is a pity that the Nizam did not listen to those who urged him to negotiate a voluntary accession to India. In the end India compelled his accession by force, but fortunately without any serious bloodshed or disturbance.

The future of Kashmir is still unsettled in 1956. The state borders on both Dominions and, as we noticed above, its strategic and economic importance to Pakistan is so great that she could hardly allow it to fall under the control of a potentially hostile power. Moreover, the arguments which in Hyderabad favoured

India's case favour Pakistan on balance in Kashmir. The dispute has already led to fighting on the scale of a local and undeclared war between the two Dominions.

The best hope of settlement seems to lie in the fact that in all other respects relations between India and Pakistan are already much better than anyone could have expected at the time of partition. The mere passage of time and the ultimate withdrawal from the political scene of individuals with bitter personal commitments on the Kashmir issue may solve a problem which, so far, the United Nations Organisation has been totally unable to control.

Both Pakistan and India have serious problems to face in common with the other peoples of the Far East. If the two Dominions can co-exist, however, or, even better, ultimately co-operate, they have one great advantage over all other countries of south-east Asia which they owe to the British policy of gradual transference of power. This is a body of trained administrators far more equal to their task in numbers, skill and experience than could be found, for instance, in China. It is to them that the steering of Pakistan through its incredibly difficult inaugural period is due, and they may yet prove the saviours of their country. No better proof could be found of the value of associating Indians with every stage of the government while it was still in its British stage.

## BIBLIOGRAPHY

*India in Outline.* Lady Hartog.
*Economic Problems of Modern India.* R. Mukherjee.
*The Unity of India.* Jawaharlal Nehru.
*India, a Restatement.* R. Coupland.
*India and the Indian Ocean.* K. M. Panurkar.
*Kim, Plain Tales from the Hills, etc.* R. Kipling.
*A Passage to India.* E. M. Forster.
*The Village.* Mulk Raj Anand.
*India Since Independence.* R. Trumball.
*The Communist Party of India.* M. R. Masani.
*The Horned Moon.* I. Stephens.
*India, Pakistan and the West.* P. Spear.

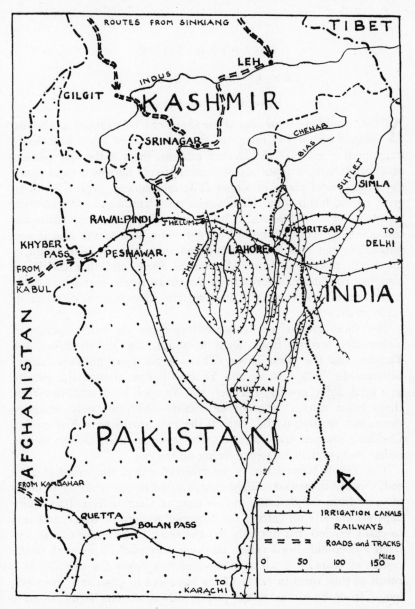

V. Western Pakistan and Kashmir. Note the course of irrigation canals.

# CHAPTER FOUR

## CHINA: THE BACKGROUND

### STRUCTURE AND CLIMATE

YOU would get some idea of the shape of China proper, excluding Manchuria, if you imagined the east coast of India immensely magnified: in place of the Deccan plateau, there is the vast plateau of Central Asia; in place of the comparatively narrow coastal plain, the wide coastal plains of China. The escarpment, broken by three great rivers, forms a barrier between the plateau and plain country running north and south. The people of plateau and plain are consequently very different. You get some idea of the size if you remember that it is further from Canton in the south to Pekin in the north than it is from Moscow to Paris, and that the River Yangtse, running eastwards from Szechuan to the sea, is navigable from Szechuan's capital, Chunking, to Shanghai, a distance of 1,400 miles.

The three great rivers whose valleys form the coastal plains of China are, reading from north to south, the Yellow River, the Yangtse and the West River. There is no great physical barrier between the Yellow River and Yangtse basins, though the climate and land differ greatly; between the Yangtse basin and the West River basin runs a range of mountains which not only separates them, but, turning north, cuts off the two provinces of Fukien and Chekiang from central China, so that these two have always lived a rather independent existence facing on the sea.

The Yellow River basin is the greatest area in the world of loess soil; this soil is formed of light dust, carried by the wind for millions of years from the deserts—in this case, of Central Asia. Its fertility depends entirely on getting the required amount of water, and it is so easily eroded that not only has the river, in its upper course, cut itself a deep cliff-lined valley, but even cart-tracks have sunk in the course of years as much as a hundred feet below the surface. As a result of this, carts in north China have had to observe a fixed axle length from the earliest times, just as railway wagons have to observe a fixed gauge.

The delta country also consists of loess soil brought down in the form of alluvial silt, and here the river is much banked up and difficult to keep within its bounds. It has in fact changed its course

several times in history, and always with great flooding and loss
of life. Until 1858 it flowed out to the south of the Shantung
peninsula, but in that year broke through the banks and carved out
a new course for itself to the sea north of the peninsula. In 1938,
on the advice of their German Staff officers, the Chinese cut the

VI. Northern China, showing the courses of the Yellow River.

dykes in order to stem the Japanese advance; the river got out of
control and turned to its old course in the south again, killing
400,000 and rendering 1,000,000 homeless. By 1947 the titanic
efforts of American engineers had succeeded in getting it back to
its old course.

As one goes north in China, the rainfall decreases and the
temperature range increases. The West River valley and Canton
area has a typical south-east Asiatic monsoon climate, very like the
Bay of Bengal, except that, not being protected from the cold

outflowing winds of winter, it has a much colder winter, and Canton is the only place at sea-level in the tropics where ice is occasionally seen. The Cantonese, therefore, live on a rice and water-buffalo agriculture such as we have described in India. The mean annual rainfall is 80 inches. Further north in the lower Yangtse valley the mean annual rainfall round Shanghai and Nanking has fallen to 50 inches, and the rain is now partly cyclonic, as in Europe.

The country was at one time well forested, and where the forest has been cut, scrub quickly grows. Rice agriculture persists, but giving way to millets almost as soon as the river is crossed. North China and the Yellow River basin have a more continental type of climate not unlike that of Canada, with a mean annual rainfall as low as 20 inches and very dry, cold winters. The effect of the monsoon is still felt, however, on the sea-coast. The country is open and park-like, with a few trees, admirably suited for the horses of the nomad conquerors who have constantly invaded north China, but so rarely extended their sway for very long to the south.

Within the boundaries of China live one-quarter of the human race.

## HISTORY AND PEOPLE

### (a) Origin and Numbers

The Chinese are a single people, numerically the greatest on earth, not because of community of race, but because of community and continuity of culture. Many races have entered that part of the world that we call China, but all have adopted the civilisation of the Chinese; and this civilisation goes back, without any break nearly as complete as the European Dark Ages, at least to the Chou Dynasty (1122–256 B.C.). Before this comes the Shang Dynasty (traditionally, 1765–1122 B.C.) and a dynasty even before that, traditionally founded in 1989 B.C. Recent archæological finds at An Yang prove that of these the Shang Dynasty was undoubtedly historical and, what is more, already a fairly mature bronze age culture, using for its written language the ancestors of the present Chinese characters. Seeing that the bones of the 'Pekin' man appear to have been one of the nearest things yet to Darwin's missing link, it is not surprising that the Chinese have always felt their own to be the world's original civilisation and have tended to look on all foreigners as barbarians.

Whether the original ancestors of the Chinese grew up on the spot or came from elsewhere, it happened so long ago that it makes no difference now. The Chinese are members of by far the world's oldest civilisation and one which for many centuries has been the world's most happy and prosperous. They cannot be expected to forget it. Professor Toynbee may well be right in suggesting that the brief history of the West may form a subject of enquiry in centuries to come for the historians of China.

Nobody knows exactly how many Chinese there are. Almost certainly there are more than 400 millions at this moment; what is more doubtful is how many there were in the past. It would be as well to put in a caution here, which refers to all population statistics in this book or any other book about the Far East.

Census figures of Far Eastern peoples are always largely guess work, because:

(a) There are often superstitious reasons for concealing deaths or births. The Chinese, for instance, fear that evil spirits may hear of the child's existence and carry it away. (For this reason, it is also polite to say 'horrid baby' and not 'nice baby' in China, since this discourages any evil spirits who may be within earshot.) It is not only evil spirits who are feared. Sometimes it is the government. One Hong Kong census was badly held up because the rumour had gone round that a new bridge was to be built and that a baby would have to be sunk at the base of each pier. The census, of course, was believed to be intended to ascertain the whereabouts of available babies.

(b) Villagers often fear (certainly with justification in the past) that a census is taken only for purposes of taxation, military service or forced labour. They dislike all these things and therefore avoid the census.

(c) Finally, and this is most important, even where census-taking is modernised, the original figures, on which all the complicated later calculations are made, are usually furnished by a semi-literate old village policeman or headman, who has everything to gain and nothing to lose by simply making them up.

Even in a modern census, therefore, the possibilities of cumulative error are enormous. In ancient censuses, which were certainly taken in China, the Emperor was really concerned to know, not how many people there were in each province, but how many soldiers or forced labourers or families owning property to tax. It must be assumed therefore that any ancient census will be very inaccurate, probably an underestimate, except when it is based on boasting for military propaganda.

G

The traditional view of China's population is that it fluctuated between 60 and 100 millions from the establishment of the Empire until the Ming Dynasty (1644), and then began to grow by leaps and bounds until it reached 300 or 400 millions in the nineteenth century. This seems extraordinarily improbable. We know that the Indian population made such a leap in the nineteenth century, but there was no sudden imposition of law and order to account for such a population increase in China. Neither the conditions nor the character of the Chinese changed radically during the Ming or Manchu periods and the increase of cultivated land between 1661 and 1833 was probably not more than 35 per cent.; why, then, should the population have rocketed up? It is universally admitted that the Chinese over centuries have changed very little in character, and one of their outstanding characteristics is their boundless vitality. They never leave any slack to take up. Visitors to China have often noticed that every receptacle, basket, cart or tramcar is filled to capacity and just over capacity. Every coolie is expected to carry a little more than he can really manage; every father brings up a family a little larger than his economic resources will really allow. Surely in view of this it is much more reasonable to assume, as Mr. Jaffe in a recent article in *Population Studies* suggests, that the land of China has usually contained just a few more than its agricultural capacity could support. When a dynasty collapsed, the resultant battle, murder and sudden death reduced the population, which grew again as soon as a new dynasty restored order. This would mean revising very considerably upwards previous estimates of Chinese population under the earlier dynasties; and this, in turn, would help to account for the fact that all invaders, such as the Mongols and Manchus, have been racially swallowed up by the vast mass of the conquered.

Finally, in considering the numbers and distribution of the Chinese people, we must remember that the Empire expanded and contracted very greatly under different dynasties. Two and a half million square miles under the great Han Empire, which was contemporary with the Roman, it had shrunk to little more than 1 million under the Sung (A.D. 960–1279), was one and a half million under the Ming and reached over four and a half million under the Manchus (A.D. 1644–1911).

Yet this expansion and contraction has left less impression on the Far East of to-day than might have been expected, since, China being a culture and not a country, areas which had once accepted

16. China: Kwangsi Province. Rice terraces in the Lu country, the result of centuries of work.

Chinese culture did not abandon it, though for many centuries they were outside the control of the Chinese Emperor. It is impossible to overestimate the importance to the Far East as a whole of this persisting civilisation, which, apart from its own territories and Manchuria, founded the cultures of Korea, Tibet, Japan and Tongking, and profoundly modifies to this day those of all surrounding countries. From the point of view of world history, the last 200 years may come to be regarded as a freak period, when for a short interval China was not one of the great leaders of civilisation.

### (b) *Political History to the Fall of the Han Empire* (A.D. 221)

The essential political features of this continuous civilisation were the position of the emperor, the unified centralised State and the educated bureaucracy. Chinese civilisation did not in fact display all these three features continuously from 1122 B.C. to A.D. 1911, but by a process of reinterpreting the past the Chinese scholars of the last 1,000 years had persuaded themselves that it did. Since what matters for understanding the present-day Chinese is not so much what actually happened 2,000 years ago as what they and their immediate forbears believe happened, it is this reinterpretation and not the historical facts which is important. If in point of fact China was a unified Confucian Empire for a thousand years up to 1900, that is long enough in all conscience, and the fact that the unification and Confucianism of the 1,000 years before that were somewhat imperfect may be neglected.

Chinese civilisation began in the north on the upper reaches of the Yellow River. One of the oldest and most profound of Chinese beliefs is the interpretation of the world as the interaction of the Yin and the Yang, the positive and the negative factors, Heaven and Earth; and the Emperor seems to have been, like so many primitive kings, in the first place a priest king. It was he and he only who could perform the sacrifices necessary to secure that harmony between the interacting forces of Nature which would ensure the crops. During the whole so-called Chou Dynasty the Emperor was little more than this; the period is called feudal, and treated by some orthodox Chinese historians as if it were a break down of the unified Empire. It is more probable that the establishment of a unified state by the Ch'in in 221 B.C. was in fact an innovation and that the central power of the Emperor, if it existed at all before that, was purely religious or magical.

The Ch'in Empire certainly was a centralised State, accepted

probably for the same reasons as the Empire of Augustus Cæsar—
sheer exhaustion. Its rigid totalitarianism was modified by the Han
Dynasty, who succeeded in 206 B.C. and ruled with a short interval
until A.D. 221. It was during the Han Empire that the political
basis of Chinese culture was laid, and so firmly laid as never to
be forgotten. They took over the position of the Emperor as sovereign
of all Chinese and representative of the people in all their relations
with 'Heaven'; from the time of the Han onwards this was never
forgotten, and to all Chinese—that is, all who accepted Chinese
culture—the normal organisation of the world consisted of the
Middle Kingdom—that is, the Chinese Empire—and outside that a
ring of more or less, but usually less, civilised barbarians. Any other
state of affairs was a temporary breakdown. The Han also introduced
the educated bureaucracy, the governing class, who took the place
of the feudal nobles; it is even possible that it was they who introduced the system of selecting the members of this civil service by
means of an examination in the Confucian classics, in which case
the examination, when it was finally abolished, was nearly 2,000
years old.

This Han Empire, which moulded China more effectively than
the Roman Empire moulded Europe, was almost exactly contemporary with the Roman and came very near to establishing direct
contact. In A.D. 97, after Pan Chao's conquest of Central Asia by
methods very like those of the East India Company in eighteenth-
century India, a Chinese army advanced unopposed to the shores
of the Caspian. They had made contact with the Bactrian Greek
successors to Alexander the Great, and now only the narrow strip
of Parthian territory separated them from the Roman provinces;
but the Parthians, fearing perhaps an alliance which would have
eliminated themselves, deceived the Chinese envoys about the route,
and the direct contact was never made. It seems probable that the
men whom the Chinese Court supposed in A.D. 166 to be ambassa-
dors from the Roman Emperor An Tun (Marcus Aurelius Antoninus)
were no more than Greek merchants, who succeeded in conveying
an exalted idea of their own importance. It is difficult not to feel
of the two empires, as one sometimes does of two friends, 'What a
pity they never met'; and that the Confucian Empire of the Han
would have found more in common with the Stoic society of the
Antonines than China has found in any Western civilisation since,
so that the needless distinction between East and West might never
have arisen. Even if they had met, however, it would have been so

much at the extreme limits of their influence that it is doubtful
whether they would have affected each other at all. Both empires,
after all, were soon engaged in building walls around themselves to
preserve the area that they had got.

The Han Empire had much the same problems to face as the
Roman: palace intrigue, currency depreciation, the barbarians; the
principle of legitimacy saved them from that constant violent
usurpation by generals which beset Rome, but the intrigues of the
various empresses' families disturbed the peace of the Empire and
once actually unseated the dynasty. In intrigue the eunuchs played
the part of the Imperial freedmen. For defence against the northern
barbarians, the Han Emperors built the Great Wall (started in the
Chin Dynasty), but the cost of garrison and maintenance was a
continual drain on the economy of the country. The dynasty fell
at the beginning of the third century A.D., because the emperors
had come to rely more and more on the palace eunuchs and grown
estranged from the people and Army. When at last an open clash
between the Army and the Palace came, the Army found that once
the sanctity of the Emperor was discounted, military force decided
everything, and the Empire relapsed into a confusion of warring
generals, from which it was prevented from recovery by the invasion
of the Tartar barbarians.

These barbarians, however, did not destroy the work of the
Han to anything like the extent that their fellow barbarians did that
of the Romans. The Tartars ruled over north China much as the
Goths ruled over the Roman Empire, imitating and acquiring their
subjects' civilisation in the process. South China was not conquered
by them at all, since it was always protected against the type of
barbarian who invaded China by the fact that its climate and terrain
were hopelessly unsuitable either for the horses or men of the
north. It was in fact the flight of the Chinese from the north before
the Tartars which began the gradual shift southwards of the centre
of Chinese culture.

This period of 400 years' confusion following the collapse of the
Han was not nearly so serious a break as the European Dark Ages.
It is, like the Dark Ages, a heroic age in Chinese literature, and no
all-embracing Confucian state existed; but the continuity of culture
was not seriously affected. The political system had temporarily
broken down, but the social and religious life went on; it is a
convenient moment therefore to consider what this social and
religious system was. The clue to it lies in the persisting influence

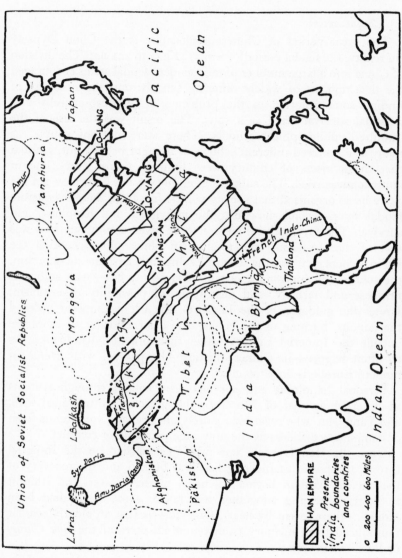

VII. The Han Empire at its greatest extent.

of Confucianism on the small, highly educated ruling class who formed the professional Civil Service.

## (c) Confucianism

The great period of Chinese philosophy is the Chou Dynasty (in reality, the feudal period), from 1122 B.C. to 221 B.C. The division of China into a large number of independent feudal states encouraged the development of widely differing schools; and the necessity of finding some solution to the problems of political anarchy and personal survival acted as a spur. The result was the rise of the 'hundred' philosophical schools. There were not, of course, as many as a hundred different schools of thought in fact, but, granted that the subjects of enquiry were limited, almost every line of approach was tried. The subjects of enquiry were, first, how can the State be so organised that society will be free from these everlasting feudal wars; second, how can the individual find happiness and survival. The first political answer to be given a complete trial was that of the 'Legalists,' the totalitarian philosophic school of the Ch'in autocracy; it was the scientific solution of absolute dictatorship, the solution of imposing a system of law—any law—with sufficient firmness and ferocity, and destroying all possibility of criticism. Under the guidance of the Legalists, the Ch'in Emperor ordered the famous 'burning of the books,' the destruction of all literature outside the Imperial Library, other than practical handbooks. As so often happens in Chinese history, the parallel with events in modern Europe is only too clear.

Personal happiness and survival were sought through systems as different as that of Mo Tzu, the preacher of universal love, and Yang Chu, who regarded a purely physical and voluptuous form of complete selfishness as the only sane principle of conduct.

Once the Han Dynasty was firmly established on the Imperial throne, the power of the Legalists was broken and the recovery of the ancient wisdom began. As usual in these cases, the attempt to destroy learning altogether had failed: some books had been hidden, others learnt by heart. One story is that an elderly scholar reproduced from memory twenty-nine chapters of the *Shu Ching*, or Book of History.

The scholars who edited the Chinese classics under the Han Dynasty were all followers of Confucius, and for 2,000 years his system was the official guiding principle of Chinese conduct. Confucius had lived from 551 to 479 B.C., nearly contemporary with

Buddha and a little earlier than Plato. His tomb is still tended by his lineal descendants, an amazing tribute to the continuity of Chinese life and the doctrines of filial piety which he taught. He was a philosopher or statesman of the feudal state of Lu, and interested therefore in the problems of society even more than of personal survival.

The great principles of Confucius' teaching were the existence of permanent moral standards and the effect of example. In his insistence on the right use of terms and on morality, he is very like Socrates; and in his practical teaching of ethics, by describing the character and behaviour of the Chun Tzu, very like Aristotle. The term *chun tzu* has been variously translated as the 'gentleman' or the 'superior man'; Aristotle's 'magnanimous man' or the Stoics' 'philosopher' are obvious parallels. One must remember, however, that the *chun tzu* was originally the feudal 'noble,' and when Confucius himself wrote of him, he was referring back to a golden age when 'nobles' behaved like 'nobles,' a doctrine very like that of our own feudal *noblesse oblige*.

The conception of the *chun tzu* as a man distinguished by his moral and intellectual qualities alone is a reinterpretation by the Han scholars, when men had practically forgotten what a feudal age was like. The *chun tzu* as we find him described in the Confucian texts is an ethical character, a rationalist, unswayed by emotion, modest, 'demanding of himself, not of others,' 'serene, not proud,' a practiser of what he preaches. Above all, he is a great observer of *li. Li* in later Chinese came to mean almost entirely 'ceremonies,' but it is probable that in Confucius' time its meaning of 'unwritten law' or 'convention' was just as strong; Lin Yu-Tang even translates it 'reason.' The change of meaning has led some people to over-estimate the importance Confucius attached to ritual for its own sake.

In addition to these purely rational qualities, we are told by Mencius, the greatest of Confucius' disciples, that the *chun tzu* will be affected also by *ching*. The exact meaning of *ching* is perhaps best explained by quoting a story with which Mencius illustrates it: this will also serve as an example of the method of teaching by illustration which the Confucian school always used. Mencius was asked:

'If the Emperor's father committed murder, what should the Chief Justice do?'

'Have him arrested.'

'Would not the Emperor forbid this?'

'How could he? The arrest would be just and lawful.'

'Then what would the Emperor do?'

'He would regard the abandonment of the Empire like throwing away an old shoe. He would secretly run away, with his old father on his back, to live along the sea-coast cheerfully and happily all the rest of his life.'

In doing this, the Emperor would be showing filial piety and moved by *ching*. Most people would agree that it is a considerable improvement on the conduct likely to have been recommended by the Stoic philosopher, who would have handed over his old father to the executioner with all the gusto of a Brutus or Torquatus executing his own sons.

To Westerners bred upon Aristotle, all this seems quite familiar; not so the importance laid on example. From a personal point of view, this is easy enough to understand: all great ethical systems have emphasised the importance of imitating the behaviour of the Master, and the Confucian combination of this with 'not letting down' one's ancestors is easy to understand. What seems much stranger is the view that the Emperor, by his own example, by leading the life of a *chun tzu*, could *ensure* that the State would be well governed. Two quotations from Confucius' *Analects* will illustrate this view, by which his admirable moral teaching was extended to provide a solution for the political problems:

'When the ruler excels as a father, a son and a brother, then the people imitate him.'

'He who exercises government by means of virtue may be compared to the polar star, which keeps its place while all stars turn towards it.'

The experience of our own times must inevitably make us ask how a political doctrine based on the assumption that 'we needs must love the highest when we see it' could persist for twenty years, much less 2,000. The answer is, of course, that it didn't. Like most ethical systems, it was revered in principle and modified in practice. This is shown very clearly by the famous debate between the Confucian scholars and the Han Emperor's minister, San Hung-Yang. The scholars found the iron and salt monopolies, imposed to defray the expenses of defence on the Great Wall, oppressive, which they were. San Hung-Yang asked them how else they proposed to defend the Empire from the barbarians. 'Your Majesty has but to manifest your virtue to them . . .' the scholars began. It has a very modern ring, and fortunately for China the Emperor paid no attention.

The explanation of the continued political favour which Confucianism enjoyed is that it suited the Emperors, their court and the bureaucracy very well: for the practical administration of the armies and the law, it never really supplanted the savage doctrines of Legalism; in the hearts of the people, it was soon supplanted by Taoism and Buddhism: but as a code of conduct for the upper class it had immense influence, particularly because it provided their dynasty and all succeeding dynasties with a principle of legitimacy which the Chous had enjoyed by right of descent.

It is often said that Confucianism is not a religion. It would be truer to say that it is an impersonal one, for it is the approval of Heaven which guarantees the code of the *chun tzu*; it is the approval of Heaven also which is secured by the emperor's personal virtue, and which by some almost magical power will therefore produce harmony and prosperity in the State. It is easy to see here the influence of the earliest mythology of the Yin and Yang and of the position of the Emperor as the high priest and son of Heaven. The Han and all subsequent Chinese dynasties justified themselves by claiming for themselves 'the mandate of Heaven,' and historians explained their fall by saying that the dynasty had lost the mandate of Heaven. There was no such thing as a successful usurper. Heaven transferred its mandate.

Confucianism thus suited the Empire very well: it based the ruler's claim to his title on the virtue of his administration and it taught the servants of the State loyalty and self effacement. Although it may not have penetrated to the uneducated, its effect through the medium of the Civil Service examinations was very wide among the upper classes, and constantly increased with the number of candidates, successful or unsuccessful. Its exponents have not always practised what they preached, any more than the exponents of any other system, and under the later dynasties of the Empire its dead hand stifled change. But it moulded the most enduring civilisation that the world has yet known.

### (d) Taoism

The second great school to arise during the feudal period was Taoism. Its followers claim as their founder Lao-tse, who is supposed to have been a contemporary of Confucius, and they have made up many imaginary dialogues between the two. This is almost certainly myth, and Lao-tse, if he ever existed at all, lived considerably later than Confucius. The *Tao Te Chung*, the main Taoist classic, dates from not earlier than 240 B.C., and in many ways Taoism marks a reaction from the teaching of Confucius and is therefore more likely to have developed after him.

It is an anarchic, personal, mystical type of belief, a typical 'escape' into the isolated personal life, almost inevitable in times of such social stress as the feudal period. In so far as it had a theory of the State and society to offer, this was the doctrine of 'government by non-action.' The early Taoists, like the early and Hinayana Buddhists, had little faith in the virtues of teaching or organised religion, and believed that it was the business of the sage to find the 'Way' or '*tao*' himself and let the rest of the world go by.

Such a doctrine in its pure form could never have found wide acceptance anywhere, but there were elements in Taoism, when popularised, which made a great appeal to the Chinese. As Confucianism grew more and more conventional, so Taoism provided an outlet for the recurrent individualism of the Chinese, and many of the great poets and artists of the T'ang and Sung periods, to say nothing of the delightfully drunken philosophers, were Taoist at heart. More important still, as Confucianism remained rigidly rational, Taoism absorbed much of the magic element in the religious consciousness of the Chinese and so gained the devotion of the mass of the people. When the Confucian order of the Han Dynasty collapsed in A.D. 221 and let in four centuries of administrative chaos, it led to a great spread of Taoism and the organisation of the cult as a predominantly magical religion for the non-intellectual. It is this development of Taoism—intimately connected with alchemy, as such religious cults also were in Europe—that has not unnaturally attracted the attention of such thinkers as Dr. Jung. Historically, it has lost much of its influence as a 'people's religion' to Chinese Buddhism.

### (e) *Buddhism*

Buddhism was introduced into China in A.D. 65, when the Han Court regarded it as an interesting foreign curiosity. With the collapse of the Han, it rapidly overran the whole Empire, and by A.D. 500 the common people everywhere are said to have embraced it—presumably along with a large dose of Taoism and lip service to Confucian principles. Like most other invaders of China, Buddhism was gradually absorbed and modified by the Chinese, until it became far more Chinese than Buddhist. In the first place, they accepted it in its Mahayana or Greater Vehicle form. Mahayana Buddhism turned the Gautama's lofty and impersonal philosophy into an emotional, personal religion by the doctrine of the Bodhisattva, the individual who, on the point of attaining Nirvana or impersonality, turns back in pity for all living things and postpones his Buddhahood until by his labours he can raise all of them to his own state of bliss. Such individuals could and did become the objects of prayers and cults of the very type that Gautama Buddha had denounced as vain; they were credited with miracles and represented in sculpture. It is clear that once Buddhism had taken this step, the development of an almost unlimited number of schools became possible. Of these the Chinese took particularly to three—Zen Buddhism, True Word Buddhism and Amida Buddhism. Zen Buddhism is the ascetic and mystic school which, although born in China, has a far wider following and development in Japan, and will therefore be described in a later chapter. 'True Word' is really an Indian form of Buddhism, preserving much of Hindu magic, and based on the mantras, which are in essence magic spells; it has made a considerable contribution to Chinese superstition and still survives. There were also one or two Chinese schools which showed a typically Chinese attempt to combine Buddhism with Confucianism.

The really native Chinese version of Buddhism, however, and the one which, for the common people, swept all others from the board, was Amida Buddhism. This quite frankly replaces Gautama in the hierarchy by a mythical Bodhisattva called Amida Buddha, supposed to have been born from a lotus in the 'Western Heaven.' Through his compassion, the degenerate mortals of later days, who could no longer save themselves by meditation, might yet be raised to Paradise. From the simple, all that was required was to call on the name of Amida; for the more educated and the more devout there was the whole process of Mahayana Buddhism with its doctrines of service to mankind, its monasteries and its contemplatives, which remind us so much at times of the medieval Church in the West. What is most noticeable of all, perhaps, in the Chinese attitude to religion is the ease with which they seem always to have been able to combine belief in two or three religions at once. No Far Eastern religion, except perhaps the Nichiren Buddhist sect in Japan, has ever been exclusive as Christianity and Islam are exclusive, but even among Orientals the Chinese are remarkable for their broad-mindedness. I should think it probable that the average Chinese of the Sung or T'ang Dynasties reverenced Confucius and believed simultaneously in the primitive sympathetic magic of the Yin and Yang, Taoism, Buddhism, and even possibly under the T'ang Dynasty, Nestorian Christianity; his modern descendant is not entirely different.

## (f) The Empire, A.D. 618–1911

The centralised Empire was restored in A.D. 618 as a result of the work of the great T'ang Tai-Tsung, and his dynasty was known as the T'ang. From that year until 1911 the continuity of the centralised Chinese Empire was real, not a historical fiction; there were times when it fell under alien domination, there were periods of confusion on the fall of one dynasty before another was firmly established, but the Empire lived on. The life of any one of the great dynasties equals in length the life of most European states. The T'ang reigned from A.D. 618 to A.D. 907, roughly 300 years, the Sung from A.D. 960 to A.D. 1280, rather longer, and the Ming from 1368 to 1644, a few years less. The Manchus, keeping to this easily remembered three hundred year period, ruled China from 1644 to 1911.

T'ang Dynasty China was undoubtedly the most prosperous and civilised country of its time; Europeans, compared with T'ang Chinese, were hopeless barbarians and Charlemagne's Empire a league of savage tribes. Indeed it was not until the late eighteenth century, after the establishment of the Manchu Empire, that Europe began to leave China behind in organisation and technology. One result of the establishment of the T'ang Dynasty was, as might have been expected, a recovery of Confucianism at the expense of Buddhism and Taoism, and this was carried on until the next dynasty, the Sung. Nestorian Christianity was introduced under the T'ang and flourished for about two hundred years, but compromised too far with Buddhism and made the mistake of never translating the Scriptures into Chinese. It ultimately died out under sudden though not very severe persecution.

Both the T'ang and Sung periods were years of magnificent artistic achievement in painting, porcelain and poetry. Perhaps the Sung were too artistic and philosophic, perhaps the hordes of Genghis Khan and his successors were a natural force that not even a warlike Empire could have stood up to; whatever the reason, in 1280 China, after putting up a longer defence than any previous

17. A vase of Tzu-chou ware (Sung Dynasty). *From the collection of Mrs. Walter Sedgwick.*

victim, succumbed to the Mongols. For rather less than a hundred
years the Empire was governed as a Mongol Khanate, but there
must have been many regions where the Mongol writ never ran.
The period is unusually well known to Europeans because the
ravages of Genghis Khan had the curious effect of opening up the
way from Europe to the East, so that it is from this period that
the accounts of Marco Polo date; and to readers of English poetry
because the Mongol ruler whom Marco Polo found on the throne
was Kubla Khan. Northern China, particularly the plateau provinces
of inland China, never recovered from the Mongol devastations,
but once again the south received an influx of refugees, including
the people now known as Hakka, who live round Canton. Under
Kubla Khan the Mongol-Chinese Empire acquired a temporary
suzerainty over many bordering states and attempted the conquest
of Japan.

The Mongols were finally driven out in 1368 by a rising of the
Chinese under a 'war-lord,' originally of low birth, who founded
the Ming Dynasty. In some directions the Chinese people seem to
have begun to show signs of exhaustion during this period. There
was little real development in the arts of painting or porcelain, and
an emphasis on the maintenance of technical standards which is
rather unoriginal. In the political sphere they were for the first time
threatened by Japan, and the long war with the Shogun Hideyoshi
over Korea did much to exhaust the Empire and ultimately let in
the Manchus. On the other hand, there was a great new development
in the drama and in prose writing, and China under the Ming
dynasty was still probably the most civilised country in the world.

It is from the Ming Dynasty that the first Chinese contacts with
European traders date, and they found these—often no very fitting
representatives of Western culture—so barbarous and unreliable
in their conduct that they were confirmed in their view that all
foreigners were inferiors. The Chinese term for Europeans—Sea
Devils—was fully earned by some of the freebooting Portuguese,
Dutch and British traders.

The Ming Dynasty unwisely transferred the capital to Pekin in
the north, away from the Yangtse valley, which had become by
now the real centre of the Empire. It finally fell through internal
dissensions, and it was not until it had done so that the Manchus,
the non-Chinese tribes of Manchuria, who had been allied with the
rebel general, crossed the few miles from the frontier and occupied
Pekin. In the north it was an almost accidental conquest with no

18. The Ha-ta-men Gate, Pekin. Pekin is one of the great architectural treasure-houses of the world. The photograph dates from the beginning of this century.

H

resistance. Even so, they did not complete the conquest of the
south until 1682. The Manchu invasion, like previous inroads from
the north, drove a large number of refugees before it, and it is to
these that we owe the colonisation of Formosa, up till then a part
of the Indonesian culture. The island was always neglected by
Chinese central governments until its cession to Japan in 1895.
Although its inhabitants are now 94 per cent. Chinese by race, they
have never submitted very happily to Chinese control, and the
Chinese proverb about them 'In Formosa every three years a
disorder and every five years a rebellion' was almost immediately
fulfilled when the island was returned to China in 1945.

The Manchus, having occupied the north peaceably, by invitation
as it were, and conquered the south after a fierce war, not unnaturally
favoured the north. Unlike all other conquerors in China, they
determined not to allow themselves to be assimilated, and so forbade
Manchus to adopt any professions other than government and war.
They maintained, of course, all the machinery of the Chinese
State, including the bureaucracy and the entrance by examination,
but they reserved half the posts for Manchus. The Manchus were a
tiny minority of the people, so that this meant that at first at least
any Manchu, however stupid, could be almost certain of getting in;
this led to a progressive deterioration in the standard of government.

The decline of the Manchu Empire from the eighteenth to the
nineteenth centuries is easy to understand therefore: it was both a
relative decline compared with the amazing technical advances of
Europe and later Japan, and a genuine decline measured by internal
standards. What is harder to understand is why no earlier rising,
particularly of the southern Chinese, drove this decaying minority
from the throne, as the Mongols had been driven. The only people
who came near doing this were the Taiping Christians, and they
were thwarted largely by the influence of the Western powers, who
had by that time already started in China their disastrous policy of
bolstering up any *status quo*, however corrupt. It has been suggested
that the explanation of this acquiescence lies in a gradual exhaustion
of the Chinese nation. One other possibility is that the rule of the
Manchus, who had admitted a good proportion of Chinese followers
called 'Banner Men' to their ranks from the first, was so diluted by
the nineteenth century as to be scarcely perceptible: whatever the
rules for entry to the Civil Service, they must have been gradually
ignored, for this imperial race held by 1877 only 117 out of a total
of 1,757 major government posts, no governor-generalships and

only two out of fifteen governorships. Apart from the Court of Pekin, it looks as if the Chinese had, as usual, led their captors captive.

The end of the Manchu Dynasty and the Revolution of 1911 take us into modern China and must be left for the next chapter. Meanwhile, let us see what were the enduring characteristics of the Chinese and of Chinese society moulded by such an environment.

(g) *The Enduring Character of Chinese Society:*

(1) *Social Structure.* The social structure of China has endured so long that it cannot have helped modifying the character of those who built it. Whether Confucianism is in accordance with the 'natural' character of the Chinese or was introduced in order to curb their excessive natural individualism scarcely matters now: the point is that they have lived so long under a system based on Confucian principles that they have inevitably absorbed much of his teaching with their 'way of life.'

The exceptional thing about the social structure of China is its stability, and it is interesting that this was achieved mainly by the same method, though without the 'scientific' technique as was used by the designers of Aldous Huxley's *Brave New World*—the education of each individual to accept, without question, his appointed and traditional place in the social order. Within the limited range of the village and the family the organisation of this accepted system was very detailed: in every old-fashioned Chinese house there is still a traditional father's place, mother's place, children's place and visitor's place. No one would think of usurping someone else's place. And in the village much the same holds true.

To this extent, Chinese society therefore has always been governed by strict rules. These are not the rules, however, of an autocratic state, but of a traditional society. The distances involved made it inevitable that the central government should leave the villages to be mainly self-governing, and the emphasis which Confucius laid on relationships *within* the family ensured that in each village the family should be the unit. In fact the central government never expected to exercise more control over the provinces, nor the provinces more control over the villages, than the minimum required to ensure that taxes were paid to the Treasury, and soldiers, when necessary, produced for the Army. To this extent the Taoist principle of government by inaction was observed willy-nilly.

Consequently, the official class was small and concerned only with extracting the men or the money that the government required;

the vast unofficial masses accepted their obligation to produce these as due service from people in their place. They accepted it the more readily perhaps because China under the Empire really was a classless society, in the sense that there were no hereditary class distinctions. Anyone could, by passing the examinations, enter the official governing class, and the cost of the necessary education was not so high as to exclude the son of poor parents. It was the failure to accept this feature of Chinese life that wrecked the Chinese system when adopted in Japan.

(2) *Family Structure.* For more than 2,000 years, therefore, the family has been the real centre of Chinese social life. Confucius himself considered relationships within the family far more important than any outside tie, and in this respect at least all China has agreed with him. It is, of course, true that when he practically reduced all virtue to filial piety, he at the same time expanded filial piety to include all virtue, by indicating that the man who was actuated by true filial piety would do nothing shameful, lest it bring dishonour on his parents. The whole ethical code is included, therefore, but the mainspring of action is reverence for ancestors on earth and not a Father in Heaven.

All Chinese want to marry and have families as soon as possible, not merely in order that their descendants should keep up the ancestral worship, but because it is in family life that all the sources of happiness they know are found. It is a patriarchal, close-knit and conventional family, where the young are kept very much in their place.

The position of women is definitely lower than that of men; and under the Manchus their feet were bound so tightly from birth to keep them small that they suffered agonies of pain in childhood and grew up incapable of walking more than a few yards. It was supposed to give them a toddling gait which was very captivating, but it was even more injurious to health than the Indian *purdah*. Age, on the other hand, was revered in China as it has never been anywhere else, and this reverence meant that by the time a woman reached middle life and was the mother of a family, her position within the house was not a bad one. Outside the home she had none; nor was she expected to complain if her husband took second wives or concubines, though she very frequently did. Two points will serve to illustrate the relative positions of members of the family: the young wife arriving in her husband's family is expected to worship his ancestors and not her own; and a traditional young Chinese would consider it good manners to fetch a footstool for his mother, but degrading to do the same for his wife. Half outside and half inside the family circle are friends: and the Chinese, following Confucius and agreeing with Aristotle, attach a great deal of importance to friendship.

(3) *Individual Characteristics.* The most noticeable characteristic of the modern Chinese to those who, crossing the 'Hump' in the late war, saw them first after some experience of the Indians, is their cheerfulness. No doubt they have no business to be happy under the conditions in which they live, but, unlike the northern Indians, who look on the whole justifiably sulky and miserable, the Chinese radiate practical good sense and happiness. It is relatively certain that this 'feet on the ground,' matter-of-fact good sense has been a Chinese characteristic as long as human memory goes back; and it seems likely that happiness has. Those psychologists who emphasise the great importance of a safe and predictable background for the young child should draw great encouragement from the rarity of neurotic complaints among the Chinese.

In so far as one may generalise at all about a whole race, the Chinese know where they are and like it: they enjoy life on earth, and because they enjoy it as a whole they have almost unlimited patience to endure the individual physical hardships that they meet, and an almost unlimited capacity for taking pains to make life more enjoyable. They are either the best or the second best cooks in the world, and their rivals in this sphere, the French, are probably the most like them of European races in other respects. The Chinese have always been consummate artists—painters and potters in the early dynasties, the inventors and the world's greatest masters in porcelain, novelists in the Ming and Manchu periods, poets always; but although their art has been often lyrical, imaginative and filled with a love of Nature, it has always remained classical and humanist. There is no romantic period in Chinese literary history, and the enduring Chinese love of man and of his life on earth was never touched by the romantic disease which has coloured all European thought from the twelfth century onwards.

We shall see in the next chapter how this permanent, stable and humanist civilisation has fared under the impact of the West.

BIBLIOGRAPHY

*China: A Short Cultural History.* C. J. Fitzgerald.
*The First Holy One (Confucius).* Maurice Collis.
*Peasant Life in China.* H. T. Fei.
*Chinese Thought.* H. G. Creel.

# CHAPTER FIVE

## MODERN CHINA

### POLITICAL

### (a) *The Revolution of* 1911

TO understand modern China, one must realise that the
revolution of 1911 is still going on. It would have been strange,
in fact, if an upheaval as drastic as this could have been finished
in less than fifty years. When the Republicans, whose spiritual
leader was Sun Yat-Sen, overthrew the Manchu Dynasty in 1911,
they aimed at something which had not happened in China for
2,000 years, a radical change in the social system. The mere political
overthrow of the Manchus might in the past have led to no more
than the establishment of a new dynasty; and this in fact is what
Yuan Shih-Kai, the Manchus' general, who became President of
the Republic after Sun Yat-Sen, tried to do. But the real strength
of the revolution lay in the young Westernised Chinese, and they
were not merely anti-Manchu: they had come to the conclusion
that if China was to survive and not be split up among the great
powers, she must modernise on Western lines, as Japan had already
done. At the same time they remained as resolutely anti-foreign as
ever: they wished to Westernise Chinese life in order to protect
China from the foreigner—and initially this meant from the
Westerner.

Until the collapse of the Manchu Dynasty, it was an axiom of
official Chinese thought that traditional Chinese culture was the
only true form of civilisation, and that China had nothing to learn
from Western barbarians. It is clear enough, therefore, that the
effects of a revolution whose object was to modernise China on
Western lines could not help but be felt in every part of her political,
social and economic life.

Had the fall of the Manchus been no more than the normal
collapse of a Chinese dynasty after outliving its strength, one of
two things might have been expected: either a strong man among
the original rebels would have seized the throne and established
himself as Emperor, or there would have been a period of 'troubles'—
that is, of conflicting war-lords and provincial governors—ending
with the establishment of a new dynasty in the line of the most
successful rival. The first solution failed in 1916, when Yuan Shih-Kai,

who had secured almost dictatorial powers as President, failed to get the necessary support to establish himself as Emperor. The second, the period of war-lords, followed as usual, but instead of the strongest war-lord ultimately uniting the Empire under his own dynasty, the strongest force turned out to be Sun Yat-Sen's revolutionary party, the Kuo Min Tang, and ultimately its Communist wing.

## (b) The Kuo Min Tang

The Kuo Min Tang party, familiarly known as the K.M.T., consisted of the original supporters of Sun Yat-Sen's Westernising revolutionaries. During the dictatorship of Yuan Shih-Kai and the period of war lords in the north, they could do little more than keep alive the progressive revolutionary faith in Canton, and work out a plan for ultimately unifying China as a republic. In doing this they had from 1923 onwards the advice of Borodin, one of the leaders of the Russian Revolution, and a mission consisting of technical revolutionary experts from Moscow: the plan, as finally worked out and accepted by Sun Yat-Sen before his death in 1925, has obvious similarities with Communist theory. The Republic was to be established in three stages: first, a military stage, to last until the war-lords were conquered; second, a stage of 'political tutelage' under the K.M.T., during which the K.M.T. was to be the only political party and was to educate the people for the third stage; the third stage was to be full popular representative government on what we should now call Western democratic lines.

Such a plan was obviously much more realistic, particularly in its first stage, than most of the 'progressive' constitutions which were devised in the nineteenth century by young oriental reformers in love with Western political theory; these tended to imagine that the principles and practices of the English Parliament in the time of Burke could be applied immediately to the central government of Tibet. The difficulty in Sun Yat-Sen's three-stage plan lay at the end, in the transition from the second stage to the third. No one really believes now the classic Communist doctrine that once the dictatorship of the proletariat has been established, the State will wither away: and it is equally difficult to suppose that the K.M.T. or any other 'monolithic' party which has monopolised the government for many years, will, at the end of this period of political tutelage, freely resign its powers and privileges and go into voluntary liquidation. The process of history is in fact showing already that the end of the 'period of political tutelage' is a constantly receding mirage.

The first part of the process, however, was completely successful, and between 1926 and 1928 armies of the K.M.T., who had established their capital in Nanking, overthrew or absorbed the northern war-lords and unified the country under a republican government. But it was not merely the war-lords who threatened the unified control of the K.M.T. Even granted that there was only one party, there were obviously possible rivalries within that party, and in 1927 these reached a head. The excesses of extreme Communists in the K.M.T. shocked more moderate supporters and seemed likely at one point to lead to intervention against the K.M.T. by the Western powers. Chiang Kai-Shek therefore expelled the Russian advisers, and the Communist elements in the original revolutionary movement set up their own administration in retaliation, at first in the south round Canton, the original revolutionary capital.

The K.M.T., true to the revolutionary doctrine that there could be only one party during the period of 'tutelage,' turned, as soon as the war-lords had been crushed, to the suppression of the Communists; and by 1934 they had made their position in the south so difficult that the Communist armies undertook the great march to join up with the other Communist area in the north-west, and perhaps to be in closer touch with support, if support should come, from Russia. This march took more than a year, and carried them over 6,000 miles in a wide arc to the west, round the fringes of K.M.T. China and Tibet, until they reached, after terrible hardships, their new capital at Pao An in the north-west—near the birthplace of Chinese civilisation. From this base they ultimately drove out the Conservative wing of the Revolution.

## (c)  The Chinese Communists

It is almost impossible to find any report on these people which is not gravely biased by the writer's own ideological background: those which purport to be 'objective records' of 'non-political' visitors are very often palpably the worst. Many of those who supported the Communists in China knew no more about Communism than William Cobbett did, but the determination of the K.M.T. government to treat all opposition as 'Communism' virtually drove them into the Communist fold. Nor is it easy to judge how much of the popular support enjoyed by Communist parties or Communist Governments is due to genuine sympathy with their aims and methods and how much to mere opposition to the existing regime.

In China there is no doubt that the Communist wing of the Revolution drove out the K.M.T. largely because the K.M.T. failed to complete the revolution in the spirit of Sun Yat Sen. His purely nationalist aims were achieved, it is true, by the allied defeat of Japan and the Western powers' renunciation of their extra-territorial rights; but too much emphasis had been laid too long on pure nationalism. In the social sphere the K.M.T. had by 1946 alienated all classes whose support was of any value: the peasants by their refusal to press land reform beyond a point where it became inconvenient to the landlord; the bourgeoisie by their corruption and incapacity to stabilise the currency or prevent galloping inflation; the intellectuals by a senseless persecution and 'witch-hunt'; the Army by the same corruption and inability to pay a real living wage as antagonised the bourgeoisie; and the people as a whole by failing to control the ravages of unpaid troops who naturally turned to rapine.

When, therefore, the American attempts to achieve a compromise broke down and the struggle between Communists and K.M.T. was resumed, the overwhelming feeling among the Chinese was that the K.M.T. had failed to govern and had therefore 'lost the mandate of heaven.' In spite of the fact that they had received much more military equipment from America than the Japanese material which the Russians 'allowed' to fall into Communist hands in Manchuria, they found their armies melting away, and in some cases going over, literally lock, stock and barrel, to the Communists. This latter process was rendered easier by the fact that some K.M.T. 'generals' were in fact only the old 'war-lords' renamed; for the unity which the K.M.T. boasted in pre-war China had been achieved in certain areas only by a face-saving compromise, which left the reigning war-lord in power as governor, with a more or less nominal allegiance to the central government.

The Communists on the other hand seemed to be people who, whatever else they did, would certainly not fail to govern. Their leaders had a perfectly coherent theory of government based on what was then thought to be 'Marx-Leninism,' but worked out by the intellectuals of the party with special reference to the Chinese situation, and continually modified by the intensely practical mind of Mao Tse-Tung. In their foreign associations they naturally 'leant to one side' as Mao put it, and worked very closely with Soviet Russia; but China was never a satellite and events since the death of Stalin have quickened the pace of her movement towards independence of Russian influence. Communism in Asia is already a Chinese, not a Russian phenomenon. To the Chinese, hesitating between Communism and the K.M.T., the Communists offered the land to the peasants, a stable currency to the bourgeoisie, the hope of a real 'New China' to the intellectuals and to everybody an army that was genuinely disciplined, convinced of its mission and trained in the school of guerilla warfare not to prey upon its hosts. As a result China fell almost without a struggle into the Communist hands, and Chiang Kai-Shek, carrying with him the treasury, a small nucleus of sincere anti-communist leaders, an aging regular army and a seat on the United Nations Security Council, retired to the island of Formosa, newly liberated from the Japanese and forty miles from the mainland at the nearest point.

The Communist régime in China plans to convert the country from a backward, 'feudal,' primary producer, politically and economically dependent on the West, into a modern, socialist, industrialised, great world power. It is prepared to take a long time over the job but not too long, and it is prepared to be completely ruthless with human lives in what it conceives to be the long term interests of the people. For this programme it was first necessary to ensure the support of the masses. So the peasants were given their land-titles, the bourgeoise permitted to trade under the new name of 'national bourgeoise' and the intellectuals promised a new freedom. In each case this early compromise was deceptive: The peasants found that having received their land they were expected to join first 'mutual aid teams' and then 'producers' co-operatives,' the ultimate aim being the usual Communist collectivisation: the bourgeoisie found more and more business nationalised, until by 1954 the state controlled 90 per cent. of rice distribution and now claims to control 90 per cent. of retail trade. The intellectuals found their new freedom rapidly replaced by 'thought control' more rigid than the Japanese and by the Chinese version of socialist indoctrination known as 'brain-washing.' Such policies, and the violent transformations in society on which the Communists had set their heart, naturally produced opposition both among their original supporters and among the classes to be transformed. This opposition was met with ruthless repression through the 'peoples' courts,' mainly in the course of two ideologically blameless campaigns, the 'three-anti' and 'five too many' movements, which were in reality mass purges of all opponents. An official American estimate is that 15 million people lost their lives through these and other repressive measures. There is no reason to suppose that it is exaggerated but, horrifying though these figures are, it is perhaps relevant to remember that, proportionally to the population, they are not much worse than the casualties in India and Pakistan at the time of the partition. What has horrified Western opinion is that they resulted from the deliberate policy of a government determined to brook no opposition.

That repression on this scale did not destroy the credit of the Communists in China itself is probably due partly to fear, partly to the puritan streak which, still persisting in the Communist programme, enlists the sometimes reluctant sympathy of the social reformer.

### (d) Nationalism and International Relations

The revolutionaries of 1911 had been deeply impressed by the threat to China from abroad. Up to the middle of the nineteenth century the traditional Chinese view of foreigners was that they were inferior barbarians: Westerners were just one type of barbarian who might, if they wished, be allowed to present the Emperor with occasional tribute in the form of ingenious mechanical devices.

The forcible expansion of Western trade in the Far East, the rapid subjection of countries like Burma and Indo-China, which were technically tributary to China, and the sudden Westernisation of Japan made it clear that physical force if nothing else lay with the barbarians.

At first it was the Westerners who seemed to present the greater threat, and Sun Yat-Sen seems to have expected that the European threat to China's integrity would have that effect of unifying under pressure which was in fact left to Japan. Actually, Sun Yat-Sen misread the temper of the West: the French acquisition of Indo-China was the last Far Eastern move in the great game of imperial grab, not the first. Provided that the 'concessions' at the Treaty ports ensured adequate opportunities for trade, there was little likelihood that they would spread, as the earlier British concessions had spread in India, into political empires. These 'foreign concessions,' of which Shanghai was far the most important, were a necessary stage in the modernising of Chinese trade. The mere fact that they attracted to themselves a vast proportion of the sea-borne trade of the country shows that ports operated under local Chinese control were not yet capable of dealing with world traffic; and Sun Yat-Sen himself observed that the Chinese should be ashamed that the foreigner, whom they despised, had been able to

turn a rocky island into the thriving port of Hong Kong, while the
ancient cities of China remained primitive and corrupt.

It was natural that as Chinese nationalism and modernism
increased, so also should resentment at these foreign-controlled
ports; and, beginning with the Russians in 1919, the foreign governments have one by one handed them back to China. Hong Kong,
a colony rather than a concession, is the only remaining port in
foreign control. It is an interesting indication of the truth about
Treaty ports that, whereas the revolutionary student type of Chinese
clamour for its return to China, the trading interests have always
preferred that it should remain British. In troubled times in China
the foreign-controlled ports were a useful factor making for stability
and a refuge for capital. A trade outlet may well prove valuable again,
and meanwhile the development and recovery of Hong Kong since
the war has been phenomenal, local light industry having largely
replaced direct trade with China.

By the time of the First World War it was becoming clear that
the political danger to China would come, not from the European
powers, but from Japan. Japan's initial reasons for seeking to
control China seem to have arisen partly from her own resurgent
nationalism, partly from economic causes; to these after 1919 was
added fear of Russia. It must be remembered that the Japanese,
far more than the Germans, have believed themselves to be a
'master race': their theory of the nature of the world included the
view that Japanese were by nature a primary and superior people.
Their defeat of Russia in 1905 marked them out as the leaders of
Asiatics against Europeans, and it was natural enough, therefore,
that they should feel an increasing desire to assume the leadership
and control of all the peoples previously subject to the Chinese
Empire. This almost paternal nationalist sentiment first became
clear in the famous Twenty-one Demands made on China in 1916,
then in the 'Asiatic Monroe Doctrine' first promulgated in 1934,
and, finally, in the theory of the Co-prosperity Sphere, which
formed the basis of Japanese propaganda to Asia during the last
war. The essentials of the doctrine were that the Japanese, as the
natural leaders of Asia (and ultimately perhaps of the world), were
entitled to control the policy of all other Asiatic nations, including
China, and to supply them with the necessary advisers and technical
experts to enable them to carry out their policy; in return, the
Japanese would recognise their nationality, protect them and
generally treat them kindly like good, obedient children. The

Chinese refused to accept this doctrine when it was put forward diplomatically in the Twenty-one Demands, and the long history of Sino-Japanese conflict from 1931 to 1945 was the story of the Japanese attempt to impose it by force.

The almost mystical view of Japan's 'manifest destiny' fitted in extremely well with her economic requirements. As a highly industrialised capitalist power she required a large primary producer as a market, and control of China would give her this. Consequently, the nearer China got to modernising her own industries, the more essential it seemed for Japan to secure control and keep her in what from the Japanese point of view might be described as her proper place in the Co-prosperity Sphere—and that was not competing with Japanese industries.

Finally, from the time that Russian power in the Far East began to recover from the Revolution, and particularly from the time of the Borodin mission to Canton, the Japanese feared that Russia, by winning China for Communism, might be able to take her revenge both for 1906 and for the Japanese attempt between 1919 and 1921 to seize Vladivostok and the Maritime Provinces. The steps taken by Japan to assure herself against Russian attack included the seizure of Manchuria and the establishment of a Russo-Japanese frontier along the Amur River, where previously there had been a Russo-Chinese one. World history brought it about that Japan's military power should be destroyed without the second Russo-Japanese war which so many Japanese had considered inevitable, and which looked at one time like being fought over the body of China.

With the Western Treaty rights relinquished and Japan eliminated, the important questions remaining to be solved were China's relations with Russia and the U.S.A.

Russia had been a neighbour, and a neighbour regarded with some suspicion, on the Manchurian border since the eighteenth century. That story is told in Chapter XI. Since the latter half of the nineteenth century, however, the two great powers have been in uneasy contact in Central Asia also. The regions involved are Mongolia and Sinkiang. In Mongolia a *modus vivendi* was reached in 1911, at the time of the Chinese Revolution, by which Outer Mongolia, with an area of 600,000 square miles and a population still probably numbering little more than a million, became a Russian satellite, while Inner Mongolia, with a much smaller area but about equal population, was in the same relationship to China. This arrangement has persisted, unaltered either by the Russian Revolution, the temporary Japanese occupation or the desire of the two populations to merge in a single, greater Mongolia. It is perhaps a sad augury for Korea and Viet Nam, and an indication of the abiding policy of both Russia and China not to encroach upon each other.

The history of Sinkiang seems to confirm this interpretation. This long tongue of 700,000 square miles, separated into two valleys by the Tien Shan range, has obviously strategic boundaries with China,

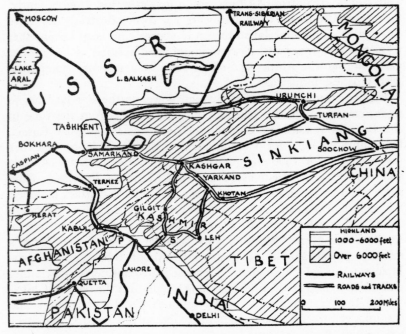

VIII. Sinkiang: routes to China, Russia and India (S=Srinagan, P= Peshawar).

Russia, Afghanistan, India, Pakistan and Tibet. It has always commanded a Central Asian route into China and its capital, Urumchi, where alone the Tien Shan can easily be crossed, has always been a centre of plots, counter plots and rumours. The mixed population are mostly Uighurs (Chinese form only 6 per cent.) and many of them have racial affinities with Central Asian minorities in the U.S.S.R. (which does not necessarily make them very pro-Russian). From 1884 to 1932 Chinese influence predominated, until a 'Nationalist' governor Shen Shih-Tsai, chose to base his power on Russian help: in 1942 Shen Shih-Tsai, thinking the Russians were about to be defeated at Stalingrad, made his peace with Chiang Kai-Shek, but was removed from office in 1944. Sinkiang was drawn into the Chinese civil war, but predictions that the Russians would take advantage of the situation to bring it within their orbit were never fulfilled, and it remains a province of Communist China, although joint Russo-Chinese exploitation of oil and mineral deposits was arranged in 1950.

Relations with the United States have, of course, become strained almost to the point of open war. (The events of the Korean war are described in Chapter XI.) American educational, social and missionary efforts in China had been very considerable throughout the century, and the emotional support for Chiang Kai-Shek in his struggle against Japanese oppression touched the whole American nation. It was natural, therefore, that in the war years America should have supported the K.M.T. (as did Russia also) and that she should have continued this support after the Japanese surrender. In the conflict between K.M.T. and Communists the U.S.A. first tried to mediate and help China to avoid a civil war. When this failed, they continued, though with lessening enthusiasm, to support the K.M.T. until the collapse. It is important to remember that immediately after the withdrawal to Formosa the intransigence in Sino-U.S. relations came more from the Communists than the Americans, and that U.S. aid and protection for Formosa was not offered until the Communists had invaded South Korea (see Chapter XI).

## ECONOMIC

The economic results of the Western revolution were at first much less important than either the political or the social. China is still a country where 80 per cent. of the population are directly dependent on agriculture, and where only 3-4 per cent. of the goods and services used are imported. The traditional self-sufficiency of the household and of the country was not therefore then seriously affected; nor has there been any great rise in the population or change in the methods of production. This is a marked contrast with conditions in either India or Japan.

## (a) Agriculture

Rice in the centre and south, wheat in the north, continue to be the main food crops—and consequently rice or noodles the main

19. Main street in China's new Detroit which produces the first automobiles ever produced in China. The basis of Soviet manufacture.

dishes. Sugar-cane, ground-nuts, cotton, tea, soya beans and oil-seeds are also grown on a large scale. In central and southern China the breeding of silk-worms and maintenance of mulberry groves is a major addition to the farmer's work, mainly carried on by the women, as an English farmer's wife will manage the hens. All these crops except tea and silk are grown chiefly for home consumption or local trading, for which they are combined with intensive vegetable gardening and pig- and poultry-keeping. Unlike the Indians, the Chinese farmer returns even human manure to the soil, so that a far greater degree of fertility is possible; but years of tree-felling without any serious replanting have sadly denuded the hillsides. The density of population in the cultivated areas is high (nearly 400 per square kilometre of *farmed* land), with the usual result that holdings are small and the standard of living low. It has been calculated—though it is difficult to extract any reality from such calculations—that the real value of the average farm incomes in northern China between 1920 and 1930 was £55 per annum, and in central China (where silk would be an addition), £71. Coolie wages in the same period were as low as 2s. to 3s. a week—very nearly as bad as India. China has, however, one great advantage over India: that, whereas only about 10 per cent. of the total area is cultivated at present, the next 30 per cent. consists of semi-arid plains, which could probably be brought under cultivation by modern mechanical methods. The man-land ratio, therefore, is not so insoluble a problem.

The main farm animals are pigs and ducks (the Chinese are the best cooks of pork and duck in the world), with horses in the north and water-buffaloes in the south for work. The cultivation of vegetables is so intense that Chinese farming has often been described as medium-scale market gardening. One further factor in the Chinese farmer's self-sufficiency is the bamboo. Like the coconut along the tropical sea-coast, the bamboo in China is the universal provider. From it the Chinese peasant makes houses, rope, furniture, raincoats, cooking-pots, charcoal, drain-pipes and a good many other things.

All this is a picture of an extremely stable and self sufficient system. How far it has really been affected by the Communist agricultural policies is very difficult to assess. It is undoubtedly true that in some parts of China, as in India, agricultural efficiency required a change over from purely individual peasant farming to more co-operative effort on larger units of land. It is clear that there

I

was at first violent opposition to the compulsion exercised on peasants to enter co-operatives and that in many places this opposition continues. The Chinese Government claim that whereas the Five Year Plan envisaged only one-third of all peasants entering co-operatives, in fact nine-tenths have done so willingly, is palpably exaggerated. Nevertheless it is probably true that the worst period of the 'socialisation of agriculture' is over.

### (b) Mineral Wealth and Industry

In mineral wealth, too, China is better adapted for self-sufficiency than most countries of the Far East. The coal deposits in the north once worked by the Kailan Mining Administration are very rich and easily reached; and the anthracite field in eastern Shansi is the largest in the world. It is on this coalfield that Japanese industry has always depended. There is adequate iron and probably large, as yet undeveloped, supplies of lead and copper. Silver, on which the Chinese currency has always been based, is also abundant. Of one of the main steel alloys, antimony, China has enough to supply the whole world, and her south-west provinces are among the main sources of another, tungsten or wolfram. The mountainous districts of western China have abundant potential water power.

The only serious mineral deficiency in China is oil, which is the great deficiency of the whole Far East. Apart from Burma, Indonesia and Sakhalin, there are no known oilfields of any importance in the Far East, and the only consolation to the Chinese must be that their very limited supplies of oil are found in Kansu and Sinkiang, where petrol for the immensely long cross-country journeys would scarcely be worth transporting if it were not available on the spot.

There is still little heavy industry in China, and even with Russian help the process of industrialisation will take many years. The main industry is cotton-weaving, and to this iron and steel is being added. Even in Formosa, where the Japanese ostensibly pursued a policy of industrialisation, approximately nine-tenths of the wealth produced still consists of foodstuffs and roughly half of rice.

The large-scale production of sugar cane and tea accounts for only 17 and 2 per cent. respectively of the island's output, and its industrial and mineral productivity is negligible.

### (c) Communications

Apart from Manchuria,[1] where a fairly elaborate railway system has been developed, mainly by foreigners and for strategic reasons,

[1] For the Manchurian railway system, see Chapter XI.

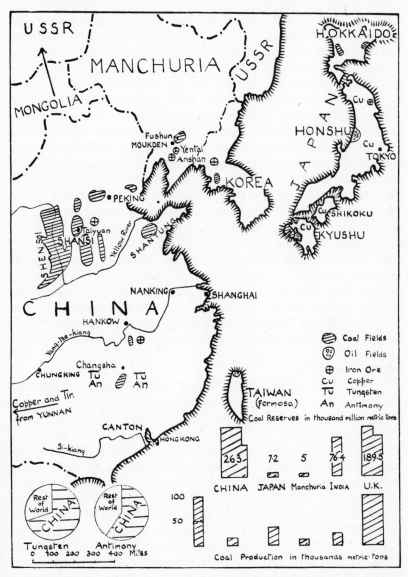

IX. China: Mineral resources. Note the proportion of worked coal to
estimated reserves.

China was poorly supplied with railways. There is one great north-south line, linking the three great districts of China from Pekin through Hankow to Canton; there is another from Pekin to Shanghai.

The Communist government, with Russian help, has started on a great railway building programme mainly designed to link China with Asiatic Russia. The new line from Ulan Ude to Peking shortens the old Trans-Siberian route by 1000 kilometres. A whole new system starting from Lanchow on the borders of Inner Mongolia has been already started and will link central China with the East and also, through Sian, Chengtu and Kunming, with the south-west. Infinitely the greater part of all goods traded within China (and therefore at least 90 per cent. of the trade done) is carried by the traditional methods—on the coolie's back, supplemented by cart and wheelbarrow in the north and barge in the south. For more valuable and perishable goods a modern innovation is the truck. Roads are mostly dirt, very poor after rain, and in the loess country so deeply sunk in the friable soil as to give the impression of miniature canyons. In such circumstances water transport is always much cheaper than land, and low freight rates in southern China account to some extent for its rather higher standard of commercial life. The Yangtse and West rivers are navigable for almost their whole length, the Yellow River only for a short part of its upper course.

### (d) External Trade

Before the war trade was almost entirely sea-borne and the blockade meant that China was entirely cut off from imports except (a) through Hong Kong (later captured); (b) by rail through Indo-China (later closed); (c) by road from Burma (later closed: see Chapter VI); (d) by air from India; (e) by road from Asiatic Russia through Sinkiang. None of these routes could handle really heavy traffic, but, apart from the supply of foreign war materials, foreign trade was not really essential to China's economy. Britain, reduced to such a trickle of imports, would have been compelled to surrender in a matter of weeks; China could carry on indefinitely. What small foreign trade there was was always centred on the former Treaty ports, and China has appeared to the foreigner more as a vast potential market for Western goods than as a source of supply. In one respect only has this potentiality been fully exploited: the almost missionary activities of the Standard and other oil companies have revolutionised Chinese domestic lighting, even in the far-away villages, and built up a market for kerosene which is of the utmost importance to the

companies. Travellers to the Far East will also have noticed that
empty kerosene tins beaten flat make a surface for temple roofs very

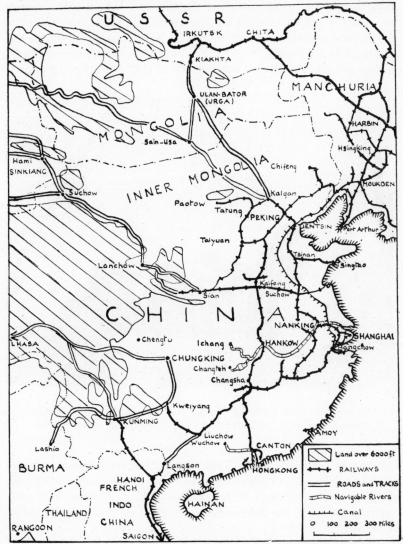

X. Communications in China and Manchuria.

little inferior to silver plating. The tobacco companies, too, have
succeeded in popularising the cigarette in China, and kerosene and
tobacco, together with small quantities of cotton and cotton goods,

foodstuffs and machinery used to form the bulk of China's imports.

Originally China's foreign trade was almost monopolised by Britain, and up to the last war Britain still led all other foreign countries in China in shipping, banking and capital investment; in the general volume of trade, however, both Japan and the U.S.A. had outstripped Britain by 1931. The establishment of the Communist régime completely altered this pattern of trade, and by 1953 three-

20. Young engineers read the Works Newspaper. Equality of status for women has been one of the most popular revolutionary moves.

quarters of China's foreign trade was carried on with countries of the Soviet bloc. It is believed that the bulk of the trade with Russia consists of an exchange of heavy industrial equipment and arms against foodstuffs, the deficiency on the Chinese side being made up by a loan.

## (e) *Finance and Currency*

From the time of the Han Empire empty treasuries and depreciation of currency have crippled successive Chinese governments. The Westernising revolution, alas, did nothing to alter this. No

Western economic or industrial revolution was possible without large accumulations of capital, and these were not available in China; partly because, as we noticed in the last chapter, the Chinese always live so near the margin that nobody can be expected to save; partly because political conditions were so disturbed that, except under the protection of the Western powers in the Treaty ports, capital was hopelessly unsafe. Why build up an industry merely for to-morrow's war-lord to seize. Consequently, modern capital development and large-scale industry was only just possible in and round the Treaty ports, and was there controlled very largely by foreign capitalists. The attempt to provide China with a national 'paper' currency on Western lines also broke down before the combined difficulties of the war, the political unrest and the national tradition of currency debasement. Under the Empire the tael, which is a weight of bar silver, not a coin, was the standard measure for large transactions, and the Mexican or Chinese silver dollar for small ones. Chinese currency remained on the silver standard while the rest of the world was on gold, and this meant that the 1929 slump, which was associated with a 'gold famine' (and therefore a drop in the world price of silver) brought a temporary rise in the Chinese price level and an artificial boom: the slump did not come for them until 1934, when the world price of silver rose rapidly.

Unfortunate as the silver standard, with its dependence on uncontrollable world prices, has been for China, the Chinese irresponsibility with paper currency has caused even more trouble. This is in a way strange in the country which invented the bill of exchange, but the temptation to every war-lord and provincial bank to issue their own currency was too great; and the tradition of inflated and worthless paper was set up long before the catastrophic inflation recently practised by the National Government in Chungking, when hard pressed to finance its war expenditure. This then led to the final situation, when the Chinese national dollar, in spite of every attempt at currency reform, commanded no confidence at all, and all wages had to be multiplied at each payment by an ever-increasing cost-of-living index. That the whole economy of the country did not break down seems to have been due to three factors:

(*a*) The vast majority of the farmers are virtually self-supporting, and have never lived on a money economy, anyhow.

(*b*) For medium-scale business in the interior, the small merchants can always in the last resort dig up their buried taels and organise a silver medium of exchange of their own. They did this under the worst inflations of the war-lords.

(c) For large-scale transactions in such places as Shanghai, the medium of exchange was long either Hong Kong dollars, American dollars or sterling paid abroad, or Chinese dollars valued at a rate fluctuating in accordance with the black market value of American dollars and the cost-of-living index.

Finally, it should be noted that industrial conditions in Manchuria (the Japanese puppet state of Manchukuo) differed considerably from those in the rest of China; they are described in Chapter XI.

SOCIAL

### (a) The Social Revolution in Peasant Areas

The aim of the revolutionaries of 1911 was to modernise Chinese society; for this purpose, certain economic changes were desirable, but they were treated as a means to a social end, not the primary development from which social changes naturally followed. This may seem queer to believers in the strict materialist doctrine, but the whole of Chinese history must seem equally queer, based as it is on an economic society which regarded 'breaking another man's rice bowl,' i.e. pressing an economic advantage too far, as one of the unforgivable crimes. It is a peculiarity of the dialectical materialist, among others, that he never seems to have considered the economic history of any part of the world except Europe. If the inevitable processes of economic development are really inevitable, it is difficult to see why over 2,000 years they never happened, or even possibly happened backwards, in China. The social changes brought about by the Revolution were not only the main object of its promoters, but proved in historical fact far more important than either the political or the economic changes. They were concerned primarily with the Chinese attitude to the outside world, with education and with religion.

Before describing the effect of the Revolution on these three aspects of Chinese life, it is worth while emphasising that the life of the peasant farmers who form the vast majority of the nation was, perhaps is, too self-sufficient, too simple in its constituents, and too limited to its own locality to be suddenly and radically affected by any revolution whatever.

In the north the peasant farmer has always lived in his one-room house of loess mud brick or cave in a loess hill; the caves are popular, being cool in summer and easily heated in winter by a stove, whose flue runs under the sort of magnified window seat, where in winter the women sit by day, and the whole family unroll their beds and sleep very snug at night. The farmer himself is busy enough fetching water, which is scarce, looking after his few pigs or sheep, growing, threshing and milling his own corn for his wife to make the noodles; she too is busy spinning and weaving all the cloth and helping in the fields. One thing only they may owe to the social revolution, and that is a kerosene lamp.

In central and southern China there will not be the problem of keeping warm, but there will be all the rice-planting, and perhaps the ploughing too, to do by hand, the water to be pumped for the irrigation channels, the incredibly voracious silk-worms to be fed, the roofs to be repaired against the monsoon rains.

How far all this is altered by becoming a member of a 'co-operative' is hard to say. You can mechanise grain farming, but there is a limit to the number of ducks that one man can look after.

Nevertheless the Westernising revolution and subsequently even more the Communist revolution have profoundly altered even the common life of the people. In the first phase the things which really touched the ordinary family were the abolition of such anachronisms as the queue (pigtail) among men and foot-binding among women, the introduction of the kerosene lamp and the bringing of the western and south-western provinces, Szechuan and Yunnan, into far closer touch with the rest of China. Apart from this the visits of young enthusiasts, imbued with the new spirit of modernism, to their old villages began the gradual process of infiltration.

All this was immensely stepped up by the Communists. It was natural that the new revolutionary creed should appeal to the young, and to young girls in particular. The complete emancipation of women was one of its most attractive features. In the years of war, first against the K.M.T. at the time of the Long March, and then against Japan, the Communists were compelled to withdraw from the big cities and concentrate on the rural areas. As a result they touched and transformed the life of the peasant as no one has done for hundreds of years. As a result many of the age-long traditions of the family have been broken up: there seems to be a 'drift' to the towns similar to that in all rapidly developing countries: and a good proportion of the thousands of young men and girls now clamouring for a higher education seem to come from the countryside. How great is that demand and its effects in draining the countryside of talent may be judged from the following figures: the quota for a year's output from institutions of higher education is fixed at 70,000, 29,000 studying engineering, 18,000 teaching, 4,000 Science, 3,000 Arts, 2,000 Economics, 1,000 Law, 300 Fine Arts and only 3,000 Agriculture. Interesting as well as the small proportion allowed to agriculture is the even smaller number of embryo lawyers, a marked contrast with the countries of emerging political freedom, where the proportion of lawyers usually seems far too high.

### (b) Westernism in the Big Cities

The extravagant admiration for everything Western, which was so noticeable in and just before 1911, did not last very long; the last great war did, in fact, more than half convince the majority of educated Chinese that they have more to teach the West than to learn from it. As a result the 'New Life' movement laid great emphasis on a return to the typically Chinese virtues, and the Communists in their social propaganda are at pains to emphasise that theirs is Chinese Communism, not merely a copy of Russian.

It would be a mistake, however, to write of the impact of the West as if it were entirely or mainly a spiritual matter. To the young Chinese in the great cities the West meant cinemas, cigarettes, trains, electric light, new clothing styles and a hundred other things. It meant overwhelmingly America, and all these everyday things were bound to instil in the semi-educated a general feeling of American superiority in other respects. It is a freak of geography, and one very little realised, that in Central Asia, Sinkiang and Mongolia such things as cigarettes and cinemas mean not America, but Russia; so that the normal propaganda situation is reversed, and the Mongolian equivalent of the flash corner-boy is likely to be an ardent supporter of Communism. This accounts for an illuminating wisecrack about Soviet Central Asia which circulated in Afghanistan: in Bokhara, they say, there are now no men over forty left alive; they have either been liquidated or died of shock at the behaviour of the young.

### (c) Education

One of the peculiarities of Confucian civilisation was its immense respect for the art of writing. Early Chinese scholars were so much impressed by the importance of this central civilising discovery that the written word, any written word, was treated as semi-sacred. A traditional Chinese scholar was horrified at old newspapers being used for wrapping-paper, simply because of the dishonour done to written words. The great drawback of this view was, not unnaturally, that once the impulse of the founders had died away it left knowledge static; there was no opportunity or encouragement for new ideas or discovery, and no life left in the inherited system.

The educational revolution was first and foremost, therefore, a revolt against Confucius, as the Renaissance was in some sense a revolt against Aristotle. In 1905 the famous Civil Service examinations were abolished after at least 1,500 years' continuous service, and in 1926 Confucius was actually burned in effigy. For some time even those who felt that the basis of the new educational system must be Chinese and not Western went back to the greater freedom and experimentalism of the Hundred Schools. But most at first turned to the West, for in the two decades between 1911 and 1931 there was a great outflow of Chinese students bent on acquiring the new learning, particularly in the natural sciences. Many went to Europe, more to the U.S.A., and most of all to Japan, where a second-hand Western education could be acquired more cheaply than anywhere else. It is important to remember that in this respect, as in the general social influences affecting family life, the ultimate source of Westernisation was the U.S.A. In point of size, Dr. Latourette (*Short History of the Far East*) estimates that this was the greatest student migration in history.

At the same time, two educational developments of the greatest importance were going on in China: the first was the establishment of modern secondary schools and universities throughout the country, including schools for girls. This introduced into Chinese life a new class, the young 'progressive' student, often no more than fifteen or sixteen years old, and filled with great enthusiasm, patriotism, self-esteem and irresponsibility. Much of the education they got was, of course, superficial, and many of the political agitations in which they took part unjustified and silly; but it would be a great mistake to underestimate their idealism and their importance. This class of young student, both girls and boys, provides the dynamic force of the Communist society to-day. The new universities of China seem some of the most hopeful places there and it is planned to reach in 1957 a university population nearly two and a half times the size it was in 1952.

The second movement, in which both Communists and New Lifers took their part, has been the drive for universal literacy. The Chinese language is so great an obstacle to civilisation that it may be rated as their greatest triumph that they have established what is probably the world's most successful culture in spite of it. Unlike all the other great languages of the world, written Chinese never developed an alphabet; each letter or character was originally a picture of the object it represented, and remains a symbol, having one meaning only and representing one syllable. To read school books in China it is necessary to memorise at least 2,000 of these characters, and an educated man will need to learn 5,000. Learning to write them is even worse, since each character has to be accurately painted with brush and Chinese ink.

This complication of the written language, which is a great disadvantage to both China and Japan, springs from the stabilising of the written word, through reverence for its sanctity, at too early a stage in the history of the race. Both countries are now trying to devise means of dealing with it. In China the two main systems have been:

(*a*) The introduction, mainly by missionaries, of a forty-character phonetic script. This is sometimes printed alongside the text, as the *kana* are in Japan, in government school-books, but the remedy seems too drastic and less likely to be effective than its rival;

(*b*) The rival method is a sort of 'basic Chinese,' which preserves the old characters, but limits the number which it is necessary to learn to 1,200. It is estimated that 10 million people have learnt to read on this system since 1926.

Finally the Communist Government is now considering the appallingly drastic measure of Romanising the written language.

In spoken Chinese also changes are being made: since it is a syllabic language, the same syllable has to do service for a wide variety of meanings, and which meaning is intended depends on the other syllables with which it is combined and on the tone of voice used: *fan* in a high tone means 'food,' in a low tone, 'tumult.' Before the Revolution, although *written* Chinese was the same all over the country, spoken Chinese differed so much that Cantonese and Mandarin (northern Chinese) speakers were incapable of understanding each other. Part of the new educational drive has been the introduction of a national spoken Chinese.

## RELIGION AND ETHICS

The shattering effect of the anti-Confucian Revolution on educated Chinese society can best be realised by remembering that the

Confucian classics enshrined not only the whole tradition of literature and history, but also of morality and ethics. It is as if the classics *and* the Bible had been simultaneously discredited in England. It might be thought that the attack on the Confucian tradition would be the opportunity for a revival in one of the two other great systems, but Chinese Buddhism had long been in decline and counted for nothing in the life of the nation, while Taoism had completely degenerated into superstition and magic. The one new factor in China was the spread of Christianity. This had, of course, been due to some extent to the same factors that favoured Christianity elsewhere in the East: that it was the religion of the successful Western powers and the easy way to secure a Western education. There is more than that, however, in the spread of Chinese Christianity; where there were less than 1 million Christians in 1896, there were well over 3 million by 1932. More significant than the numbers was then the quality of those adopting Christianity, who have included Sun Yat-Sen, the founder of the Republic, Chiang Kai-Shek and the famous Soong family of sisters.

The Communist Revolution has, temporarily at least, altered the whole situation. Christianity has been treated much as capitalism was. Since a direct frontal assault would probably have provoked more opposition than it was worth, the Christian Church in China has been tolerated on two conditions: that its members became 'national' Christians, like the 'national bourgeoisie,' and that it severed its connections with the West, accepting the gradual expulsion of Western missionaries, doctors and teachers. Christianity is alive in China still but the pulse is beating low.

Communism itself, on the other hand, as practised by the Chinese, has much of that combination of moral precept and social science which characterised Confucianism. There are individual elements in 'Marx-Leninism' which are alien to the Chinese temperament, but it is surely unhistorical to see anything contrary to the main trends of Chinese thought in the idea of a central government which controls, mainly by moral suasion, every facet of the individual's life. And this, now that the days of the great purges are over, is how Chinese Communism seems to be developing. To the young the great public campaigns against moral and social evils, whether it is corruption or house-flies, are one of the great attractions of the Communist programme. And this attraction affects very strongly the Overseas Chinese. It is for the moment, at any rate, a new religion and can call forth from some of the best of them the devotion and self-sacrifice that one associates with religion.

### BIBLIOGRAPHY

*China's Destiny.* Chiang Kai-Shek.
*My Country and My People.* Lin Yu-Tang.
*Journey to Red China.* R. Payne.
*The Challenge of Red China.* G. Stein.
*Land and Labour in China.* R. H. Tawney.
*Village and Town Life in China.* Y. K. Leong and L. K. Tao.
*The New Culture in China.* Lancelot Foster.
*China: Her Life and People.* Mildred Cable and Francesca French.
*The Good Earth.* Pearl Buck.
*A Leaf in the Storm.* Lin Yu-Tang.
*Government and Administration in Communist China.* S. B. Thomas.
*The Prospects for Communist China.* W. W. Rostow.
*A History of Modern China.* K. Latourette.
*Formosa To-day.* A. J. Grajdanzev.

# CHAPTER SIX

## BURMA AND CEYLON

BURMA and Ceylon have from the point of view of physical
geography no connection with each other. Ceylon is structurally
a part of India, Burma of the Indo-Chinese peninsula. The reason
for treating them together in this chapter is the similarity of their
cultural history and background. In the past they have been linked
as centres of Hinayana Buddhism, which still flourishes in both
countries; more recently both have been administered by the
British, first as parts of India and then as separate dependencies.
Since 1945 both have attained independence, Burma as an isolated
republic, Ceylon as a member of the British Commonwealth. Even
this similarity is limited, however, by the fact that Ceylon, being a
tropical island, has many features in common with Malaysia rather
than Burma or India. The two halves of the chapter will therefore
be treated completely separately.


## BURMA

### STRUCTURE AND CLIMATE

The first thing to remember about Burma, one which many
soldiers of the British 14th Army will never forget, is that most
things—mountains, rivers, and therefore the people—run north
and south. To move east and west in Burma usually seems contrary
to the course of Nature.

The geographical divisions of the country reflect this fact; the
heart of modern Burma is the lower Irrawaddy valley and delta,
in which more than half the people live. To the north of this is the
dry zone, on the middle course of the Irrawaddy; to the west the
Irrawaddy valley is cut off from the coastal district of Arakan by
the mountains of the Arakan Yoma, and to the east from the Sittang
valley by the Pegu Yoma. Arakan is in some ways a sort of miniature
Burma itself: it has its river, the Mayu, and its rice-growing area in
the river delta; it even has, in Akyab, a miniature rice-exporting
port like Rangoon. Otherwise it is mostly jungle, and more easily
approached from Eastern Pakistan than from Burma, since the
Arakan Yoma is very difficult country, with only one tolerable pass,

the Taungup, into central Burma. The main-land route from India
to Burma is from northern Assam across the mountains to the
Chindwin valley and then down the Chindwin until it reaches the
plain of the Upper Irrawaddy near Mandalay. This, the route of
the 14th Army and the route by which the Japanese attempted to
invade India, is again so difficult that there is no railway from India
to Burma and until the war no practicable road existed.

To the north of the Mandalay plain Burma is separated from
southern China by country so difficult to cross that no more than
a track existed until strategic reasons compelled the building of
the Burma Road in 1937 (see illustration on p. 156). This and other
recent additions to Burma's communications are treated separately
in a later section.

To the east of the Irrawaddy and Sittang valleys lie the Shan
plateau and Karen Hills, cut by Burma's third great north-south
river the Salween. Across these again difficult and ill-frequented
tracks lead to the sparsely populated and isolated northern province
of Siam.

To the south of the rest of Burma, elongated like the forefinger
of a signpost hand, stretches the district of Tenasserim. Geographically, Tenasserim is the north-western coast of the Malay Peninsula;
politically, it has been attached to Burma since the late eighteenth
century. The political boundaries of Burma, Siam and Malaya in
this area are complicated and justifiable neither on grounds of
physical structure nor of race. The sketch map on p. 194 shows
how they run in reference both to these considerations and to
natural resources.

The climate of Burma is, of course, very much like that of India.
The Arakan and Tenasserim coasts get the full force of the south-west
monsoon and both have rainfalls of over 200 inches. Rangoon and
the Irrawaddy delta have a rain distribution not unlike Bengal's,
except that the drying winds from central Asia at the peak of the
hot weather are perhaps more marked. Northwards from the delta
the rainfall decreases rapidly, until it falls in the dry zone of central
Burma to as little as 20 inches; beyond that, again, the effect of the
northern mountains begins to be felt and the figure rises again to
over 80 inches.

## HISTORY AND PEOPLE

The Burmese are a group of Mongolian peoples akin to the
Tibetans, who seem to have entered the Burmese plains from the

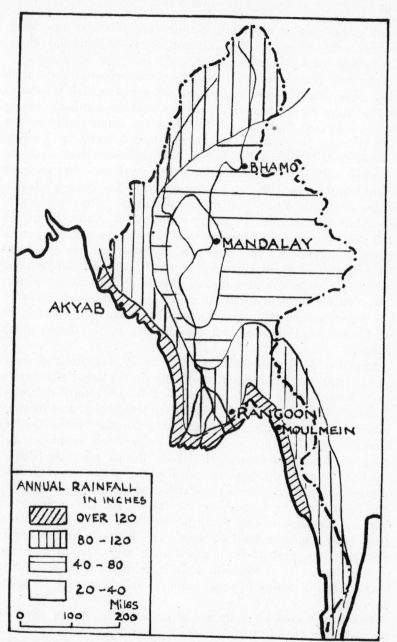

ANNUAL RAINFALL
IN INCHES

OVER 120

80 - 120

40 - 80

20 - 40

MILES

0    100    200

XI. Burma, showing variations of rainfall. Note the 'Dry Zone' in
the middle.

K

north some time in the ninth century A.D. Those tribes which stayed in the surrounding hills, Karens, Chins, Kachins and others, are by now markedly different from the Burmans of the plains.

Originally there were two kingdoms, a northern and a southern, as in Siam, and of these the northern followed the Mahayana form of Buddhism which flourished in Tibet, and the southern, having been evangelised from Ceylon, the Hinayana. In 1057 Burma was unified under the northern kingdom, but the country as a whole adopted that Hinayana Buddhism which has been ever since the strongest abiding force in its culture. In 1287 Burma, like so many other oriental countries, was subjugated by the Mongol Chinese armies of Kubla Khan, and the usual shadowy Chinese claim to suzerainty (see Chapter VII) dates from this conquest. From this time also dates the southward move of the Thai people, one branch of whom spread into the Shan plateau. From the time of Kubla Khan to that of Akbar there was no strong central Burmese state, but in 1550 there arose the first of a series of Burmese conquerors who made the Burmese hated and feared among all their neighbours. His empire extended to Manipur on the Indian side, Yunnan on the Chinese, and included both the northern and southern capitals of Siam.

After his death there was another period of chaos and internecine strife until the revolt of Alaungpaya in 1750. Alaungpaya made himself King of all Burma, sacked and utterly destroyed Ayuthia, the capital of Siam, and, in the words of J. L. Christian, 'established a bloody sort of unity from Yunnan to the Gulf of Martaban.' He founded a dynasty of kings, cruel, tyrannous and many of them half-insane, who ruled Burma until the British expelled Thibaw, the last and possibly the worst, in 1885. The only possible exception to this condemnation was Mindon (1853–78), who tried rather inconclusively to preserve the last remnants of Burmese independence by methods not wholly unlike those of the great King Chulalongkorn of Siam. The Burmese as conquerors were the curse both of Siam and Assam; they seem to have had no constructive ideas whatever in their military campaigns, but to have confined themselves to plunder, massacre and complete destruction.

The British control of Burma began with the war of 1824. In the eight years before this date, the Burmese raids are said to have reduced the population of Assam by half, and it was clearly impossible that they and the East India Company should fail to come into conflict. The position was not helped by the completely romantic view which the Burmese rulers held—and always seem to have held—of their military power compared with that of other nations. As a result of the Burmese defeat, Arakan and Tenasserim were ceded to the Company and the Burmese promised to refrain from further attacks on Assam and Manipur.

War broke out again in 1852 over the usual question in those times of the harsh and contemptuous treatment of European merchants. There was no serious resistance, and Lower Burma was annexed to British India almost without fighting, but after heavy losses from disease. One year later, as the result of a *coup d'état*, Mindon became King of Upper Burma and peace and order were maintained until his death in 1878. In 1885, his successor, King Thibaw, made the mistake of granting considerable concessions to the French while discriminating against the British. Franco-British colonial rivalry was strong at the time and Britain firmly established in Lower Burma. Thibaw himself was a cruel and degenerate tyrant, like so many of his line, and in the circumstances the Government felt they had every excuse for forestalling the French by absorbing Upper Burma. This they did with little trouble and to the great relief of most of the inhabitants of Lower Burma.

Until 1937 Burma was governed as a province of India. The arrangement was never popular, partly because of national pride, partly because Indians, many of whom were moneylenders, were becoming increasingly unpopular in Burma. In any case, it was difficult to avoid the suggestion that Burmese interests were being sacrificed to Indian. In 1937, therefore, Burma was separated from India and had, by the outbreak of war, progressed a long way on the road to independence, the whole government of the country, other than defence, foreign affairs, monetary policy and the Anglican Church, being in the hands of democratically elected Burmese ministers.

In spite of this progress, there was, of course, a radical nationalist party who clamoured for immediate independence and who conspired with the Japanese; later in the war, finding that the Japanese sort of independence was a fraud and that the British were likely to win, they changed sides and formed a rather more successful conspiracy against the Japanese. From their own point of view, of course, they were never 'pro' either side, but simply pro-Burmese. The help of these Burmese nationalists and even more of the Karen, Chin and Kachin hill peoples undoubtedly saved a great many Allied casualties. It was not, of course, in any way decisive, but it would have been utterly out of character if the Burmese nationalists had not imagined it so, and many of them to this day believe that they freed the country on their own. Immediately after the war, Britain implemented her promise to grant complete independence, and Burma, foolishly, in my opinion, chose to leave the Commonwealth. The country is now constituted as a republic, the 'Union of Burma,' the hill peoples being represented by their own ministers in the Union Parliament. Whether the Union can hold permanently together is still in doubt.

The reasons why all previous independent Burmese governments have been so violent, and why the new Union came to birth in a fog of assassination and rebellion, seem to lie in the Burmese character. Before separation, the murder rate in Burma was higher than in any other Indian province, and some have claimed that her general crime rate was the highest in the world. Burmese youth seem to have a very marked taste for violence of all kinds. They have been called the 'Irish of the East' and this in part at least conveys some idea of the national character—that is, if you remember what people usually mean by calling others 'Irish.' The violence seems mainly a characteristic of the 'lads of the village,' a phase through which many young Burmans go and which is good-humouredly deplored by their elders on the 'boys will be boys' principle. The good humour, on the other hand, which also seems 'Irish,' is very general. They are fond of all pretty things and often vain of their own extremely attractive appearance, courteous, kind when they are not being cruel or angry, intelligent, fond of intrigue, superstitious, with an eye to the main chance and a 'realistic' attitude about the dignity of labour. Above all, they are fond of fun and probably find political gangsterism exhilarating. It is an understandable mixture of characteristics and seems to make a happy race who are certainly good company, and whose sense of humour particularly appealed to the British; but it does not seem a very stable basis for democratic political institutions. Even under British control there was a rebellion as late as 1931.

It may seem queer that such people should be devout Hinayana Buddhists, but Buddhism probably appeals to the good-natured side of their fluctuating character and is certainly the kind of religion that the commonest national weaknesses seem to demand. If the Chinese adopted Confucianism to curb their natural individualism, the Burmese may have adopted Hinayana Buddhism to curb their natural violence.

## Modern Social and Economic Structure

### (a) Natural Resources

The natural wealth of Burma consists primarily of the great rice-growing deltas, the forests and the mines. Only in the 'dry zone' is mixed farming of any kind carried on and diversified crops of cotton, groundnuts, millet, etc., grown. Fruit-farming has also been started on a small scale in the high uplands of the Shan plateau. No further description of the rice agriculture of the deltas is needed, since it does not differ materially from that of Bengal.

The forests of south-east Asia are commonly divided into three groups:

*Tropical Rain Forest.* This occurs mainly where the rainfall is over 80 inches per annum. The trees are of many different species, mainly of very hard woods, and not of great commercial importance. Walking through a tropical rain forest, you never see the sun; you do not even see the tops of the trees. There are, in fact, three layers of life: the ground, where quantities of animals, flowers, orchids and tree seeds struggle for existence; the middle layer, perhaps no more than 50 to 60 feet high, where the ordinary trees reach the limit of their growth and spread out half in vain, still shut out from the sun; and the top layer, where the crowns of giant trees, having outstripped the rest, spread out wide and luxuriate in all the sun and air they require. The best description of this sort of forest is in John Still's *The Jungle Tide.*

*Monsoon Forest.* This occurs in areas where there is a long dry season and a rainfall of 40 to 80 inches. The trees shed their leaves in the dry season and are usually much more widely spaced than in tropical rain forest. This is the home of teak and of most of the other valuable timbers used in construction. Forest fires are frequent and therefore fire-resisting trees such as teak establish a gradual predominance over other species.

*Mangrove Forest.* The name 'mangrove' covers a number of trees which grow in narrow strips of tidal swamp along the sea-coasts. The tangle of twisting and protruding grey roots emerging from the slime is an eerie and unpleasant sight, but the trees often reach a considerable height and the timber is quite valuable. Landing from the sea through mangroves is never pleasant and rarely practicable.

Burma is more than half covered with forests of all three types, and timber, mainly teak from the monsoon forests, came third in her list of exports before the war. The forests are government-preserved and controlled by government forest officers. The teak is mainly floated down the Chindwin or Irrawaddy to Rangoon, though a certain amount comes down the Sittang to Moulmein. A log may sometimes take as long as two years on the journey (see photograph).

Burma's mineral wealth is very great. In historic times this

21. Teak rafts on the Irrawaddy. The man in charge builds himself a little house on the raft itself.

sentence would have referred to the famous ruby and jade mines in northern Burma. Nowadays these are of little real importance compared with the oil-fields of Yenangyaung and Chauk, which had an average yearly output of about 285 million gallons before the war,[1] and the silver lead mines of Bawdwin. The Tenasserim coast also gives Burma a share in the great tin- and tungsten-bearing area, which she shares with Siam and northern Malaya. There are very considerable deposits of brown coal, mainly in the Chindwin valley, but these are not yet worked to any serious extent. The positions of these mineral deposits is shown on the sketch map. Note also on Map 24 (p. 329) the scarcity of petroleum in the Far East as a whole.

[1] The output since the war has been approximately one-tenth of this.

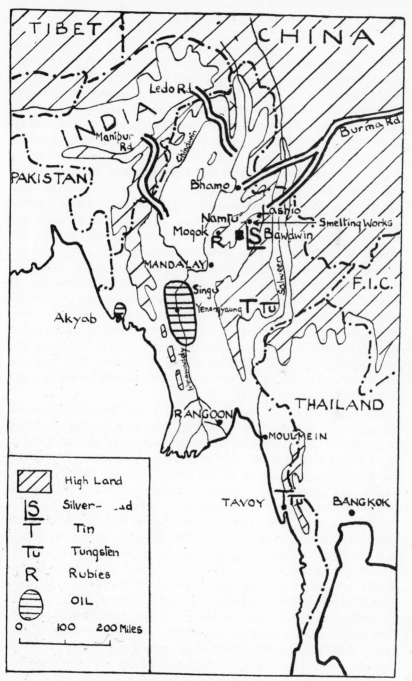

XII. Burma: Minerals and Land Routes.

## (b) Distribution and Occupations of the People

The population of Burma has more than doubled since 1891, and according to the census of 1941 was nearly 17 million (probably about 19 million in 1956). Of these over 10 million are Burmans, 1¼ million Karens, just over 1 million Shans, 350,000 Chins and 150,000 Kachins. It should be noticed that 'Burmese' is a political term denoting a citizen of Burma, 'Burman' a racial term denoting the Burmans of the plains, as opposed to the hill peoples. The 10 million Burmans live mostly in the large cities and the river valleys and deltas; they include the Arakanese, who have rather the same sort of reputation as the Scots—not quite a different nation, shrewd and inclined to take more than their fair share in running the country. Originally the Burmans were not prepared to take the trouble to develop the rice-lands of the Irrawaddy delta, and the British Government encouraged Indian immigration to work the land. There used to be annual immigration from Chittagong, in eastern Pakistan, down the Arakan coast to work the rice-fields. Most of the Burmans, nowadays, except the town-dwellers, are rice-producers, and the prosperity of the country before the war depended overwhelmingly on rice crops and prices. Since the war there has been a tendency for the Indian labourers to drift back and the area under rice to contract. The danger which this means for Burma's standard of living is obvious.

The Chins, Kachins and Karens live in the hills that surround Burma, and it is some help in placing them to remember that they go clockwise in alphabetical order, the Chins in the north-west, the Kachins in the north and the Karens in the east. The rest of the population is made up of the Shans, who are racially a Thai people, and various more primitive tribes, such as the Wa and the Nagas. Unfortunately, this simplification is not the whole truth, for the Karens, apart from inhabiting the Karen Hills in the east, are also inextricably intermingled with the Burmans in central Burma and particularly in the south-west around the port of Bassein.

The Karens are a simple, hardy, industrious and largely Baptist people who were on extremely friendly terms both with their American missionaries and with the British. Consequently, they did not really wish to leave the Commonwealth, but, particularly in view of their scattered position throughout Burma, they somewhat reluctantly agreed that the path of common sense seemed to point in the direction of co-operation in the new Union of Burma. Unfortunately the immediate post-war Government of Burma suffered from a combination of unrealistic optimism in its plans with failure to establish its real authority throughout the country as a whole. This is a not unnatural weakness of States emerging from colonialism in a period of general unrest and dislocation: but it encouraged the Karens in their desire to set up a separate and, by their standards, better organised Karen State. In the first clashes between the Socialist Government and the militant Communists it was the Karens who came to the defence of the Government: but subsequently, in spite of considerable concessions to Karen racial separatism, a large

22. Rangoon today. Western office blocks are being swallowed up again in an Eastern city.

number broke with the Central Government and tried to set up a separate Karen State, which at one time controlled both Moulmein and Toungoo. The Central Government, however, showed a remarkable mixture of steadfastness and conciliation, and from 1950 onwards the Karen revolt gradually died away. The other hill peoples have perhaps accepted rather than actively co-operated with the Union. The Kachins are now probably more concerned about the capacity of the Central Government to halt Chinese encroachment than about the possibility of undue interference from Rangoon.

The largest alien minorities are the Indians, nearly 1 million, and the Chinese, probably about 350,000. Apart from the immigrant Indian cultivators whom we have noticed, the Indians are mainly mechanics, business-men and moneylenders; the Chinese small *entrepreneurs* or plantation growers. Neither community is very popular with the Burmese and anti-Indian riots were not uncommon. This was not surprising in view of the extent to which Indian financial control had spread. By the outbreak of war in 1942, 58 per cent. of the total foreign capital in Burma was Indian, and 60 per cent. of Burma's exports went to India. The Burmese share of India's export trade was 7 per cent. Since the war, however, feeling against Indians seems to have declined. The position of the Chinese in such countries as Burma is more fully described in the next chapter. Two points are worth noting here, however: first, that the Sino-Burman mixture of blood is like the Sino-Thai—often a very happy one; and, second, that, if foreign colonies are not very popular in Burma, the same may be said for Burmese colonies abroad. The only considerable group of Burmans outside Burma are a small colony at Pursat in Cambodia, who, not surprisingly, have the reputation among the somewhat easy-going Cambodians of being violent and troublesome.

## (c) Commerce and Communications

Before the war Burma's three great exports were rice, petrol and timber. Imports consisted, as usual, mainly of cotton and other manufactured goods and machinery; Burman fashions made it inevitable that there would also be a considerable import of silk.

The recovery of Burma's rice export was of immense importance to south-east Asia, left after the Japanese occupation on the verge of starvation. Rice exports from 1934 to 1938 averaged just over 3 million tons out of a crop of about 6 million: in 1946 the total crop was less than half what it had been, and although the I.E.F.C. hoped for an export of 1½ million tons for 1948, that figure had not in fact been reached even by 1951-2, the years for which the Burmese Government had planned an export of over 3 million. The place of rice imports from Burma and Indo-China has, however, been largely filled by improved rice-production in the former importing countries.

The traditional line of communications in Burma is the Irrawaddy River, which is navigable for 900 miles from its source up to Bhamo: its main tributary, the Chindwin, is navigable for 300 miles from its junction with the Irrawaddy. The other great north-south rivers, the Sittang and Salween, are too fast-flowing and obstructed with rapids to be of much use for navigation, but throughout the delta country, round Bassein in the south-west and Akyab on the Arakan coast, almost all transport is water-borne, and a maze of channels connects the villages in the rainy season. The loss of country craft and river steamers during the war was therefore a great blow to commerce.

Such railways as Burma had before the war were mainly supplementary to the rivers; the main line and the main motor road in the country connected Rangoon and Mandalay, which were already connected by steamer.

The war added three important routes to Burma's external communications, the Burma-Siam Railway, the Burma Road and the Manipur and Ledo Roads, connecting Burma by road for the first time with Siam, China and India respectively.

The Burma-Siam Railway had been considered before the war on the grounds that it would shorten the journey from Bangkok to Europe by five days. It was never built, presumably because those who were in a hurry were going more and more by air, and because the freight charges on goods would be so high that the long sea journey would still be cheaper. Also the country through which it would have to be built presented appalling problems. The Japanese, having lost command of the sea, built it as a route for the supply of Burma. They used as labourers British and Indian prisoners of war, of whom it is estimated that nearly half died as a result. The railway ran from Kanchanaburi in Siam to Thaton in the Tenasserim province of Burma.

The Burma Road was also built for strategic reasons, and opened for traffic in the autumn of 1938. It runs through appalling mountainous country from Lashio in north Burma to Kunming in Yunnan, a distance of 726 miles. In this distance there are no less than 289 bridges and 1,959 culverts. The average width is 9 feet, with bays for trucks to pass, and the mortality rate of trucks has always been very high, although the average speed was not more than twelve miles an hour. During the monsoon landslides are frequent (see illustration on p. 156). The whole of this amazing road was built by hand by the pressed labour of literally hundreds of thousands of coolies, working partly from genuine patriotic enthusiasm, partly for 4d. a day and partly from compulsion. No other country but China could have done it, and in the end, even when it was reopened, it carried less supplies than the American air-lift over the 'Hump.'

The last of these three strategic routes, the Manipur and Ledo roads, linked Assam with northern Burma through the state of Manipur. The Ledo Road was essentially a new cut to connect the Burma Road with India, and the Manipur Road the route by which the 14th Army re-entered Burma. It was built by a mixture of the most modern American and ancient Indian methods, bulldozers and elephants.

23. Repairs after a landslide on the Burma Road. Note the wild country between Burma and China.

All three of these strategic routes have now relapsed into the jungle or slithered, in a series of land-slides, down the hills. The railway might have been useful in a period of settled government and expanding trade; but their fate, and the fate of Burma's world trade in rice, oil and timber are symptomatic of the break-up of South-east Asia as an economic whole. The real benefits to their peoples which the successors to colonialism can confer will depend very largely on their ability to re-establish it.

## (d) Post-war History

The post-war history of Burma exemplifies most of the dangers which threaten a country moving from a colonial to an independent status. The new government inherited three acute problems: its population was not homogeneous but consisted of different elements who had been jointly governed but not welded together by Great Britain; the war had impoverished the country and disrupted its foreign trade; and the resistance movement, both anti-Japanese and anti-colonial, contained a strong Communist element whose intention to overthrow the new Independent Government of Buddhist-Socialists was clear. All these problems the Government of Premier U Nu successfully tackled with help from the U.S.A., India and Britain. At first separatist and Communist risings threatened the very existence of the Government. The Arakanese on the west coast, aided by the militant Red Flag Communists, were the first to break away: they were followed, after the Calcutta Conference in 1948 (see Chapter XII) by the White Flag Communists, who had many supporters within the Government itself, and by the Karens. By 1949 things looked very black indeed: Karens and Communists, acting together, controlled Mandalay, Maymyo and most of North and Central Burma, and Karen troops were encamped within eight miles of Rangoon; 40 per cent. of the members of the existing Parliament were either in open revolt or in gaol; foreign trade was virtually non-existent. But the Karen-Communist alliance was an unnatural one, and the steadfastness of the Government, backed both by the U.S.A. and the Colombo Plan powers, gradually triumphed. Direct Rangoon-Mandalay communication was restored in 1950 and in 1956 it was possible for the Premier to accompany the Chinese Foreign Minister on a tour of the disputed frontier in the extreme north.

Commercially, however, the pattern of trade was broken, and when in 1954 Burma regained her place as exporter of 35 per cent. by volume of the world's rice, she found that few of her old Asian customers could afford the price. A barter deal for cement from Russia did not prove a great success. Such cement as arrived did so unexpectedly in the monsoon and got stuck on Rangoon wharves.

## CEYLON

### STRUCTURE AND CLIMATE

Ceylon is a pear-shaped island with a mountain core slightly south of centre and an area of just over 25,000 square miles. It lies south-east of the southern tip of India, to which it was once joined and to which it is still almost connected by a chain of islands and sandbanks. The connecting straits are, in fact, so shallow that the steamer service between Danushkodi in India and Talaimannar in Ceylon operated regularly on schedule throughout the war: there was no point in concealing the times of sailing because the water was too shallow for submarines to operate in it.

All round the mountain core and particularly in the north are flat plains, and round most of the coast coconut-fringed lagoons merge into a shallow sea. Trincomalee on the east coast is the only good natural anchorage, but the construction of breakwaters to fend off the south-west monsoon has produced a good harbour also at Colombo on the west. The highest peaks in the central mountain mass rise to over 8,000 feet, but the foothills are not very extensive, and only a comparatively small proportion of the island as a whole is over 2,000 feet.

The rainfall is governed by the position of the mountains. Ceylon lies in the direct path of both the south-west (June to October) and north-east (November to December) monsoons. In the extreme north and south, there are no mountains to break the monsoon clouds and the rainfall there is as little as 20 inches in the year. In the mountainous centre of the island, and particularly on the south-western edge of the mountain core, the rainfall is very heavy and in places exceeds 200 inches. The rivers are short and useful for irrigation rather than communications.

The southernmost tip of the island is only just 6 degrees north of the Equator and there is therefore very little difference in temperature between winter and summer, nor, along the coast, much between night and day. The average temperature at Colombo only varies between 79° in the coldest and 82° in the hottest month and the difference there between night and day is never more than 12°. It is a not unpleasant, monotonous kind of climate, and it is remarkable how refreshing it makes even the slightest sea breeze appear. To the European it is the lack of difference between night and day that is perhaps most trying, and one great pleasure of going up the mountains to a hill station is certainly that of getting a night cool enough to endure a blanket on the bed.

## HISTORY AND PEOPLE

### (a) Early History to the Arrival of the Portuguese in 1506

Ceylon, like Burma, is a country of many communities and the history of the island can still be traced in their differences. Like many parts of the Far East, it still harbours remnants of the aboriginal small, dark race, akin to the negrito or Australian bushman; these, in Ceylon, are called the Veddas, and a few scattered families still live their primitive life, preserved nowadays like a rare and almost extinct animal. The first people of whom we have anything like recorded history were the Aryan ancestors of the present-day Sinhalese and they certainly established in the first centuries of the Christian era the most flourishing civilisation that Ceylon has ever known.

This civilisation centred round Anuradhapura in the northern half of the island and well to the north of the mountain core. It is difficult to disentangle legend from history, and the story that the housetops of Anuradhapura stretched all the way to the sea is pretty obviously legend. The story that the population of the island was ten times what it is to-day might almost be true. The remains of buildings in the 'lost cities' of Ceylon certainly show that it was very much greater.

This great civilisation was built up on an elaborate system of irrigation from 'tanks.' The largest of these tanks covered areas up to twelve square miles and were based on dams as much as seven miles in length. More remarkable perhaps than their size was their frequency, and in some river valleys they averaged one to the square mile. The water collected in the tanks was distributed among terraced rice-fields attached to each tank, and this distribution must have demanded a very high degree of social organisation.

This tank civilisation was Buddhist in culture and in fact preserved that form of Buddhism which Asoka practised in India and which was so soon to die out in its native land. It was from Ceylon that this 'Hinayana' Buddhism spread to Burma and Siam, and Ceylon has always remained the most important centre of its influence. Communications were maintained at this time both with China and the West, though in both cases they were probably rather tenuous and intermittent; it is interesting to note, however, that practically all of over 1,000 coins found in the excavations of the rock palace of Sigiriya were Roman.[1] The great tank civilisation was destroyed partly by civil wars, but mainly by invasions from the Tamil kingdoms of Southern India between A.D. 300 and 1500. As soon as warring forces adopted something approaching modern 'total' war and destroyed the enemy's tanks, its doom was sealed; for the rebuilding of the tanks and even their maintenance was too big a task for the local inhabitants to undertake, particularly with

[1] I am indebted for this piece of information to Lord Holden's *Ceylon*.

the threat that the next campaign would mean renewed destruction. The loss of the irrigation water was not the only result of the destruction of the tanks, for the swamps which spread in their place bred mosquitoes and mosquitoes spread malaria; so that this, once the richest and most populous area of Ceylon, is now thinly inhabited by a fever-stricken remnant. This is not, as is sometimes suggested, a result of European exploitation. An Italian traveller who visited Ceylon before the Portuguese ever arrived reported that the tanks were then broken down and rice so scarce that it was imported from India.

### (b) Malaria

The depopulation of the tank country by malaria is, of course, no isolated example. Malaria causes more deaths than any other disease in the world, and south-east Asia is one of its worst breeding spots. Worse even perhaps than the direct deaths caused is the general weakening of resistance to disease and will to live which endemic malaria produces. This means that the peoples of south-east Asia are unusually easy victims to other deadly diseases—Rangoon before the war had one of the highest tuberculosis rates in the world—and unusually helpless in defence against disease. And the more malarial the district the more helpless and apathetic the victims; so that only an enthusiastic force from outside can really fight the disease.

The disease can be fought. As everyone knows nowadays, it is carried only by one or two species of mosquito, and strict control of the breeding grounds of these species, coupled with treatment of existing cases, can actually stamp it out. This was best exemplified perhaps in Malaya, where the condition of an enthusiastic external anti-malaria service was best fulfilled. The first serious attack on modern lines was carried out at Klang (in the F.M.S.) between 1902 and 1905 and brought the death-rate from malaria down in three years from 368 per 1,000 to 45 and simultaneously the rate from other diseases from 214 to 68.

Much has been done in Ceylon, and in the Matale area, for instance, oiling of the main streams in 1940 produced an immediate reduction by two-thirds of the incidence of the disease. There is a great deal yet to do, however, and this, with the repair of the tanks, would appear to be the first step in rendering the island independent of food imports. The chief difficulties are the usual apathy of the local inhabitants in the worst affected areas, and religious opposition from most strict Buddhists to any policy which involves the wholesale taking of life, i.e. mosquito life.

## (c) The Portuguese and Dutch

The first Europeans to arrive in numbers were the Portuguese in 1506. They were allowed to found a trading factory at Colombo, and soon the island became a centre for their spice trade and a valuable staging post on the way to the East Indies. As elsewhere in the Far East, the Europeans soon extended their trading post to a fort and gradually acquired political control of the low country, those Sinhalese who were determined not to lose their independence retreating to the hills. We shall see in later chapters that the Portuguese and Spaniards differed from the British and Dutch in attempting seriously to convert the people of their oriental dependencies to Christianity and so creating a much more genuinely fused Euro-Asiatic society. This was done more easily in Ceylon than elsewhere because of the comparatively small and isolated population whom the Portuguese found. You will find a far higher proportion of Sinhalese with Portuguese blood or Portuguese names than Indians, for instance, with British blood, and parts of Colombo are still not unlike parts of a Portuguese city. Portugal has also left a legacy to Ceylon in the number of Roman Catholic Christians in the island to-day.

In the seventeenth century the Portuguese were driven from Ceylon and all their Eastern conquests by the Dutch, and for 150 years the Europeanised parts of the island—mainly the coast-line from Colombo to Galle—were ruled by the Dutch. The Dutch, too, intermarried with the Sinhalese, as they did in Java with the Javanese, and have left a small community of mixed blood. Roman Dutch law is still strongly represented in the legal system of Ceylon. During the Napoleonic Wars the island was seized by the British, like Java, but was not, like Java, returned to Holland at the peace.

## (d) The British Period (1796-1948)

For just over 150 years Ceylon was governed as a British colony. At first it was administered from Madras as a dependency of the East India Company. It was the same mistake as was made with Burma, but it did not last so long. As often happens the Government in Madras completely failed to understand their new province; by abolishing overnight the ancient Sinhalese system of land tenure for service, which had been left untouched by both Portuguese and Dutch, they provoked rebellions sufficiently serious to induce the Home Government to remove Ceylon from their sphere of control.

L

At first the British writ ran no further than the Portuguese and Dutch had done, but after a second war in 1815 Kandy and the interior of the country were also annexed—another parallel with the gradual absorption of Burma.

The history of Ceylon during the nineteenth century shows two outstanding features, the introduction of a succession of new cash crops and the growth of a genuinely Ceylonese urban middle class.

Ceylon was originally one of the spice islands and its importance to the Portuguese and Dutch was based on cinnamon. Although cinnamon, cloves, nutmeg, citronella and other spices are still exported from Ceylon, their importance to the Western world had already greatly diminished by the beginning of the British period, and early in the nineteenth century Ceylon developed a new cash crop, coffee.

In 1835 the duty on Ceylonese coffee entering Britain was reduced, and this led to a rapid boom, annual exports rising from 1,000 tons in 1828–35 to 10,000 tons in 1845. It was the coffee boom which first led to the importation of Tamil estate workers from India, although certain trades which were contrary to Ceylonese caste customs had been exercised by individual Tamils for some time. The collapse of the coffee trade in the 1880s thus not only ruined many planters, but brought misery to many imported labourers. This collapse was not due entirely to the blight which attacked the plants, but partly at least to world monetary conditions and the development of Brazilian competition—just as the first cultivation of rubber in Ceylon and Malaya broke the great Brazilian rubber boom and ruined the city of Manaos.

New cash crops were ready, however, to take the place of coffee, and of these the most important was tea, which had been introduced in 1883 just before the great coffee failure. Tea, as we buy it in the shops, is the withered and dried leaf of a particular kind of camelia. The bush, if left to itself, would grow into a tree about 20 feet high, but it is constantly pruned to a height of 3 or 4 feet in order to promote a continual supply of fresh young shoots, and it is the leaf buds of these which are picked for drying. Consequently, tea-picking has to be done by hand and the tea plantation requires a large labour force, averaging one to the acre as opposed to 1 to 3 acres in rubber plantations and 1 to 4 or 5 acres in peasant coconut groves. This labour force has been supplied by the importation of more and more Tamil labourers from South India, and the tea-plantation manager has to be a man well skilled in looking after people.

Tea grows best at a height of 3,000 to 5,000 feet, and the orderly plantations form a monotonous kind of scenery; to prevent soil exhaustion and erosion, the tea bushes are usually interspersed with 'shade' trees and sometimes with leguminous weeds. The withering, fermenting and drying are simple processes and are completed in a 'factory,' usually situated in the middle of the tea plantation itself and close to the manager's bungalow.

Second in importance to tea came rubber, which was first introduced to Ceylon in 1876. Its cultivation is described in Chapter VIII, since it plays a far greater part in the economy of Malaya than of Ceylon. It is only necessary to say here that Ceylon was the centre from which the Brazilian rubber tree reached the rest of the Far East, and to note that, while Malayan rubber plantations are mostly flat, those in Ceylon cover the lower slopes of the mountains up to approximately 2,000 feet. The rubber-tappers are, again, Indian Tamils.

The third crop which was developed for its cash value in this period was the coconut. It differs from all others, however, in that it is primarily a consumption crop which was later expanded for its cash value as an export. Coconuts are, like the bamboo in South China and Kaoliang in Manchuria, an 'all-purpose' crop. They provide the villager with almost all that he needs: timber and thatch for his house, food and drink (both alcoholic and soft), oil for his lamp, fibre for mats and clothing, shells from which pots and vessels can be made. They had been cultivated, therefore, from time immemorial before the Western demand for oil and fibre made it worth increasing the acreage to provide an export crop. In Ceylon this increase simply meant that the villagers and small planters grew more coconuts; it did not lead to the establishment of large-scale modernised plantations, as it did in the Philippines.

The rise of a genuine middle class in Ceylon was largely the result of the economic conditions created by the development of cash crops and a connection with the world market. It did not really start until the last decade of the nineteenth century, when it profited from a steady expansion of education which had been going on for fifty years. Any country whose economic development followed the path of Ceylon's in the nineteenth century would inevitably begin to produce an urban middle class, but the peculiarity about Ceylon is that this class was Ceylonese and not Chinese or Indian, as it was in the other Buddhist countries, Burma and Siam. Moreover, the degree of urbanisation among Ceylonese is higher than that of almost any other Far Eastern people—13 per cent. in 1931 and 15·3 per cent. since 1946

This urban middle class live mostly in Colombo and its environs (361,000 population), but Jaffna, Mt. Lavinia, Kandy, Moratuwa and Galle all have populations around 50,000 to-day—quite a high figure for a country whose total population is only 8 million.

It seems probable that the growth of this middle class was partly made possible by the fact that the island was a more manageable size than most areas of the Far East. As a result, the impact of the Portuguese and Dutch rule had really made an appreciable effect on the people before the British arrived, and when the British administrators set out to create roads, and the missionaries to build schools, they did not feel themselves faced with an impossible task. The standard of road communication in Ceylon was always high relative to India, and it is perhaps significant that the first stage coach to run in the Far East was from Colombo to Kandy.

Education was also well ahead of India. An excellent foundation had been laid during the Dutch administration, and a great missionary effort was made throughout the nineteenth century. Partly in reaction to this, there was also a strong revival of Buddhist learning from the middle of the century onwards. By 1911 the literacy figures had passed 25 per cent.—a figure they have never reached in India— and the literates were not merely illiterates crammed with a simplified form of reading for propaganda purposes, but people who had enjoyed some years of real education. In 1921 a University College was formed, and in 1942 this was promoted to the full status of a University. The existence of this middle class, small though it was, had a considerable effect on the political development of Ceylon. It meant that there was never any lack of responsible Ceylonese to fill either administrative or political posts and the progress from colonial to independent status was carried through with an unusual degree of common sense and practicality. In 1948 the Ceylon Independence Act came into force and Ceylon became a fully independent member of the Commonwealth. With a more varied social structure than most of her neighbours, she has a better chance of a stable and prosperous future.

MODERN SOCIAL AND ECONOMIC STRUCTURE
(a) *Natural Resources*

Ceylon has no mineral resources of any importance, though she has long been famous as a source of precious stones and pearls. Graphite is mined when the world price makes it profitable, and just before the war Ceylon was supplying 14 per cent. of the world's needs. The forests, although extensive, are not of any great commercial value, being mostly tropical rain forest, badly suffering from

24. Fishermen with catamarans near Colombo. This coconut-fringed coast is typical of Ceylon.

*chena* cultivation (i.e. shifting cultivation with burning) and not yet adequately controlled. There are a few rare trees, like satinwood, which are valuable when they can be readily extracted.

The fisheries could perhaps be of some importance and could certainly provide enough fish to render the present imports unnecessary, but the Ceylonese are not a seafaring race, and the native craft, the catamaran, is totally unsuitable for large-scale fishing. Since 1947 the Government has been developing inland as well as deep-sea fishing.

*(b) Distribution and Occupations of the People*

Considering that its total population is just over 8 million (an increase of 21·7 per cent. since 1946) the number of separate racial communities in Ceylon is high. These are usually listed as: Up-country or Kandyan Sinhalese, Low-country Sinhalese, Jaffna or 'Ceylon' Tamils, 'Indian' Tamils, 'Ceylon' Moors, 'Indian' Moors, Burghers and Europeans. The figures given in the following brief list are simplified estimates based on the 1953 Census. It is note-worthy that this census shows an increase of 25 per cent. between 1931 and 1946 and 21 per cent. between 1946 and 1953. The growth of population in Ceylon since the early nineteenth century has been as remarkable as that in Malaya—from less than 1 million in 1823 to 6½ million to-day. Nevertheless, only a quarter of the land is cultivated and there is still plenty of additional land which could be brought into production. The pressure of population, therefore, is not so serious as in India, Java or Japan.

*Sinhalese* (5,600,000). The Sinhalese are by tradition divided into Up-country or Kandyan Sinhalese and Low-country Sinhalese. The difference is not so great as that between the hill peoples and the Burmans, but the principle of differentiation is the same. The Kandyan who lives in the mountain core of Ceylon has preserved a more conservative tradition, less affected by Westernisation and more tribal in organisation. Kandyans probably do not account for more than one-third of the total number of Sinhalese, and as their rate of increase is less than that of the Low-country Sinhalese, this proportion is continually decreasing.

The Low-country Sinhalese have the highest reproduction rate of any community in the country, and as the combined Sinhalese already account for two-thirds of the total population, Ceylon is not, like Malaya, faced with any possibility of an immigrant community ultimately outnumbering the native stock. The Low-country Sinhalese are also the most Westernised community, apart from the Burghers and Europeans, and inhabit the richest and most urbanised part of the country. It is mainly from them that the urban middle class of which we have spoken are drawn.

*Jaffna Tamils* (700,000). The Jaffna or 'Ceylon' Tamils are the descendants of the Tamil invaders from South India who destroyed the civilisation of the tank country. When the economy of this area broke down completely, the population receded before malaria and the jungle northwards and southwards, the Tamils to the north and the Sinhalese to the south. The Jaffna Tamils are physically difficult to distinguish from the Sinhalese. Culturally, they have preserved many features of a more rigid Hinduism, including caste and *purdah*, and an Indian rather than Ceylonese form of dress. The Jaffna Peninsula is not a fertile part of the island and the Jaffna Tamil is noted for his industry and simple style of living. A number have emigrated to Malaya, where these qualities have enabled them to compete even with the Chinese, mainly in clerical positions.

*Indian Tamils* (985,000). The Indian Tamil community is made up almost entirely of labourers brought over within the last fifty years to work either on plantations or for the Public Works Department. Conditions of recruitment and work are now pretty good and the scarcity of labour during the war years greatly increased the bargaining power of the tea-pickers and rubber-tappers. Since the establishment of Indian and Ceylonese independence, the political future of this community has given rise to considerable dispute between the two Dominions, since the Government of Ceylon is reluctant to grant them Ceylonese citizenship.

*'Ceylon' and 'Indian' Moors* (475,000). Both these communities are descendants of the Arabs who have left their mark all over Malaysia. As in the case of the Tamils, the 'Indian' Moors are simply later arrivals who are not permanent inhabitants of the island, but come over from the Malabar coast for trade. The 'Ceylon' Moors, on the other hand, like Arab communities in Singapore and Java, are on the whole prosperous above the average and have contributed in many ways to the life of the island. The fact that the Ceylonese are not themselves seafarers was originally an additional reason for the attraction of a strong Arab community; but many of them now are settled on the land.

*Burghers* (44,000). The Burghers are the descendants of the Dutch settlers, and almost all Burgher families now have a proportion of Sinhalese or Tamil blood. On the whole, they maintain the Western rather than the Eastern mode of life, but they have completely accepted Ceylon as their native country. They are mostly occupied in trade or Government service, and help to swell the numbers of the urban middle class.

The other Europeans in Ceylon cannot really be counted as part of the permanent population at all, since they rarely if ever come to regard it as their home. They are the planters, business-men and officials who spend their working lives in Ceylon, but do not bring up their families there, and usually retire to their native lands when they give up work.

This diverse population is occupied in two different economies which run separately, side by side, but almost out of contact with each other. The life of the Sinhalese and of the Jaffna Tamils is based on a typical Eastern subsistence economy ; that of the Europeans and Indian Tamils on a Western plantation economy. You do not find Sinhalese working as labourers in the Western economy nor Indian Tamils settling down in the villages and small towns.

There are, however, one or two important points of contact. Ceylon, in spite of its fertility, is not self-supporting either in rice or fish, and these imports are paid for by the export of cash crops produced by the plantation economy. This is more clear now that the plantations are being rapidly bought up by Sinhalese, so that the old accusation that their wealth was drained from the country can no longer be made. That part of the community which practises the subsistence economy cannot therefore be considered separately, since it would not be able to subsist on its unaided efforts.

The chief subsistence crops are rice and coconuts (palmyra taking the place of coconuts in the north). The standard of rice cultivation in Ceylon is not very high, and it is generally agreed that the yield per acre, the lowest of any Far Eastern country, is considerably lower than it need be. When you add to this the loss of great areas of potential paddy land by the destruction of the tanks and the large number of unproductive Buddhist priests, it is not difficult to see why Ceylon has been for the last 300 years at least an importer of rice, at first from southern India, and later from Burma.

During and since the war this subsistence economy has been diversified by the establishment of small local industries, designed originally to supply imported goods that could no longer be brought from abroad. Of these the factories for the treatment of coir (coconut fibre) and plywood, which are based on Ceylonese crafts and raw materials, are likely to prove a permanent addition to the wealth of the country; whether others, which produced shoes and glass, can stand up to foreign competition when conditions of normal trade return is more doubtful. The quality of their output was not particularly good.

After the war the Ceylon Government, like many others in the same position, was perhaps rather over-optimistic in the 'plans' for nationalised industrialisation which were approved. Factories for the production of cement and plywood were, however, established and at least a beginning has been made of a national hydro-electric power scheme and very small steel and textile industries. Anything which will diversify the economy of the island and reduce its dependence on one or two cash crops is clearly sound economics, but Ceylon suffers from the general shortage of capital; and the aid so far given under the Colombo Plan has not been enough to do more than touch the fringes of the problem.

## (c) Communications and Commerce

It is clear from the briefest glance at the map that Ceylon is a natural centre of sea communications, and since the eighteenth century Trincomalee has been one of the natural naval bases which command Far Eastern waters. Trade, however, centres on the modern harbour of Colombo, with a dry dock capable of taking vessels up to 10,000 tons and berths, even during the south-west monsoon, for thirty-five vessels. Ceylon lies on the direct route from the Suez Canal to Calcutta (1,250 miles), Rangoon (1,235 miles), Singapore (1,577 miles) and Fremantle (3,100 miles). Its greatest importance, perhaps, is as a refuelling point on the route to Australia. Air routes do not pass through Ceylon, but cross northern India to Burma and then run either via Bangkok to Hongkong or down the Malay Peninsula to Australia.

Ceylon's exports consist almost entirely of tea, rubber and coconut products, with small quantities of gems, spices, cacao, graphite, etc. Of these tea is by value outstandingly the most important, the value of exports in 1954 being nearly four times as great as that of rubber exports. During the war, of course, when the Western Allies were cut off from their normal supplies of natural rubber in Malaya, Sumatra and Indo-China, Ceylon rubber became very important, and its value as an export had climbed to more than half that of tea. In recent times, however, it has not always been possible to find a ready market for Ceylon's rubber except in China when that country was similarly excluded from the Malayan market. It seems likely that for some considerable time the tea plantations, exporting nearly half their output to Great Britain, will remain the basis of the country's economy; and this would appear a strong reason against any hasty plans of nationalisation.

Copra and other coconut products suffered severely in the great slump of 1929, and even by the beginning of the war there was very little demand for Ceylon copra. The post-war shortage of fibres and oils changed all that and there is now a steady demand and an even more valuable export of desiccated coconut. The main import continues to be rice and paddy, as it was before the war, but Ceylon is also still a large importer of cotton piece goods and, comparatively speaking, of coal.

The political development of Ceylon since the war has followed the same sort of lines as that of the Philippines, with which the island has many affinities. Independence was reached without any bitter struggle against the colonial power and the first elections returned a 'national front' with a group of splinter leftist parties in opposition.[1] Unlike most South-east Asian countries, Ceylon never suffered from an armed communist rising. She has, however, had her share of the usual troubles with minorities, in her case South Indian Tamils rather than Chinese. Good sense on the part of the Indian and Sinhalese Governments has prevented really serious clashes, but if this community is to be absorbed as citizens of Ceylon they will have to be assured of equal rights.

Relations with Britain have remained good, although the new Government is anxious to limit very strictly the existence and use of British bases in Ceylon. Since the decision to establish an R.A.F. base on a virtually uninhabited island in the Maldive group this should not present any great difficulties.

### (d) Hinayana Buddhism

Ninety-one per cent. of the Sinhalese are Hinayana Buddhists. The main principles of the Hinayana system have been outlined in Chapter I. Unlike the Mahayana in China and Japan, which has been in decline for many years, Hinayana Buddhism is a powerful social force to-day in Ceylon, Burma and Siam. This is largely due to the revival in Ceylonese Buddhism during the nineteenth century, when, faced with the strong counter-attraction of an enthusiastic Christian mission, the Buddhist leaders adopted many Christian practices, including the communal singing of hymns and the establishment of Young Men's Buddhist Associations.

The social effect of Hinayana Buddhism in the villages is mixed: it is a conservative and traditional force, valuable in its stabilising effect, but, like all such forces, apt to oppose changes, such as malaria control, which have nothing genuine against them but their novelty. Its doctrines of peace, kindliness, learning and generosity have undoubtedly done much to soften the naturally violent Ceylonese nature (like the Burmese, they have a very high murder rate). On the other hand, the proportion of unproductive males maintained

---

[1] The Ceylon elections of 1947 returned: 42 United National Party, 21 Independents, 10 Trotskyists, 7 Ceylon Tamil Congress, 6 Indian Tamil Congress, 5 Leninists, 3 Communists, 1 Labour.

in the priesthood is certainly one cause of the island's poverty in food, and Inner Mongolia is a living example that this withdrawal of manpower, if carried beyond a certain stage, can destroy a country's economy. In Burma before the war it was already becoming doubtful whether the bad priest did not do more harm than the good priest did good; and the 'left wing' youth were almost as bitter about the priesthood as they were about the British.

Ceylon also has her share of 'left wing' youth, divided among the usual somewhat romantically named revolutionary groups (see footnote to p. 170), but not having been occupied by the Japanese she has not suffered from any violent revolution. She seems to have a better chance than most south-east Asiatic countries of proceeding with the necessary reforms and development without such a reactionary disaster.

## BIBLIOGRAPHY

*Modern Burma.* J. L. Christian.
*The New Burma.* W. J. Grant.
*British Rule in Burma.* G. E. Harvey.
*Lords of the Sunset.* Maurice Collis.
*Grandfather Longlegs.* I. Morrison.
*Burmese Trials.* George Orwell.
*Ceylon.* Lord Holden.
*Ceylon under the British.* G. C. Mendis.
*A Geography of Ceylon.* E. K. Cook.
*The Jungle Tide.* John Still.
*The Purple Plain.* H. E. Bates.
*The Jacaranda Tree.* H. E. Bates.
*The Economic Development of Burma.* E. E. Hagen.
*The Economy of Ceylon.* Sir Ivor Jennings.
*The Village in the Jungle.* Leonard Woolf.

# CHAPTER SEVEN

## SIAM (THAILAND) AND INDO-CHINA (VIET NAM)

THIS chapter, as explained in the preface, suffers from a problem of names. In 1939 the Siamese Government announced that in future the country would be called Thailand and the people not Siamese, but Thais. This decision has been twice reversed, and it will be simpler to keep to Siam. In 1954 the Geneva agreements involved the division of Indo-China into Northern and Southern Viet Nam, Laos and Cambodia.

### STRUCTURE AND CLIMATE

Geographically, the whole Siam-Indo-China peninsula, with much of Burma, is a single entity. Culturally, it is accurately named as the place where the culture of India and China meet, and the French were well justified in referring to Burma as British Indo-China.

The life of each of the two countries is grouped around its river valleys: the Menam in Siam and the Red River and Mekong in Indo-China. The Menam and Mekong were probably one river in geological times, and the watershed between them is low; it is not remarkable, therefore, that in historical times a single empire has often embraced the upper waters of both. The Mekong (2,734 miles) is much the longer of the two; and the Menam, rising near a point almost halfway down its course, where the Mekong takes an eastward bend, flows almost due south to the Gulf of Siam. The centre of Siam's life has always been the flat plains and delta of the lower Menam, though the alluvial plain is relatively narrow and does not extend more than 100 miles inland. To the north-west the hills around Chiengmai are as sparsely populated as those of the Shan States in Burma, into which they merge; to the north-east the dry plateaux between the Menam and Mekong are more desolate still; to the east, between the mouths of the Menam and Mekong lie the almost uninhabited and unexplored Monts des Cardamomes. Except from the sea, the Menam valley enjoys a natural isolation.

Indo-China has two great river valleys, the Mekong, of which we have just spoken, and the Red River. The Mekong, in spite of its great length, is of little use for navigation, since, like the Salween, it flows mainly through mountains and is interrupted by serious rapids. On its lower course it is connected with a vast inland lake, the Tonle Sap (area over 1,000 square miles at low water and nearly 4,000 at high water), which acts as a natural flood control, filling up when the river is high and emptying when it is low. The Red River, like the Mekong, rises in China, but flows south-west through Tonkin to the sea in 670 miles, less than a quarter of the length of the Mekong. It is navigable on its lower reaches, but carries down a vast quantity of silt, so that its delta (already nearly 6,000 square miles) is building up with great rapidity.

South of the Red River and between the Mekong and the sea lie

25. Limestone rocks in the Baie d'Along, Indo-China.

the mountains of the Chaine Annamitique, an ancient eroded plateau, round which, in geological times, were formed the folded ridges of Tonkin. To the north of the river these ridges form a mountainous barrier which separates Tonkin and the Red River basin from south China. The mountains of the Chaine Annamitique are steeper on the east coast than the west (cf. the mountains of Korea), and the narrow, broken coastal plains at its foot are another of the fairly populous areas of Indo-China. The Bay of Cam Ranh on this coast is one of the finest natural anchorages in the world and of considerable strategic importance. To the west of the Chaine Annamitique and between the Red River and Mekong is a mountainous area, infertile, sparsely populated and difficult to cross.

As a whole, the climate is of the normal tropical monsoon type. The annual range of temperature in Saigon is only 6·2° F. between

April, the hottest month, with an average temperature of 85°, and December, the coldest, with an average temperature of 78·8°. Bangkok is much the same. The Red River Valley, however, is 10° farther north and not much south of the Tropic of Cancer; there is therefore considerably greater temperature range, from an average of 84·5° in June to 62·6° in January.

Rainfall is heavy during the monsoon periods, diminishing as you get farther from the sea; Tonkin (Red River valley) also enjoys a considerable amount of winter drizzle, called the *crachin*, which, with the general high humidity, makes possible an extra rice crop in what would normally be a dry season.

The coasts of Indo-China are subject to occasional typhoons, a violent form of cyclonic storm which is more fully described in the chapter on the Philippines.

## HISTORY AND PEOPLE TO 1857

### (a) The Annamites

Tonkin, or the Red River basin, was first civilised by the Chinese under the Han Empire. The Chinese ruled over the area for more than 1,000 years, from 181 B.C. to A.D. 939, and, finding it barbarous, left it indelibly stamped with Chinese culture. The very word Annam is a Chinese one meaning 'pacified south.' The Annamites are, however, not Chinese, and from 939, when a patriotic rebellion drove out the Chinese, to 1882, when the Annamite Emperor accepted a French protectorate, Annam preserved her independence: the only interval of renewed Chinese rule from 1407 to 1428 was so short as hardly to count, and was no more than an incident in the ultimately successful wars which Annam waged with the neighbouring kingdom of Champa.

Internally, the subsequent history of Annam is fairly simple: the Le Dynasty, an imperial family on the Chinese model, drove out the Chinese in 1428 and ruled, officially, until 1786: in fact, from 1527 onwards they were as much puppets as the Merovingian kings or Japanese emperors, and the real power lay in the hands of two great noble families, the Trinh in the north and the Nguyen in the south. After the expulsion of the last Le Emperor, these two families came into open conflict, and ultimately the Nguyen won the imperial throne, which they have held since 1802; in the last phase of the civil war Nguyen Anh was much helped by a French Bishop, who mustered for him a body of auxiliaries at

Pondicherry and got back to Indo-China in the significant (for France) year of 1789. Externally, the slow expansion of the Annamites over the rest of Indo-China has been one of the permanent features in its social development; for the Annamites are a hardier, more resourceful, more ruthless and harder working race than the other peoples of Indo-China; where they have conquered, they have quickly settled. Consequently, areas once included in the spreading Annamite Empire have soon become Annamite in culture and racial stock. Starting in the Red River basin and delta, they had practically absorbed the kingdom of Champa (the eastern coast of Indo-China) by 1470. By the beginning of the eighteenth century they had completed the absorption of Champa and spread also over the Saigon delta (Cochin China), so that the Annamite territory included the whole Red River basin and a narrow coastal strip extending almost the whole way round the country. Their expansion was still going on in Cambodia and Laos when the French intervention 'froze' the internal Indo-China situation; it seems probable that if the French had not intervened, the Annamites would gradually have expanded over the whole of the present area of Indo-China. As usual in such cases, they are unpopular both in Laos and Cambodia.

In race the Annamites are clearly of southern Mongoloid type, with pale, yellowish complexions, fair, regular features and an average height of 5 feet 3 inches. There may well have been intermingling with an earlier proto-Malay stock. Their culture and religion are, as we have seen, almost entirely Chinese in origin. In some respects, the 'freezing' effect of the French protectorate has meant that institutions abolished in China, such as the mandarinate, the Civil Service examinations and the Confucian ritual, were long preserved at the Court of the Emperor of Annam.

In a few respects, the Annamites appear to have been in the past either more resourceful or less bound by tradition than the Chinese. They have shown rather more ability to extend the unit of communal self-government beyond the village, and they have gone considerably farther in solving the language problem. Starting with a tonal spoken language and written characters almost indistinguishable from the Chinese, they proceeded in the thirteenth century to a syllabic system and in the seventeenth to the Romanised script, invented by a French Jesuit missionary, which is used to-day. Unfortunately, this Romanised script (*Quoc Ngu*), like many other improvements of the rational age, is falling out of favour with the extreme nationalists of Annam.

## (b) The Cambodians

By racial origin, the Cambodians of the Mekong basin are of Mon-Khmer stock; their culture is Hindu. Culturally, they therefore represent the Indian half of this joint Indo-Chinese society.

As early as the third century B.C. there were Hindu settlements in the Mekong delta, but a united Cambodian Kingdom was not

26. The ruins of Angkor Wat. For Hindu influence compare the Jagdish Temple on p. 29.

firmly established until the ninth century A.D. The hero founder of this kingdom and builder of the great temple and capital at Angkor was Indravarman, a Hindu prince of the imperial family of Sumatra. Under his descendants, Cambodia passed through the zenith of its power from A.D. 900 to 1200 (Indravarman died in A.D. 899 with Angkor still incomplete). At this time it included all western

Indo-China and most of modern Siam, the river systems of both the Mekong and the Menam. Its culture was feudal Hindu, with Mahayana Buddhism also flourishing. In Angkor Wat and the Bayon Temple at Angkor it has left one of the greatest architectural monuments of the world. The Hindu influence is clear in the illustration compared with that of the Jagdish Temple at Udaipur in central India.

From the middle of the thirteenth century Cambodia was hard pressed by the southward movement of the Thai peoples, and after Angkor had been captured and sacked four times between 1300 and 1500, the capital was removed south, ultimately to Phnom-Penh, where it remains to-day, the ruins of Angkor being left to the jungle, from which French archæologists rescued them in the middle of the last century.

The collapse of the Hindu Cambodian empire before the Thai produced profound changes in the social structure of Cambodia, the break-up of elaborate feudalism, the re-emergence of the native Khmer speech and the spread of Hinayana as opposed to Mahayana Buddhism.

Cambodia always maintained a shrunken and qualified independence although threatened often by Siam, and a vassal first of Annam and then of France. The people are rather taller and darker than the Annamites, but not so resourceful or industrious; they remain conservative, devout Hinayana Buddhists, with an unusually rigid code of social procedure and great emphasis on chastity. That their artistic gifts have not entirely abandoned them may be seen in their exquisite and highly formal dancing.

## (c) The Thais

The Thai peoples originally lived in Yunnan. They had probably started moving south earlier, but the key date for their migration into Burma, Indo-China and Siam is usually taken to be the capture of Talifu, their capital, by the Mongols in 1254. The same force, therefore, which opened China to Europe and shifted the centre of the Chinese Empire from the Yellow River to the Yangtse was responsible for the foundation of Siam.

At first there were two kingdoms, with capitals at Chiengmai in the north and Ayuthia in the south. After a series of wars, Ayuthia established control over Chiengmai, but almost immediately became involved in recurrent wars with Burma, waged over such personal matters as which king had the greater number of sacred white

M

elephants. The Burmese captured Ayuthia in 1568 and held the Siamese in subjection for fifteen years. In the mid-eighteenth century the long warfare between Ayuthia and Burma reached its climax. The Burmese captured Chiengmai in 1762 and utterly destroyed Ayuthia in 1767. The ferocity of their behaviour we have noticed in the previous chapter.

Strangely enough, this utter defeat led to the founding of modern Siam. A Siamese general (significantly enough, he was of mixed Thai and Chinese blood, usually a strong combination) founded a new capital lower down the Menam River at Bangkok. He soon drove out the Burmese, and when he himself went mad (in a somewhat Tiberian fashion) his successor founded the Chakkri Dynasty, whose descendants hold the Thai throne to this day. Under this first Chakkri king, Vientiane and Luang Prabang in the Laos area of Indo-China were brought under Thai domination, and also the northern Malay states as far south as Kelantan and Trengganu: a general Siamese suzerainty over Cambodia seems also to have been recognised.

One of the political difficulties of this whole area is that at some time or other in history almost every state has included most of its neighbours under a loose form of suzerainty, just as they almost all at one time or another acknowledged China as overlord. Tokens of submission in the form of ceremonial presents would be sent, as the Malay state of Kedah sent them to Bangkok, long after all practical dependence had been forgotten. This means that whenever any one of the states feels in a nationalist or expansionist mood, it is able to claim that territories on its frontier belong to it 'by virtue of the suzerainty acknowledged in the year so-and-so.'

While the Nguyen were consolidating the Annamite Empire to the east of the Indo-Chinese peninsula, the Chakkri were doing the same to the west. By the middle of the nineteenth century they were already rivals for suzerainty over Cambodia. The Thai were fortunate in that King Mongkut (1851–68) foresaw the necessity of compromising with the West, and in 1855 opened the country to Western trade, signing a treaty of friendship and commerce with Great Britain. The Annamite Emperor, Minh Mang, took the opposite line of persecuting the Europeans and particularly the missionaries and converts. In 1857 the French, whose missions had been prominent in Indo-China since 1658, having failed with diplomatic protests, intervened by force. They soon occupied

Saigon and Cochin China, the three eastern provinces of which the Annamite Emperor was forced to cede to France—a belated return, perhaps, for the French Bishop's assistance to his ancestors.

## MODERN VIET NAM

### POLITICAL SITUATION

From 1858 onwards the French gradually extended their control. The steps by which they did this were reflected in the political history of French Indo-China, which showed very much the same diversity as that of Malaya and for the same reasons. The extension of European control at a time when 'naked imperialism' was becoming increasingly unfashionable, produced in both countries a mixed system of direct government and protectorates, starting in Indo-China with the direct cession to France of the three eastern provinces of Cochin China in 1862 and ending with the establishment of the Indo-Chinese Union at the end of the century. The constituent members of this Union were:

(*a*) Cochin China (eastern provinces ceded in 1862; western annexed in 1867), governed directly as a French colony.

(*b*) Cambodia, a protectorate established in 1864.

(*c*) Annam, an empire of the Confucian type, under French protectorate from 1874.

(*d*) Tonkin, nominally a subsidiary protectorate to Annam, but governed as a direct colony from 1897.

(*e*) Laos, officially a protectorate from 1893, but actually governed directly, except for the kingdom of Luang Prabang in the north.

In establishing this political position, France faced possible conflict with three other powers, China, Siam and Great Britain. The possibility of conflict with Great Britain arose in the period of Anglo-French colonial rivalry at the end of the nineteenth century, from the fact that the gap between British territory in Burma and French in Indo-China was obviously narrowing. It was resolved in 1896 by a convention in which both parties agreed to regard Siam as a neutral zone: a supplementary agreement of 1904 between Britain and France defined western Siam as a British sphere of influence and eastern Siam as a French. This arrangement was humiliating to Siam, but was certainly instrumental in preserving Siamese independence. The other two conflicts were resolved only by force. That with China developed from the unique conception which the Chinese had inherited of their place in the world. This conception has affected the whole Far East in two ways: in the behaviour of Chinese residents in other countries and in the diplomatic procedure of the Chinese Government. Both factors will receive their fullest treatment in this chapter, but are relevant to other chapters.

The Chinese emperors, as we have seen, regarded themselves as the natural rulers of mankind; they accepted embassies from other nations, including Western nations, only under the guise of emissaries paying tribute. Any area, therefore, which at any time during recorded history had been tributary to China was regarded by the Chinese court as legitimately part of their Empire. The duties of the vassals were often kept up, since they consisted of no more than the presentation of ceremonial tribute and the receipt of often more valuable 'presents' in return. From the international point of view, the infuriating thing about this claim was that while China hotly resented any interference with her 'vassals,' she also disclaimed any responsibility whatever for their behaviour. Although Annam had been in practice independent of China since A.D. 939, she was still a technical vassal of this kind in 1874, when the Emperors accepted the French protectorate. On these grounds, the Chinese opposed the expansion of French control in Tonkin, and a desultory, undeclared war dragged on between 1884 and 1885, before the French position was recognised. There was some apprehension that in 1945 the Chinese might renew this claim, but the Chinese troops which had taken over Tonkin from the Japanese were in fact withdrawn in accordance with their agreement.

The conflicts between France and Siam arose from the fact that about the middle of the nineteenth century Annam and Siam were rivals for control of the declining kingdoms of Cambodia and Laos, regions where no boundaries had ever been fixed. France took over the Annamese claims. The first dispute arose in 1864, when envoys of both countries claimed the right of crowning the new King of Cambodia: the French envoy did it and the Siamese acquiesced. In 1893 it was the expansion of Siamese influence in Laos (the Lao people are racially Thai) which induced the French to establish their protectorate and expel all Siamese garrisons east of the Mekong by force. Geographically, it would seem reasonable that the main stream of the Mekong should form the boundary between the two countries, but the Siamese have some justification for resenting the way in which the French established themselves on, and in one place beyond, this boundary. France got her way in 1893 by the despatch of gunboats to Bangkok. The negotiations were then dragged out so long that by 1907 the French had still not evacuated the areas which they had 'temporarily' occupied in 1893 to enforce the completion of the agreement.

To secure their final withdrawal, the Siamese had to cede the two Cambodian provinces which France had assured to them in 1867. Culturally and geographically, these provinces belong in Cambodia, and the Siamese claim is only the usual sketchy one based on the fact that all Cambodia was at one time a Siamese vassal. It is not surprising, however, that in 1941, when France was weak, the Siamese Government should have attempted first to secure the small areas *west* of the Mekong, which the French had retained, then to recover the lost Cambodian provinces and, finally, that protectorate over Cambodia as a whole which they had failed to establish in 1864. The Japanese award in this case was a compromise, giving Siam much, but not all, that she asked for. It was naturally annulled on Japan's defeat, and the final agreement then left the boundary where it was in 1939. It is not surprising, however, that there were rumours of an attempt by the Communists under Ho Chi Minh to purchase Siamese support by the offer to cede these non-Annamite provinces to Siam.

### SOCIAL AND ECONOMIC STRUCTURE

#### (a) Population

In view of the diversity of races and political systems in French Indo-China, it is important to stress first of all the overwhelming preponderance of the Annamites. It is not only that they are the most vigorous among the different peoples, and, but for the French, would have engulfed the rest; but they are also far more numerous than all the rest put together—19 millions out of a total of 24 millions. They inhabit all the most fertile and populous areas, Tonkin, the eastern coastline and Cochin China.

Of these, Tonkin is one of the most densely populated areas in the world. Even its mountainous areas are not so deserted as is usual in the Far East, and in the Red River delta the density is over 1,000 per square mile. In the delta region of Cochin China, the Annamite settlement is more recent, and the density of population is only just over 250 per square mile. This great difference between areas almost equally suited to rice cultivation is one of the anomalies of Indo-Chinese society, and many schemes have been attempted to drain off some of the surplus population from Tonkin to Cochin China or the other areas. The non-Annamite areas, for instance, are very sparsely populated indeed. The total population of Cambodia is about 3 millions, while Laos has a population of no more than a million. In the long run the migration of 900,000 refugees from the Communist North to Southern Viet Nam after the partition in 1954 may prove a blessing.

## (b) Occupations

The vast majority of the population of Viet Nam, like most Far Eastern peoples, were peasant farmers before the partition, most of them owners, except in Cochin China, where tenant farmers and landless labourers were ·common. Rice is overwhelmingly the most important crop, forming, as usual, nine-tenths of the peasant's diet. As often happens, it is frequently supplemented by fish, of which great quantities are caught in the Tonle Sap, where the fish density is said to be higher than anywhere else in the world. Beyond this so great a surplus is grown that French Indo-China was one of the world's great rice-exporting areas, and rice formed 70 per cent. of its export trade. Other less important crops are maize, sweet potatoes, sugar, tobacco and a little inferior silk. A purely export crop of pepper, making this area the world's second most important source, is raised in Cambodia: this crop is entirely in the hands of the Chinese. The standard of living is very low—probably not quite so low as in peasant China, but rather lower than in Thailand.

There are few large towns: only four with populations of over 100,000, Hanoi, Phnom Penh, Saigon and Cho Lon. Cho Lon and Saigon are now administered as one area, but the two were once separate towns, Cho Lon being a Chinese commercial settlement of long standing. The government of South Viet Nam have this year (1956) made a determined effort to absorb their overseas Chinese, declaring all Chinese born in the country to be Vietnamese citizens and banning to 'foreigners' all the most lucrative trades in the country. So far the effect of this Draconian measure has been the usual black-market scandals, a drying up of rice exports and a drop in the price of domestic rice to the lowest level ever recorded.

## (c) Education and Westernisation

The original French policy in the colony of Cochin China was one of assimilation to France, on the model of French colonial

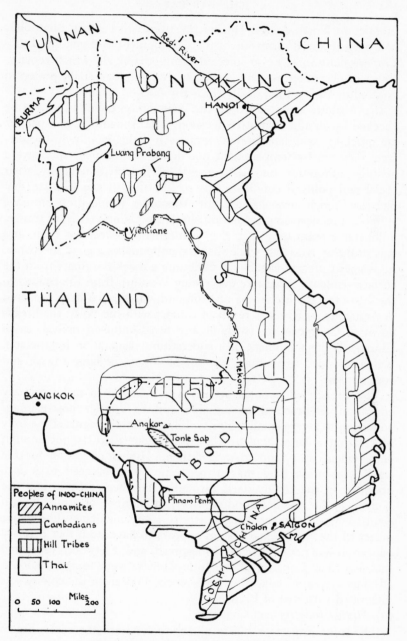

YUNNAN

CHINA

Red. River

BURMA

TONGKING

HANOI

Luang Prabang

Vientiane

THAILAND

R. Mekong

BANGKOK

Angkor

Tonle Sap

CAMBODIA

Phnom Penh

Peoples of INDO-CHINA
Annamites
Cambodians
Hill Tribes
Thai

Miles
0 50 100 200

Cholon SAIGON

COCHINCHINA

XIII. Racial distribution in Indo-China.

practice in North Africa. During the twentieth century this policy had been reversed in favour of the development of a genuine Indo-Chinese culture. It never affected Cambodia at all, which remains a sort of charming museum piece, an Indo-Chinese Bali, protected both culturally and politically from any outside influence.

In Annamite lands, however, the assimilation policy could not be checked by an administrative decision. The Annamites, as a people, are quick to assimilate foreign ways, even if this is only on the surface; they are by temperament not unlike the French, and have a genuine admiration for many aspects of French life; finally, their social and political condition was so like that of the Chinese that had the French never existed, the Annamites would probably have suffered a modernising revolution similar to China's. It is, of course, a debatable point how deep the 'Westernising' effect has been, and it is probably true that while the Annamite makes a good mechanic, he is not at present capable of designing a machine. Apart from the surface tendency to admire everything Western, from the cinema to the cigarette, three changes of profound significance have occurred in Annamite society as a result of contact with the West: the breakdown of Confucianism (without any neo-Confucian revival, as in China); the abandonment of a superstitious veneration for the soil, which impeded agriculture; the establishment of large towns; and communism.

The French educational system was intended to make primary education as practical as possible and to restrict post-primary education to a very small minority. This at least recognised the folly of creating a large student class for whom there is not enough employment of a kind to satisfy them. Higher education for the small proportion (less than 1 per cent.) who proceed to it was provided in the colony itself through a number of *lycées* and the University of Hanoi (founded, 1917); a number of students also went to French universities, mostly to study medicine. The major defect in the educational system appears to have been that primary education was not sufficiently widespread, and it has been estimated that less than a quarter of the Indo-Chinese went to any school at all. The system of education for French children in the colony was integrated with that of France.

(d) *Mining Industry and Commerce*

The most important mines in Indo-China are the coalmines of Quang Yen in the Red River delta. They produce virtually all the coal in the country, $2\frac{1}{4}$ million tons a year, and the seams are so thick in places and so close to the surface that all the mining was originally open-cast. The coal is a good, smokeless anthracite, and, being so near the sea, is easily transported. The over-population of the Tonkin delta provides an endless fund of labour. Tin, zinc and gold are also produced in small quantities, and iron ore is available. There is plenty of potential hydro-electric power, which has not been developed.

The most important manufacture, and the only one providing any quantity of exports, is the great cement industry of Haiphong, which supplied almost all the countries of South-east Asia, and is therefore of considerable strategic importance. It is based on the Tonkinese coal and the limestone of the eastern Annamese coast. Output in 1937 was 235,000 tons. Besides this there are one or two match factories and a small cotton-spinning industry, for local consumption.

Plantation agriculture is represented mainly by rubber. Since the fillip imparted in 1922 by the Stevenson restriction scheme, which did not include Indo-China and therefore left her free to compete against the older and now restricted areas, the rubber plantations in the south have provided an increasing proportion of the world's supply. By 1938 Indo-China was producing 60,000 tons a year and supplying all the needs of France. There are no other plantation crops except the coffee and tea grown for local consumption.

Indo-China normally had a surplus of exports over imports and a Budget surplus. The volume of foreign trade per head, however, was not great—less than that of Java or the Philippines. By far the most important single export is rice, of which Indo-China provided before the war about a quarter of the world market:[1] maize was also exported in large quantities to France, and rice, rubber and maize provided three-quarters of the total.

Imports consist mainly of normal manufactured goods, with textiles forming roughly a quarter of these.

Before the war most of the rice went to China through Hong Kong or to France; the maize to France; the rubber to the U.S.A.; and about half the coal to Japan. The natural direction of trade for Indo-China is with other countries of the Far East, but the trade depression of 1930 hit the country as hard as it did other primary producers: in 1928 France had introduced a policy of reciprocal free trade within her Empire, and the result was that from 1930

[1] The post-war exports of rice in a good year (1954) were only about one-third of what they had been in 1938: but rubber exports had increased by nearly 50 per cent.

onwards the proportion of Indo-Chinese trade which was carried on with other countries of the French Empire increased, and soon outstripped her trade with the rest of the Far East. This economic link with France was of great value and as late as 1954 three-quarters of all imports were French; one-third of all exports went to France or the French Union.

## (e) The Annamite Nationalist Movement

Considering the state of Asia, the disruptive social changes mentioned in Section (c) and the Annamite tendency to be influenced by events in China, the growth of the Annamite nationalist movement in the late nineteenth and twentieth centuries is not surprising. At first the leaders were mainly intellectuals, who found it easier to arouse sympathy in France or Russia than in French Indo-China itself: it should be remembered that one of the strongest elements in that French 'way of life' which Annam was assimilating was the passion for liberty and approval of revolutions. Colonisation had always had its left-wing opponents in France, and Tonkin has always been one of the least popular colonies. The effective life of the movement dates, however, from 1925, when Ho Chi Minh, an Annamite Communist, arrived in Canton from Moscow, ostensibly to work for Borodin's mission to Nationalist China, but actually to organise the Annamite Communist Party.

Ho Chi Minh has proved a resistance organiser of great skill, and as a result of his work the Communist Party has long dominated the Annamite nationalist movement. In 1929 an attempt at a terrorist revolution was started with the assassination of the Director of the Labour Recruiting Bureau, followed in 1930 by mutinies at Yenbay. As usual, this outbreak was mixed Communist-nationalist in its origins and support, and the justice or injustice of the severity with which it was repressed cannot be calculated in individual cases. The mutineers at Yenbay killed their own officers with savage cruelty and then could think of nothing further to do; on any scale of justice, they deserved what they got. Elsewhere unarmed crowds demonstrated, like the Koreans in 1919, and like the Koreans or the Indians at Amritsar, were fired upon; many individuals among them may well have been innocent dupes.

In general, it is true that the French executed far more than the revolutionaries killed; and it is equally true that had they failed to suppress the rising, the country would almost certainly have been plunged into an orgy of cruelty and massacre with which the occasional savageries of the repression could bear no comparison.

Those who are horrified by the economic exploitation or cruel repression of Asiatics by Westerners have the right to be so only on the grounds that Western standards and political experience should have devised some method of eliminating the necessity for such methods. By Asiatic standards, the Western administrations of America, Britain, Holland or France have been probably the most just and certainly the most merciful in the history of the Far East. It is reported that of 200 political prisoners sent after this outbreak to the French prisons, thirty died within the year: humanitarian circles in France were justifiably shocked, but the average Asiatic government, unaffected by the West, would have considered such a death-rate remarkably low.

The suppression of the Yenbay mutiny and of the Communist disturbances which followed it drove the Communist leaders into exile. They still retained their position, however, as the hard core of the nationalist movement.

## War and Post-war Developments

The post-war recovery of Indo-China was rendered impossible by the struggle between the Viet Nam, or Annamite nationalist government, and the French. When France surrendered in 1940, Japan was quick to demand military concessions in Indo-China, and the Vichy Government preferred the policy of collaboration with the aggressor, in the hope, no doubt, of affording as little real help as possible. From then until 1945—that is, throughout the critical part of the Far Eastern war—Indo-China was in effect a Japanese dependency. In 1945 the Japanese decided to take over direct control, and, in spite of sporadic acts of heroic resistance by individual companies of French and Annamite troops, they were obviously able to do so quite easily. The blow to French prestige inflicted by these events and by the defeat of metropolitan France was even more severe than that suffered by the Dutch, whose Navy had put up a gallant resistance. Consequently, when Indo-China was liberated, the nationalist movement was relatively much stronger and more confident.

Two groups of Annamite nationalists had their headquarters in southern China during the last years of the war: the Communists under Ho Chi Minh, and the non-Communists, who enjoyed the support of the Chinese Government. The Communists were, however, very much the better organised, and when the Chinese occupied north Indo-China and permitted the establishment of an

independent Annamite state of Viet Nam, it was they who secured
the dominant part in the various 'united front' governments which
were set up. In the south the British occupied Cochin China, and
under their ægis the French were soon able to turn out the Viet
Nam officials and restore, not without some fairly fierce fighting, their
own administration.

Cambodia and Laos were on the whole glad to see the French
back, and the original French plan was for a federation, within the
French Empire, of Cambodia, Laos, Cochin China and Viet Nam,
allowing considerable independence to Viet Nam. This solution is
almost exactly the same as that proposed later by the Dutch for
Indonesia.

Agreement was first blocked by the proposal to separate Cochin-
China from Viet Nam, and negotiations between the French Government and Ho Chi Minh dragged out for many months in an
atmosphere of growing distrust on the Vietnamese side. In spite of
this, Ho Chi Minh signed the agreement for a truce in September
1946, but there was no real good faith, and after sporadic breaches of
the truce on both sides, general hostilities began in December and for
eight years plunged the country in civil war. As long as China north
of the border was controlled by Nationalist forces, the war was a
stalemate, with the French controlling the towns and the day, the
Vietnamese the countryside and the night. Gradually the Annamite
nationalist movement became more completely Communist dominated, and the establishment of a friendly Communist China over
the border, ready to help with training and material, enabled them
to take the initiative. In 1954 a large French force, surrounded at
Dien Bien Phu, was forced to capitulate.

France was weary of a war which was draining the best of her
manpower to no purpose, and the Great Powers feared the outbreak
of another Korean, or even global, war. It was not difficult, therefore,
for the Conference called at Geneva to achieve not only a cease-fire
but an agreement to a temporary partition of the country between a
Northern (Communist) and Southern (Democratic) Viet Nam,
leaving Laos and Cambodia as independent states. As in similar
cases elsewhere this temporary partitioning seems to be hardening
into permanent hostility.

## MODERN SIAM

### (a) Political

We have seen that the foundation of modern Siam (Thailand)
was the acceptance of the West by King Mongkut. He was succeeded

in 1868 by King Chulalongkorn, who reigned for forty-two years, abolished slavery and steered the country with great skill through the period of adaptation to an Asiatic world ruled by the West. As a result, Siam emerged as the one country of south-east Asia which retained its independence. The main principle on which Chulalongkorn worked was to accept Western advice, but not Western control, to give way when, as in 1893, it came to a trial of force, and above all to balance one Western power against another (e.g. France and Britain between 1890 and 1900).

The Westernisation of Siam's administration was carried on largely through 'advisers' attached to the various government departments, and in the selection of these the principle of balance was carefully maintained. The chief or general adviser was always an American, presumably because the U.S.A. was considered the least dangerously imperialist power. The Financial and Judicial Advisers (including Police, Customs and Inland Revenue), were usually British, the Legislative Adviser, French. A Dane was head of the Provincial Gendarmerie; there were Germans employed in the Railways, Posts and Telegraphs, and Italians and French in the Public Works. All these foreigners were individual servants of the Siamese Government, not agents of the Western Powers.

We have already noted the disputes with France over the Indo-Chinese boundary. In 1909 Siam's southern boundary was also adjusted when she surrendered to Britain her suzerainty over the northern Malay states of Kedah, Perlis, Kelantan and Trengganu. This arrangement was not particularly unpopular in Siam, since the inhabitants were Malays and the suzerainty had been for many years a very shadowy one. There was no dispute or resort to force in the discussions, and Siam received in return the abandonment of certain extra-territorial rights by Britain and the grant of a loan for railway construction. In view of the trouble which Siam has experienced with Malay irredentism in the remaining southern Malay states, the line might well in fact have been drawn farther north with advantage to all parties (see sketch map, p. 194).

In spite of the gradual Westernisation of administrative methods, Siam remained an absolute oriental monarchy until 1932. In this year a bloodless *coup d'état*, partly inspired by the Army and partly by liberal politicians, forced the King to accept a constitution on 'democratic' lines. The cause of this *coup* was mainly that the new King was reverting to an older Siamese custom of reserving all important posts for members of the Royal Family: its authors, whether of the liberal or military wing, were called the 'Promoters.' Although theoretically democratic, the new Constitution allowed for a temporary period during which half the Assembly were to be appointed by the Government; this period has been continually prolonged, and all Thai governments have in fact been confined to one or other group of the original 'Promoters,' constantly jockeying against each other for power. The two most prominent men in this struggle have been Pibul Songgram, the present Premier and Chief of the Army, and Nai Pridi Panomyong, the original leader of the left-wing intellectuals and widely believed to be a Communist.

## (b) Social Structure (including the Overseas Chinese)

Siam is a country of one great city, Bangkok, with a population of 900,000, and beyond that nothing very much except villages. Similarly, there is a small community of highly educated and cultured Siamese grouped round the Court and Government, and beyond that nothing very much except peasants. The middle class consists almost entirely of Chinese, who number about one-fifth of the total population (3 million out of 16 million), and control virtually all the trade. The country is not over-populated and the standard of living of the Siamese peasant farmer is probably slightly higher than that of his neighbours. He is also one of the few people who has gained rather than lost from the war.

The problem of the overseas Chinese concerns almost every country in south-east Asia, and is in many ways comparable to the problem of the Jews in Europe. Except in Malaya, where large numbers were brought in as coolies in the Chinese-owned tin-mines, the overseas Chinese usually devote themselves to 'business,' shop-keeping and market-gardening. The great majority of them come from Kwantung and Fukien on the south-east coast of China. The Chinese from these provinces are particularly quick and adaptable and they prove so much more industrious, enterprising, daring and commercially minded than the majority of Malays, Thais or Mon-Khmers that in areas populated by these peoples they soon get control of virtually the whole commerce of the country.[1] In Indo-China only the Annamites have been able to compete with them. This produces a position where they enjoy all

[1] Actual numbers of overseas Chinese are very hard to calculate. The best modern estimate is probably that of a Royal Institute of International Affairs Study Group and is as follows: Malaya and Singapore 3,300,000, Siam 3,000,000, Indonesia 2,000,000, Viet Nam over 1,000,000, Burma 350,000, Philippines 300,000, British Borneo 275,000.

27. Bangkok from a B.O.A.C. plane. Note the pinnacles of the ancient wats and the modern town planning.

the profits and all the unpopularity of the middleman and money-lender in an agricultural society. Not only are they unpopular with individual peasants, but they earn the enmity of the governments where they live by remitting a large proportion of their earnings to China for the upkeep of their families: that, after all, was what the came abroad for; but it means that most of the wealth earned in a country's retail trade is steadily drained away beyond its frontiers.

This flow of wealth was very much discouraged after the war by the Communist policy of confiscating the remittances on arrival; present Chinese policy is trying to rectify this mistake. Too often they import their own Chinese secret societies with all their attendant disturbances; recently they have tended to import also their own Chinese civil war, so that both in Malaya and Siam Chinese Communists are a serious menace to public order. This attitude is supported by the Chinese Government wherever it feels relatively strong enough to do so, and every overseas Chinese is encouraged to claim dual nationality, Chinese and that of the country he lives in—but Chinese first.

Clearly the existence of such a minority in Siam is a serious social problem. It is no new one, for of the 3 million Chinese in Siam about 2½ million were born in the country. Siamese governments recently have tried to meet it by limiting further immigration, by controlling the curriculum of Chinese schools with a view to seeing that the children are educated as Siamese citizens, and by encouraging Siamese to enter the commercial professions, which have previously been a Chinese monopoly. It is doubtful how far such artificial measures will be successful, and in the economic sphere the Government has already been driven to the establishment of State trading concerns in order to compete with the Chinese. For a long time Siam refused to establish normal diplomatic relations with China, on the grounds that Siamese citizens of Chinese race would claim the protection of the Chinese diplomatic and consular representatives.

The fact that this 'overseas Chinese' problem, which affects the whole Far East, is more serious in Siam than anywhere else except Malaya is a sufficient refutation of the curious view, sometimes put forward, that it is a product of Western colonialism. The Chinese had spread in this way far and wide over south-east Asia long before the Westerners arrived, and are just as much attracted to independent areas as to colonies. It is in fact conditions in China and not in the receiving countries that have been responsible for the emigration.

Siam avoided serious implication in the Far Eastern war. After offering token resistance, Pibul Songgram accepted the Japanese invasion and made formal declaration against Britain and the U.S.A. Siam engaged in no warlike acts, however, other than the acceptance at Japanese hands of Burmese and Malayan territory, which was restored after the war. As the tide of war swung in favour of the West, real power in Siam passed into the hands of Nai Pridi and the 'Resistance Movement,' although no overt resistance was offered, or required by the Allied High Command.

At the end of the war Pibul was relegated to comparative disgrace, and from 1945 to 1947 Pridi held office as Premier with a moderately left-wing Government, such as was common at that period. This position was reversed by a *coup d'état* in November 1947, since when real power has been in the hands of Pibul, with the backing of the Army. Pridi is believed to be in exile in China.

The government of Pibul has proved stable and acceptable to the Siamese people. It has joined the Manila Treaty and with the Philippines takes an active part, supported by the U.S.A., in resisting Communist expansion.

## (c) Commerce and Industry

We have seen that the Siamese does not take naturally either to commerce or industry. Like Indo-China, Siam has always been an exporter of raw materials, rice, tin, rubber, teak and tungsten, and an importer of manufactured goods, chiefly textiles and foodstuffs.

Bangkok is connected by rail with Singapore, and the Japanese built, with prisoner-of-war labour, a strategic railway, now disused, through some of the world's worst country, to link up with the Burmese system in Tenasserim: the junction with the Cambodian system through Battembang, though contemplated, has not yet been achieved. It is doubtful whether the Burma-Siam Railway will ever be restored now, and the main foreign trade of the country is likely always to be seaborne. What is more important is that Bangkok is an ideal staging point for all air routes from the Far East to Africa or Europe, and already an important air junction. The B.O.A.C. photograph opposite p. 190 gives a very clear picture of the mixture of ancient and modern in the city.

Since the 1932 revolution, the attention of successive Siamese governments has been increasingly drawn to the extent to which the country's exports are foreign-controlled or exploited. The rice was almost all processed and marketed by Chinese; the teak-

N

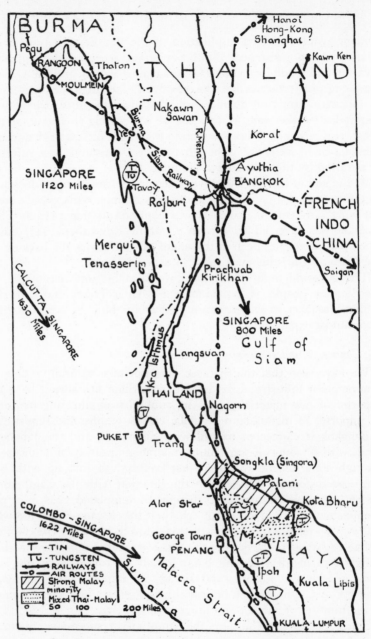

XIV. Burma, Thailand and Malaya: the complication of routes, races, tin, tungsten and frontiers. Note Bangkok's central position as an airport.

extraction companies were 88 per cent. foreign owned (mainly British and French); the rubber, which in 1939 had reached 40,000 tons, putting Siam fourth in the world's rubber producers, was mainly planted and marketed by Chinese immigrants from the Malayan plantations. The Government has tried to meet this situation by such moves as the establishment of the Thai Rice Company and the Government petrol monopoly, and by banning foreign-controlled companies from coastal shipping.

This first type of reaction, the attempt to secure for Siamese nationals the control of already existing commercial operations, has some chance of success. Against it, however, must be counted the indifference, and therefore often incompetence, of the Siamese nationals themselves, and the serious blow to all foreign confidence and investment which is dealt by such actions. A country must be very sure, for instance, that its own nationals will provide an adequate coastal shipping service before it drives out the foreigner: for the foreigner who has once seen his property expropriated or rendered valueless will be in no hurry to return if it proves that the native article is too costly or inefficient.

The second type of reaction—the attempt to develop entirely new and quite inappropriate industries on Western lines—is still mainly in the visionary stage and likely to remain there. This type of superficial Westernism is on a par with the importance attached to the cultural regeneration which, during the Fascist dictatorship, was expected from the compulsory adoption of Western hats.

Nevertheless Siam remains one of the most stable, happy and least overcrowded countries of South-east Asia. Her overseas trade is expanding; in 1954 she exported, by volume, 24 per cent. of the world's total exports of rice, 6 per cent. of the rubber and 6 per cent. of the tin; and unless her future is threatened by subversion or aggression from without, she has an economy and an administration (including the Police Force) capable of preserving order and sustaining a reasonably rapid improvement in the standard of living.

## BIBLIOGRAPHY

*Siam: Past and Future.* Sir J. Crosby.
*Thailand: The New Siam.* V. Thomson.
*French Indo-China.* V. Thomson.
*Little China: The Annamese Lands of Indo-China.* A. H. Brodrick.
*Economic Changes in Thailand since 1850.* J. C. Ingram.
*Public Administration in Siam.* W. D. Reeve.
*A Dragon Apparent.*
*The Struggle for Indo-China.* E. J. Hammer.

# CHAPTER EIGHT

## MALAYSIA

### STRUCTURE AND CLIMATE

WE shall include in the term Malaysia the Malay Peninsula and that wide subcontinent of innumerable islands now known as Indonesia which lies to the south and east of it; the greater part of these islands were more familiarly known to the British reader before the war as the 'Dutch East Indies.' The Philippine Islands, in spite of certain geographical and historical connections, we will leave to the next chapter.

The Malay Peninsula itself is the northern land-based end of a chain of islands connecting Asia and Australia and separating the Indian Ocean from the South China Sea and the Pacific. Looking at it from north to south, the peninsula slants slightly eastward of a due north-and-south line, and this slant is carried on and accentuated until by the time you reach Java or New Guinea the island chain has become more like the circumference of a vast circle, and has wheeled almost due west and east. Within this circle, east, therefore, of Malaya and north of Java, is an area of sea larger than the Mediterranean and more thickly dotted with islands than any other sea in the world. These islands vary in size from Borneo, the fifth largest in the world, to tiny clumps of palm or strips of beach. The beauty and diversity of them is indescribable in a few words, but those who have read the stories of Joseph Conrad will remember the picture he paints of palm and sand and river mouth, hidden and inextricably interlaced in an uncharted labyrinth of blue sea-lanes. You will get some idea of what one of his rivers looks like from the illustration of the Rajang River on page 234.

There are only two gaps in this outer circumference of islands that afford a practicable passage for shipping between India and China. Every ship that sails between these countries must pass either through the Straits of Malacca, between Malaya and Sumatra, or the Sunda Straits, between Sumatra and Java. The Straits of Malacca route, past Singapore, is 1,200 miles the shorter, and when you consider that India and China have long been the two most populous areas of the world, it is not difficult to account for the strategic and commercial importance of Singapore. One of the bogies which for a long time haunted certain sections of the British

Press was the fear that someone—presumably the Japanese—might cut a canal through the Siamese part of the Kra Isthmus, where southern Siam overlaps with northern Malaya, and thus render Singapore itself 500 miles too far south. Such a canal would in fact have had no value either strategic or commercial, since its exit would have been commanded from Burma and its running costs too high to be profitable.

This geographical position, like a fence with gates in it, has had a profound effect on the history of Malaysia, at once the barrier and the link between two great civilisations.

Now let us consider what the lands that form this barrier are like themselves. To the north-east of the Straits of Malacca stretches the Malay Peninsula, to the south-west Sumatra. Malaya (the peninsula) is a small country, a little larger than England without Wales, and provided, like northern England, with a backbone of mountains. These parallel mountain ranges are a good deal more formidable than the English Pennines, rising in places to over 7,000 feet and covered with thick jungle. As in Burma, they make east-west travel in the north of the country very difficult and divide the country into two quite separate areas. The eastern coastal plain is wider and flatter, as in India, but the western lay closer to the original British settlement at Penang; add to this the fact that the north-east monsoons make the eastern seaboard very dangerous to shipping, and it is not difficult to see why the modern development of Malaya has been almost entirely along the west coast. Even on this western coast there are few good harbours, for the land shelves away very gradually into the sea.[1] The one great port and city of Malaya, Singapore, has been built on an island just off the southern-most tip of the peninsula; incidentally, it lies almost exactly on the Equator.

Sumatra is a very large island, smaller than Borneo but high on the world's list, being just over 1,000 miles long and 284 miles across at the widest point. The spine of mountains that we have found in Burma and the Andamans and again in Malaya, is carried on in Sumatra and runs the whole length of the island, in this case close to the west coast. The highest peak is over 12,000 feet, and many of them are volcanic. Incidentally, this great mountain range is carried the whole way round the circumference of Indonesia to

[1] When the liberation of Malaya was being planned, it was found that there were very few points where a submarine could approach close enough to the shore to land a beach reconnaissance party, and few if any beaches firm enough to support an armoured landing.

New Guinea, where it has been so little surveyed that rumours
were always recurring of a peak in the Owen Stanley Range there
higher than Mt. Everest. The chain is carried on after the break
of the Sunda Strait by Java and then the islands of Bali, Lombok,
and Timor, until you come within 300 miles of the northernmost
territory of Australia. North of this chain lie the Celebes Islands,
stretching northwards to meet the southernmost outliers of the
Philippines. The climate is of the tropical type described in Chapter I.

## History and People to 1824

The Malays and Indonesians are of a single racial stock and have
as much right as any of the settled races of the Far East to consider
themselves the native inhabitants of the countries to which they
have given their names. It is probable that they drifted south in
prehistoric times, when Malaya, Java and Sumatra were a single
land mass with no intervening straits at Sunda or Singapore. Even
so, there are, as in India, survivors of earlier aboriginal races in
Malaya, known as the Sakai and Semang tribes.

Malays tend to have clear brownish complexions, slightly flattened
noses, brown eyes, finely proportioned but small figures and cheerful
dispositions. Like the Burmese and Sinhalese, they seem always to
have been both friendly and quick-tempered, very careful both of
their own dignity and of their guests', conservative and often lovers
of beauty, utterly uninterested in acquiring more money than they
actually need.

The Malay Peninsula itself seems never to have developed any
high degree of civilisation before the coming of the Westerners,[1]
but Java and Sumatra were from the seventh century A.D. within
the orbit of the great Hindu civilisation of Sri Vijaya, centred probably at Palembang in Sumatra. The last remnants of this culture
survive in Bali, the island to the east of Java, where they became a
stock attraction to Western expatriates and world-cruise tourists
between 1930 and 1939. Taken all in all, however, the contribution
of Malaysian civilisation to the world's sum of beauty in dancing,
music and the plastic arts has been great in the past and may well
be great in the future.

This Hindu civilisation was gradually taken over and modified
by the Moslem Arabs between the twelfth and fifteenth centuries,
and the whole of Malaysia with the exception of Bali is now Moslem

[1] It is possible that evidence of such a civilisation is now beginning to be found.

28. Rice-fields and coconut palms in the hills of West Java.

in faith and culture. There have, of course, been Christian influences, as everywhere else in the Far East, and it is remarkable that although modern Indonesian nationalism might well have drawn on Moslem fanaticism from the first, two of the main leaders of the 1946 Republican government in Java were Christians.

The social structure on which the European powers impinged for the first time when the Portuguese fleet arrived at Malacca in 1509 was therefore the more or less homogeneous Arab-Malay Moslem world which covered the whole of Malaysia and the Philippines. The vast difference in social structure and density of population between Malaya and Java to-day seems to have been a creation of the period of European rule.

It is perhaps as well to state this difference at the outset. In 1821 the population of Java was $4\frac{1}{2}$ millions and that of Malaya unknown, but probably well under 1 million. By 1935 the population of Java had increased tenfold to 42 millions, while the Malay population of Malaya had scarcely reached 2 millions, although its area is about the same. This difference was partly due to the greater fertility of Java's volcanic soil, partly to the fact that whereas Java was from the first the centre of Dutch power in Asia, Malaya was on the very fringe of the British sphere of influence. In the history of Western dominions in the Far East, the true comparison is between Java and India rather than between Java and Malaya. It may in fact come as a surprise to many British readers that the Dutch used always to refer to 'British India' as distinguished from Netherlands India, just as we have seen many Frenchmen used to call Burma 'British Indo-China.'

The Portuguese then, after their great but short heroic age in the sixteenth century, when they controlled the Indian Ocean, had been driven out by the British and Dutch merchants by 1641, and the newcomers shared the spoil between them. Yet the Portuguese influence in Malacca, as in Ceylon and southern India, has been, considering the shortness of its impact, curiously strong; for, as we noticed in the last chapters, they came to give as well as to receive. Like the Spaniards in the Philippines, they came primarily as missionaries of Christianity and Western civilisation, not as merchants to make as much money as possible before returning home.

With the Portuguese out of the way, the Dutch were free to deal with the British, whom they finally drove out of Java in 1684. The British for the next 150 years found their time fully occupied in India; and until Sir Francis Light committed them to the acquisition of Penang at the end of the eighteenth century, Malaya, apart from the Dutch trading station at Malacca, was left almost untouched by European influence.

In the East Indies the Dutch Company, putting out its major effort in the seventeenth and early eighteenth centuries, extended its interests widely over the Malaccas as well as Java; but by the end of the eighteenth century it was bankrupt, and by a mixture of oppression and corruption had so far lost its hold that its influence was virtually confined to certain parts of Java. At this moment, when reforms similar to those made in the administration of the British East India Company were already contemplated, and when the startling principle had been laid down that 'the welfare of the East Indies' was to be the Company's first concern, Holland itself was incorporated in Napoleon's Empire. As in 1940, the exile government called on the colonies to join in the fight against the tyrant and to admit British troops; but, as happened in most of the French Empire in 1940, the colonies refused to do so. They were therefore occupied one by one by force. It was thus that the first major appointment of Sir Stamford Raffles, founder of Singapore, co-founder of the London Zoo and perhaps the most attractive of all British Empire-builders, was the governorship of Java in 1811.

Britain at this time had no interests of her own in Malaysia except a new and tenuous foothold at Penang and an old and decaying trading post at Bencoolen, on the west coast of Sumatra. The Home Government's intention in occupying Java was merely to expel the Dutch and French, who might be a menace to India, and then, if possible, return the island to the Javanese.

Raffles, however, had quite different plans. He combined with his genuine belief in the superiority of Western civilisation a deep sympathy with the Malays and a hatred of tyranny, slavery and monopoly. It was a curious coincidence that though he hated the Dutch as monopolists and slave-traders, his work as the only British Lieutenant-Governor of Java has always been linked with that of Daendels, the Radical Dutch Governor-General, who immediately before him represented the Napoleonic 'Batavian Republic.' Between them these two introduced to the Dutch possessions a system of direct government instead of 'company' trade. This direct system was closer to that of British India than it was to either the later British system in Malaya or the later Dutch system in the Netherlands East Indies. It reflected simultaneously the

Napoleonic faith in reason and organisation of Daendels, who was a former Dutch Jacobin general, and Raffles' conviction that the oriental peasant was better off when efficiently governed by Europeans than when badly governed by his own leaders. Unfortunately, it also reflected Raffles' Liberal and Free Trade principles, admirably suited to British colonies, which were primarily ports of commerce, but not to Dutch, which were plantations.

At the end of the Napoleonic Wars, Britain handed Java and all her former rights in Malaysia back to Holland. This decision infuriated Raffles, who had visions of a great Malaysian empire, stretching under Britain's beneficent control from the Bay of Bengal to Australia; but it adequately refutes the cynical twentieth-century legend, so widely believed in the U.S.A., that the British Empire in the heyday of its power never relaxed its grip on any territory which it had once acquired.

Baulked in Java, Raffles turned his attention to the establishment of some point of power and influence in Malaysia which should enable Britain to keep a share in the East Indies trade and at the same time allow him to put into practice his Liberal theories. He chose as second best, after failing to get the Riouw Islands, the almost uninhabited swamp of Singapore, where the British flag was raised on January 29th, 1819. Being a very far-sighted man and convinced that the principles of Free Trade, which were rapidly gaining support in England, were right, he insisted that from the first his new city should be a free port—that is, that everyone, British, Chinese or Dutch, should be free to trade there on an equal basis without hindrance. The result was immediate; few men can ever have founded a city and seen it grow more visibly under their eyes. Singapore, when Raffles picked on it for the site of his trading post, was a swampy island which had once had some importance, but now harboured no more than 200 or 300 Malay or Chinese villagers. Within the first six months 5,000, mostly Chinese traders, had flocked to the new colony. Within a year its revenues covered all its necessary expenditure—a matter of considerable importance to the Home Government. By 1825, six years later, its trade was more than double that of Penang, the older settlement, and seven times that of Malacca. This process has continued since, until now Singapore is one of the greatest entrepôt, or redistribution, centres in the Far East, where goods from every source are transhipped into smaller vessels for distribution through south-east Asia. Its population to-day has reached almost a million—that is

between one-fifth and one-sixth of the population of Malaya, and
the vast majority of these are Chinese.

The occupation of Singapore was finally recognised by the Dutch
in the treaty of 1824, by which Holland gave up all possessions in
India and Malaya and Britain all possessions in Sumatra. Holland
also agreed by this treaty to do an impossible thing—to put down

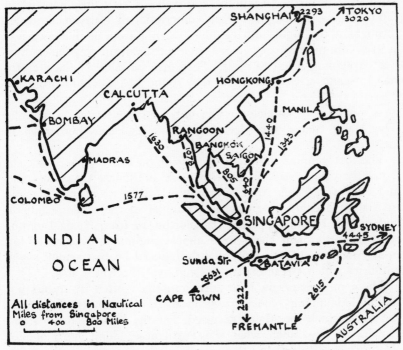

XV. Singapore. The natural centre of entrepôt trade.

the Achinese pirates, who lived in the northern tip of Sumatra,
without depriving the Achinese of their independence. From this
time onwards Malaya and the Netherlands East Indies are best
considered separately.

## THE NINETEENTH CENTURY IN MALAYA

For many years after the foundation of Singapore the Malay
inhabitants of Malaya pursued their old course, not greatly influenced
by the two trading islands of Singapore and Penang, which, under
British rule and populated mainly by Chinese immigrants, formed

purely mercantile outposts of the nineteenth century at the gates
of their disturbed Malay feudalism. Some 'anti-imperialist' writers
have suggested that the presence of Europeans in these trading
posts and their interference in local politics somehow stifled the
growth of a unified Malay civilisation. The history of those areas
in Borneo and north-eastern Malaya which were untouched by
Europeans until the twentieth century lends very little support to
this optimistic theory. Dr. Purcell's description of Malayan chronicles
throughout the eighteenth century, when European influence was
at its minimum, probably gives a truer picture of the way the country
was developing if left to itself: 'They give no sense of the life of a
social organism. Read seriatim, they sound like a column from the
*News of the World*. . . . Intrigue, murder, flight follow one another
in a monotonous catalogue. The only constant factor is misrule.
The Malay States were decaying into a feudalism bordering on
anarchy.'

The first genuine impact from outside on this society, if society
it may be called, was the great increase in Chinese tin-prospectors
and miners in Perak from 1850 onwards. The profits to be made
in Malaya had always attracted a number of the bolder Chinese,
and it soon became apparent that northward from Kuala Lumpur
right up into Siam there were almost unlimited chances of big
money in tin, with the risks slightly reduced by the general vague
authority which Great Britain wielded over the whole area.

These prospectors in their turn imported—often by means not
far off kidnapping—coolie gangs of their own countrymen to do
the work which the Malay despised. For the Malay remained and
remains to-day much what the Portuguese found him, one of
'Nature's gentlemen,' and the essential definition of a 'gentleman' is
that he does not have to work if he does not wish to. At the time
we are speaking of, the only forms of work which he found consonant
with his dignity were farming, fishing and fighting; but when he
resorted to the latter in the form of piracy, the Chinese prospectors,
many of whom were Straits-born British citizens, appealed to the
British for protection; these appeals, combined with the necessity
of suppressing the internal gang warfare of the Chinese, led to that
intervention which ended with the creation of a mixed population
under British protection. At first the British policy was to limit
their commitments to the Straits Settlements of Penang, Malacca
and Singapore, which were directly governed from the Colonial
Office; but in the end, partly on purpose, partly through 'absence

of mind,' the British Government came to exercise through advisers an effective control over all the Malay States, though the nominal independence of the Sultans was maintained.

The average Malay, as soon as he saw that he could not by plunder or piracy derive any profit from the Chinese tin-miners, left the unpleasant business of tin-mining to them and returned to the occupations on his own list, to which he has now added, in place of fighting, joining the police, driving buses and small-scale rubber-planting, but very rarely coolie (i.e. unskilled) labour for an employer or shopkeeping.

This, from the economic point of view, has been partly his downfall and partly his salvation. It has meant that the whole trade of the country has passed into the hands of the Chinese, but it has saved him in the main from becoming a hired rubber-tapper on someone else's estate or a hired labourer in someone else's tin-mine. On the other hand, tin and rubber require unskilled labour, and modern economic development requires shopkeepers; so that the result of the Malay's refusal to undertake what he considered unsuitable tasks was first to attract foreign merchants, who came to the ports to trade, and then to induce foreign capitalists to import by thousands the labour force they needed to work in their tin-mines and rubber plantations. At a later stage, mainly in Kedah and Kelantan, Malays did join these labour forces.

The Malay, however, did not particularly care. Those who have tried to exploit Malays as producers by offering them better wages or profits to do jobs they do not like, or, as was tried in Java, to produce heavier crops by improved methods, have simply found that as soon as the Malays have earned enough to support themselves for the next few months on their old standard of living, they stop work or go home. At this stage it is no good offering them two or three times as much to go on; they do not like the work and they do not wish to be rich.

If the discovery of tin destroyed the Malays' isolation, the planting of rubber entirely altered the face of his country and his whole economic existence. From the moment that it began to become commercially productive in 1905, rubber proved Malaya's staple crop: it has had periods of slump when the planters and investors lost most of their savings, but on the whole it has brought immense riches to the country.

Again this contact with the modern industrial world involved the import of a foreign labour force, since the Malays, as we have seen, would not undertake the coolie work of tapping the rubber trees. This time the planters turned to India, and thousands of Tamil labourers were brought in from the Madras Presidency, mostly on short-term contracts averaging about three years, though a number of them always stayed on in the country. These Tamils are on the whole an illiterate labouring community, and the few other Indians in the country are either merchants from western India or Sikhs originally brought in as police and watchmen. A number of these Sikhs have settled down as agriculturalists, particularly in Negri Sembilan. There are also a number of Sinhalese and Ceylon Tamils, attracted from Ceylon to fill minor jobs in the Civil Service, with which again the Malays could not be bothered. Finally, it should be remembered that many of the Malay inhabitants of Malaya are themselves recent immigrants from Indonesia.

By the end of the 1914 War, therefore, Malaya was organised into a loose agglomeration of Straits Settlements, Federated and Unfederated Malay States, all under the effective control of the British Colonial Office. Its population was very small for the area, anyhow, and also included a smaller proportion of native-born inhabitants than any other comparable area in the globe.

## MODERN ECONOMIC STRUCTURE OF MALAYA

The economic structure of Malaya since then has been based—and based far too exclusively for the welfare of the country—on those three factors which in historical order attracted the foreigner to her shores: entrepôt trade, tin and rubber. We have seen how in the early nineteenth century the entrepôt traders were able to establish themselves in the great ports without much affecting the life of the Malay inhabitants in the hinterland; but both tin and rubber production meant considerably increasing the population without in any way increasing its production of food or other necessaries. As long as Malaya had an assured market for tin and rubber and external sources of supply for food, this did not matter very much. But a slump in the world price of either commodity or the interruption by war of rice shipments from abroad meant serious hunger in Malaya, for it must be remembered that by 1938 rubber and tin accounted for nearly two-thirds of her total exports (canned pineapples, a subsidiary industry considered important by Malayan standards, accounted for only 1·2 per cent.), while nearly one-third of her imports consisted of foodstuffs—mainly rice. This economic structure is particularly dangerous to-day, when the balance of world prices has moved so drastically in favour of foodstuffs, and when there is a world shortage of the rice which Malaya needs to import: moreover, both tin and rubber are commodities of which the world supply even in pre-war years exceeded the world demand, and for which synthetic substitutes are likely to become increasingly available. A glance at the pre-war situation will show clearly the difficult problem with which Malaya is faced.

### (a) Tin

Malaya and south Siam are probably the richest tin-bearing areas of the world. The ore is found in large quantities in the granite rocks, and over countless ages has been washed from them into the silt of the alluvial deposits. The first miners, as we saw, were the Chinese, working on an open-cast system and without elaborate machinery. Up to the 1914 War they were responsible for three-quarters of the tin-mining in Malaya, but since then the introduction by European capital of the bucket dredge and of hydraulic mining has rendered their part in the industry less important. The bucket dredge is a horrifying and expensive object, which sucks up the tin-bearing mud, washes out the tin, and then spews forth the mud again. Hydraulic mining is carried on by directing a very powerful jet of water on to the lode and washing out the tin-bearing gravel. Installing these dredges or hydraulic plants took more capital than the average Chinese could collect, and their running cost was so high that it demanded a high and constant world price for tin. When, therefore, in the great slump of 1929 the world price of tin dropped from £284 a ton in 1926 to £120 in 1929, the big dredging companies preferred to restrict the output of tin in an attempt to keep up the price rather than to cut the costs, as the small Chinese miner might well have done by tightening his own belt.

The first restriction scheme failed because small producers had not been included, and restriction in the main producing countries merely meant that the output of the small producers increased. The second restriction scheme worked better, but while it profited the big companies by maintaining a stable high world price, it was unpopular with the Chinese miner: he considered that as the cheapest producer of tin in the world he was being unfairly treated by having his output restricted for the benefit of others. Moreover, it is doubtful whether the world demand would have been adequate to make this scheme work if it had not been for the rush to buy strategic

metals from 1937 onwards. In any case, the policy of maintaining
by restriction of output a high and stable price for tin cannot fail
to be an incentive to consumers to develop substitutes.

Not only tin-mining, but tin-smelting is a Malayan industry.
About the time that European capital was first invested in Malayan
tin-mining, the British Government was induced to place a prohibi-
tive duty on the export of raw tin ore, and so prevent the tin-smelting
industry from leaving Malaya. The tin-producers claimed that
unless Malaya had her own smelting industry, she would be at the
mercy of the U.S.A., the largest consumer, who through her
monopoly of smelting and alternative supplies of ore in Bolivia
would be able to fix the price of raw Malayan tin more or less to
suit her own convenience.

Tin from its first development has been more than a staple
industry to Malaya; it has been one of the main sources of revenue.
The fine roads, the Government buildings, the hospitals of which
Malaya is justly proud were never financed by Malayans or out of
direct taxation. Indeed, Malaya was even prouder of the fact that
there was no income tax than she was of the roads. No; all this
high level of modernisation was paid for by the rest of the world
out of export duties on tin and rubber in the Federated States and
excise duties in the Straits Settlements. They came, like everything
else in modern Malaya, including half the population, out of the
twin export commodities and the entrepôt trade. And if these fail,
then the roads and hospitals will sink back too into the jungle.

### (b) Rubber

Rubber is the sap of a tree that grows wild in the jungles of the
Amazon. In 1873 seeds were smuggled out of Brazil for Kew
Gardens by a British expedition, and eventually twenty-two rubber
saplings were raised in Ceylon. From these twenty-two are descended
all the rubber trees of the Far East, including the 4 or 5 million in
Malaya.

A ring is cut in the bark of the trees, and the thick white sap
runs out into little cups—in native plantations, coconut shells; but
this process, called tapping, cannot, of course, start until after five
or six years, when the trees are mature, so that it was not until
1910 that Malayan plantations began to supply the world with
rubber on a considerable scale. From that time onwards the rubber
industry has expanded with the growth of its one great market, the
motor-tyre industry.

29. A Tamil woman tapping rubber on an estate in Malaya.

o

A rubber plantation is a dreary sight—row upon row as far as the eye can see of straight, grey, rather ghostly trees of equal age, evenly planted, evenly grown. In the old plantations even the ground between the trees would be bared, but nowadays it has been found better to leave the natural weeds, clearing out only the few that are definitely harmful. On small Asiatic rubber plots the space between the trees is very often used for growing food crops.

The history of rubber has been very like that of tin. Everything depends on the world price, and in the boom of 1910–12, which followed the invention of the motor car, vast fortunes were made, and rubber reached 12s. a pound. By 1921, when Malaya was exporting nearly 200,000 tons a year (more than half the world's output) it had fallen to under 1s. The producers tried the usual scheme of limiting output, a system known as the Stevenson Plan. This worked fairly well at first, but, as in the case of tin, they forgot that limiting output was an invitation to other producers—in this case, the Netherlands Indies and Indo-China—to flood the market. The boom of 1928, however, saw the Stevenson Plan abandoned in a moment of false optimism, and an even worse slump started in 1929, in which the price fell to under 3d. a pound. The result of this was a new restriction scheme, including all the Far Eastern producers, Malaya, Ceylon, the Netherlands Indies, Siam and Indo-China. The objection to all rubber restrictions, however, is twofold: first, the difficulty of preventing the Asiatic smallholder from growing and marketing what is often his only cash crop; and, second, the fact that, although natural rubber is better for tyres, synthetic rubber is already in some directions preferable to the natural article, and too high a price for raw rubber will always drive the consumer either to synthetics or to reclaimed rubber.

In spite of all these fluctuations, rubber and tin have made Malaya between 1900 and 1940 one of the richest countries (considering wealth per head) in the world.

## Modern Social Structure of Malaya (including Singapore)

In considering the population question in Malaya it is essential for political reasons to distinguish between the mainland and the island of Singapore. The Federation, on the mainland, is an under-populated area of very mixed race. Although the area is almost equal to that of Java (40 million), the population is not more than

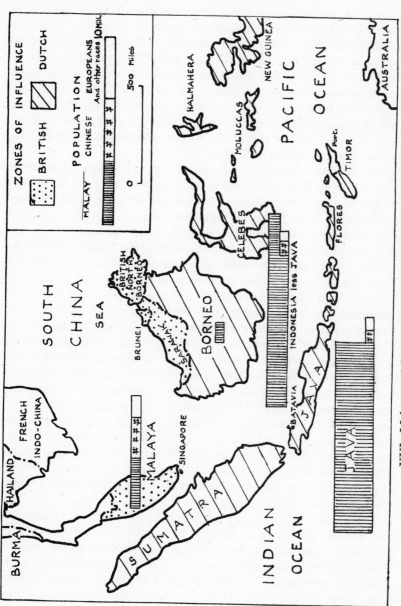

XVI. Malaya and Indonesia, distribution of population.

6½ million; and of these roughly 48 per cent. are Malays, 39 per cent. Chinese and 11 per cent. Indians; the problem, therefore, is not one of minorities but of a truly plural society. Singapore, on the other hand, is by race virtually a Chinese city with a population 80 per cent. Chinese. It is this difference in racial structure which makes union between the two so difficult to-day. The distribution of this population is governed mainly by the historical facts given above: speaking generally, where there is commerce or mining you will find Chinese, where there are rubber plantations, Indians, and where there are neither, Malays.

The Malays themselves are one of the few oriental peasantries not suffering from land shortage, though even they have been increasing in numbers during the twentieth century, largely through immigration from Sumatra. Although Malaya has been swamped with immigrant Chinese and Indians, there has never been any question of their driving out or supplanting the native race, for the simple reason that the three communities live entirely different lives. The Chinese, as we have seen, are traders and miners, the Indians estate labourers and the Malays smallholders and fishermen. Moreover, there was never any possibility of the Malay being squeezed out of his ancestral home by immigrants, because it was illegal until 1939 for anyone but a Malay to own or farm rice-land. It is doubtful, even if this had not been so, whether Chinese in any numbers would have wished to transfer their attention from the lucrative trades of market-gardening, shopkeeping, trading and mining to the comparatively unrewarding life of the peasant cultivator. The Malay peasant has therefore enjoyed throughout the British period all the rice-land that he wanted and more than he usually bothered to cultivate. He has even been assisted by considerable irrigation work in north Kedah, north Perak and Malacca. Where at present Chinese have been settled in villages, it is on land which the Malays have failed to take up.

The Malay aristocrat, on the other hand, has both gained and lost. He has had far more security and probably more money than he would have had, but much less power. Between these two, the Malay middle class scarcely exists, in spite of well-intentioned attempts to bring it into being. A small number of educated and able Malays have always been available to fill the non-European higher administrative posts in the Civil Service, the Army and the Police, none of which were open to non-Malays before 1953. But there has been no Malay Bank, no successful Malay industry and no Malay Press to

30. The village shop in Malaya. 'Overseas' Chinese and some Tamil customers.

compare with the English language or Chinese. The young student
Nationalists, common throughout the 'colonial' world, are few in
numbers among the Malays and likely to be recent Malay immigrants
living in Singapore—or London. On the other hand, it is easy to
over-estimate the traditionalism of the Malay and consequently the
political strength of the Sultans and their feudal aristocracy.

The Indian immigrants of Malaya, unlike the Chinese, were
mainly uneducated coolies brought in to work on the estates for
short terms of service; they did not, pre-war, settle down in the
country, and there was always a constantly shifting Indian population. Their conditions of work were good by Far Eastern standards,
since the Indian Government demanded a strict control over
immigrant Indian labour, and the Malayan administration was rich
enough and the planters far-sighted enough to provide good health
services. Neither are to be blamed very much for their neglect of
higher Indian education, since the population was so transitory and
the value of extended education in the present economic conditions
of Indian labourers is so doubtful. The Tamil estate schools for
primary education are compulsory on all estates and do excellent
work.

The system suffered, however, from the inevitable disadvantage
of imported labour that in times of slump the only cure for unem-
ployment was to send the labourer home to his country of origin,
probably also suffering from a slump at the same time. On the
whole, it was the Chinese and not the Indians who presented pre-war
Malaya with her social problems.

## Pre-war Political and Social Problems

The two chief problems of this type in pre-war Malaya were the
number of different political administrations in a small country
and the attitude of the Chinese to the country they were living in.

The political settlement of 1909 left Malaya with three separate
governments: the Straits Settlements, which were British colonies;
the four Federated Malay States of Perak, Selangor, Negri Sembilan
and Pahang, which were in theory independent protectorates, but
in practice a single entity controlled from Kuala Lumpur by a
Civil Service which was British at the top; and the five Unfederated
Malay States of Perlis, Kedah, Kelantan, Trengganu and Johore,
also protectorates and, apart from Johore, the most backward, the
least populated and the most Malay areas in the peninsula.

At first sight, the obvious remedy seemed to be the creation of a single authority to control the whole country; but to this two main objections were made: first, that since the relations between the British Government and the Malay States were governed by treaties, the British Government could not honourably compel the sultans to come into any scheme for a common administration against their will; and, second, that the economic interests of the different parts of the country and different communities were mutually antagonistic. As Virginia Thomson has pointed out in her *Post-mortem on Malaya*, it was difficult to make much headway with schemes for a unified administration as long as the economic interests of the tin- and rubber-producers of the Federated States were diametrically opposed to those of the entrepôt traders of the Straits Settlements.

The problems presented by the Chinese in Malaya were typical of overseas Chinese problems which we have already considered, and at first appear contradictory: at one moment the Chinese appear too anxious to be Chinese, at the next too anxious to be Malayans. These problems are easily understood, however, when one realises the determination of the overseas Chinese to get the best of both worlds. The Chinese conception of dual citizenship has in fact nowhere been better exemplified than in Malaya: as Chinese, they were responsible for a constant drain of money from the country, which they sent home to their families in China, and for the importation of Chinese domestic political quarrels into Malay society; as residents of Malaya, on the other hand, they practically created the economic life of the country and demanded in return the full privileges of citizenship.

## WAR AND POST-WAR DEVELOPMENTS

The Japanese occupation was a turning point in Malaya, as it was throughout South-east Asia. The initial blow to British prestige was offset by the successful military return in 1946, which for a variety of reasons was genuinely welcomed. The returning Government, however, faced two new problems as well as the unsolved legacies of the past.

First, the return flow of immigrants to China and India had been stopped turning Malaya into a permanently 'plural society,' with no 'majority race.' Second, about half a million Chinese, driven from the towns and mines, were 'squatting' on the fringes of the jungle as small-holders on unregistered land. The boldest among them, led by the Communist party, had established a 'resistance movement' in the jungle itself.

Since no united Nationalist movement existed, Britain at first attempted to impose a rational long-term solution. This was the unification of mainland and Singapore in a single Malayan Union, citizenship of which was open on easy terms to the Chinese. In the first flurry of post-war reoccupation the Malay Sultans agreed to this constitution, but Malay opposition to it was soon organised by the United Malay National Organisation (U.M.N.O.). Since the Chinese did not seem particularly enthusiastic about it, the British Government withdrew the new Constitution in favour of a Federation of nine Malay States and two British Settlements on the mainland, while Singapore reverted to the separate status of a Crown Colony.

The world shortage of rubber meant a fairly rapid economic recovery for Malaya, but this was interrupted in 1948 by a campaign of armed Communist violence. Though this insurrection failed, it did have a very considerable effect on the social development of the country. Much money which could have been better used was inevitably diverted to tracking and controlling the terrorist bands into which the Communist forces soon split up. Much more important, the half million new Chinese peasants from the jungle fringes were re-settled in new villages, some of which are now thriving towns.

This great piece of social engineering, which has changed the whole pattern of Chinese life in Malaya, was mostly carried out during the régime of General Templer, who brought a new sense of urgency to the whole development of the country, from local government to national parks.

The Government's urgency in pressing on with the foundations of independence was at last met by political initiatives to form a National Government, capable of negotiating the transfer of power. The first attempt to form a united non-communal party under Dato Onn, who had led Malay resistance to the Malayan Union, failed. Its place has been taken by an alliance of frankly communal parties, the Malay U.M.N.O., the M.C.A. (Malayan Chinese Association) and the Indian parties. It is this alliance who are due to succeed the British as the first government of an independent Federation of Malaya in August 1957.

They will be faced with three great problems. The first, though perhaps least permanent, will be the militant Communists, a jungle force of about 2,000. The second will be relations with Singapore. It is not unnatural that a Malay leader of territory enjoying great communal harmony, where the transfer of power has been unusually well handled, should be nervous of union with a Chinese city where students are still out of hand and independence uncertain. Nevertheless some form of union seems the only possible solution, since Singapore is neither viable on its own nor likely to accept the perpetuation of colonial status. Since a main objection to fusion is that it would upset the balance of races, giving the Singapore city Chinese a quite unwarranted predominance, a solution might be found by including the neighbouring territories of Brunei, British Borneo and Sarawak in some sort of Federal Union. Whatever form of government emerges will have to face the third and greatest problem: how can a genuinely multi-racial society of this type be governed, not by a colonial outsider, but some form of democratic national administration.

## INDONESIA FROM 1824–1901

### 1830–70: *The Culture System*

The period from the departure of Raffles to the beginning of the 'Culture System' in 1830 may well be described as 'The Years of Muddle.' Raffles and Daendels had done the Indies great service in transforming a trading company into a government, but Raffles' economic theories, based on Adam Smith and the last word in modern economics, were hopelessly unsuitable to the position of Holland. Free Trade, after all, meant that the profits went to the most enterprising traders, and at this time the British were the most enterprising traders in the Far East, and the Dutch the least enterprising. Consequently, the Indies proved a continual drain on the Dutch Treasury, until in 1830, faced with national bankruptcy at home, the Dutch Government gave Van den Bosch a free hand to reorganise the whole system. Within one year he had balanced the Budget, and for ten years, from 1831 to 1840, sent home an average profit to the Home Government of 9·3 million florins a year. This yearly payment of tribute was known as the *batig slot*, and is the most straightforward example known in modern times of the administration of colonies in the interests of the mother country. It was achieved by the Government going into trade on a really large scale: the taxes on the native population were changed to payment in kind, and the Javanese were compelled to plant a proportion of their land, varying from a fifth upwards, with those crops which the Government required; these were then shipped to

Amsterdam in Dutch ships for sale on the European market. The profits to Holland were immense, and a system which had been introduced to save the homeland from bankruptcy was prolonged as an unfailing source of too easily earned wealth.

The Culture System has had a very bad Press in world history, but as Van den Bosch operated it for the first ten years it probably brought increased happiness to the Javanese. All statistics illustrating changes in their standard of life seem to indicate this, and it is intrinsically probable that payment in labour and crops was less oppressive to the native cultivator than payment in money, which almost inevitably meant getting into the hands of the moneylenders.

Unfortunately, the temptation to squeeze so rich an orange even harder was more than the Home Government could resist, and from 1843 onwards the rapid growth of the population and the pressure to produce export crops combined to cause actual famine. The system had two other long-term disadvantages, which Raffles could have foretold: the Javanese, cut off from experience of normal economic exchange, became increasingly less able to hold his own against the Chinese in commercial matters; and the Dutch merchants, sheltered behind this vast and all-embracing monopoly, had no need to compete with the rest of Europe, and ultimately fell far behind them in productive methods and the use of modern transport. Between 1860 and 1870 the Culture System was progressively abandoned before a wave of liberal idealism and modern economic theory; but the practice of remitting a money surplus from the Indies to Holland was continued until 1877, when the increasing cost of welfare and of the Achin War swallowed up the surplus. In fact, the *batig slot* was higher under the first years of the liberal régime than it had been under the Culture System. The main crops cultivated under the Culture System were coffee, sugar and indigo, of which indigo was by far the most unpopular among the Javanese.

### 1870–1914: *The Liberal and Ethical System*

The opening of the Suez Canal in 1869 had thrown south-east Asia open to the world: the Agrarian Law of 1870 threw Java open to the private capitalist. It was clearly necessary, if the State monopoly was to be abandoned, that private business should be allowed to rent land for planting; but at the same time great care was taken to see that the rights of the native population were not infringed. To some extent, but not excessively, this care was thwarted by the very vagueness of these rights and by the money power of the

European planters. The second great change brought about in this period was the expansion to the Outer Islands. We have seen that by the end of the eighteenth century the Dutch East India Company had virtually retired to Java; throughout the Culture Period only Java was profitable, and therefore only Java was occupied. Representatives were maintained in the other territories, but mainly in order to prevent other European powers from laying claim to them.

Now, freed in 1871 from the Treaty of 1824, the Dutch began a serious attempt to pacify once and for all the Achinese pirates of north Sumatra. From 1871 to 1896 the war dragged on, fought with little success on defensive lines. Then, at last, the great soldier Van Heutz was given command, and by a policy of vigorous attack broke the Achinese power in little more than a year. In the next few years the Dutch armies transformed their nominal suzerainty into effective control, and it was said that when Van Heutz retired in 1909 'the archipelago was so different that it was as if one had come into a different world.' It is this period of hopeless resistance by Malays or desperate plotting in remote strongholds that one finds described in Joseph Conrad's novels and in Vicki Baum's *A Tale from Bali*.

A change in Dutch internal policy was also made in 1901 with the introduction of the Ethical Policy. Where the liberal policy had been designed to free the Javanese from the oppressions which had gradually developed under the Culture System (and incidentally to increase profits, which it did), the Ethical Policy was an attempt by predominantly Christian parties to make positive welfare an object of policy. In this it was a manifestation of a typically Dutch conception of colonial policy. The policy of British governments in the Far East has been, by and large, to maintain law and order and leave social organisation to the Oriental himself; to this non-interventionism, irrigation and famine control have been the main exceptions. The Dutch, on the other hand, have constantly tried to organise the everyday life of the Oriental, either in the interests of Holland or, later, in his own interests. The British official was there to see that violence was not used and to collect the taxes: he was called the 'Collector.' The Dutch official was there to help and advise the Orientals in every sphere of their lives: he was called the 'Controleur.' It is not surprising that although the domestic political problems in India are far greater than those in Java, the transition from colonial to self-governing status is likely to prove a far more difficult business in Java.

## MODERN ECONOMIC STRUCTURE OF INDONESIA

The economic structure of Indonesia is far less vulnerable than that of Malaya. Even Java, with its extremely dense population, is self-supporting in rice by means of a delicately adjusted balance of export and re-import. The dependence on an export market is therefore not nearly so complete; moreover, though Indonesia's prosperity, if not her life, depends on a world market, the commodities she has to offer are far more varied. One of the results of the abandonment of the Culture System has been a change in the crops exported. Indigo has died out; sugar, which for many years right into the twentieth century was Indonesia's largest export, has fallen right back; but their places have been taken by rubber, petroleum from the Palembang oil-fields of Sumatra, vegetable oils, tea, tobacco and quinine. The Stevenson rubber restriction scheme, as we have seen, helped Indonesia to take the place of Malaya as the world's greatest single source of rubber, so that she produced a third of the world's supply in 1925 and almost half in 1927. Rubber had in fact before the war begun to assume almost an unbalanced position in Indonesian exports, accounting for 28 per cent. by value of the whole in 1937 and 37 per cent. in 1941; similar figures for petroleum products, the second export by value, were 17 per cent. in 1937 and 20 per cent. in 1941. Indonesian petrol has a peculiar strategic importance, in view of the very scanty sources of petrol in the Far East as a whole, only Indonesia, Burma and Sakhalin producing any appreciable quantity.

Indonesia has been important in modern times not only as a primary producer but as an export market for which the manufactured goods of Holland and Japan were in fierce conflict before the war. In this respect, Holland suffered badly from the great slump of 1929, and her proportion of Indonesia's imports fell from 20 per cent. in 1929 to 13 per cent. in 1934. In 1935 the Dutch Government took steps to right this balance much in the same way as the British Government had negotiated the Ottawa Agreements; they were the more justified in that Japan was fast ceasing to provide Indonesia with any market at all for her exports other than oil, and the balance of trade was becoming entirely one-sided. Partly as a result of these measures and partly no doubt owing to Japan's concentration on war industries, Japan's share of the Indonesian market had fallen back to 15 per cent. by 1937.

Cheap goods from Japan—bicycles, rubber-soled shoes, etc.— were, however, such popular features of oriental life throughout the

Far East by this time that they undoubtedly provided Japan with one of her strongest propaganda points at the beginning of the war. To the uneducated Asiatic, whose country had not yet fallen to Japan, the prospect of Japanese occupation was mixed up with that of the return of cheap Japanese goods to the bazaar, and in fact meant little else. Nor could any economic policy which deprived those living on an oriental standard of living of those products of equally cheap oriental labour have been permanently justifiable. It would have meant protecting the standards of living of the European at the cost of preventing the Asiatic from satisfying his needs in the cheap market which his own low standard of living both produced and demanded.

## Modern Social Structure of Indonesia

In distribution of races, the structure of Indonesia is much closer to that of India than to that of Malaya. The vast majority of the people (97·4 per cent. in 1930) are native Indonesians. The Chinese, who are the largest alien group, form only 2 per cent.

Behind this statistical similarity, however, are very striking differences, and these would be noticed first of all in the great cities. We have seen that the Malay, whether in Malaya or Indonesia, is not by nature a trader or a city-dweller. Consequently, we find characteristics in Indonesian cities which are more reminiscent of Singapore than of Bombay or Calcutta. First of all there is no 'drift to the towns' comparable to that in India; secondly, the towns were run by foreigners in a way and to an extent that would be quite incomprehensible in India. There are great cities in India which were entirely Indian-run and where scarcely anyone but an Indian was ever seen. But in Java the Europeans and Chinese, although nothing like the proportion of the total population that they were in Malaya, monopolised the business world and ran the cities. The Javanese, if he lives in a city at all, seems to like behaving as if he were still a villager, and will probably live in a *kampong*, or village, enclosed within the city limits, and reminding the stranger of those 'native villages' which one sees at international exhibitions, complete in every detail, but with a giant racer or a display of the latest textile machinery housed just outside the village stockade. It is, incidentally, not unlikely that an agglomeration of villages of this sort is the true and normal oriental type of city, while Bombay, Manila and Singapore are Western impositions. In point of actual figures, the seven largest cities of Java (and two of them, Batavia and Sourabaya, are large modern cities), contained only 3·7 per cent. of the Javanese population, but over half the Europeans and approximately a third of the Chinese.

31. Market day in a West Javanese village.

Another difference between Indonesia's social structure and that of the old British India lay in the position of Europeans. The strict segregation of European and Asiatic which was one of the failings of Britain's nineteenth-century Indian Empire never existed under the Dutch. Mixed marriages were common from the first, and the growing community of Indo-Europeans added a new social problem to the administration. They were officially classed as Europeans, but not unnaturally sometimes found it difficult to find their correct social and economic niche in the 'Plural Society' of Indonesians, Chinese and Europeans. Partly owing to the inclusion of this group among the figures for Europeans, but partly also to a genuinely greater readiness on the part of the Dutch to live and settle in the East rather than work there and retire home, the figures of Europeans per thousand of the population were four times higher than in British India. This last difference should not be exaggerated, however; there have always been a number of Englishmen who have settled down and died in India, and the main increase in the proportion of Europeans in Java has been a comparatively recent affair—from 86,000 in 1870 to 242,000 in 1930.

Finally, the position of the Chinese needs to be strictly differentiated from that of the Chinese in Malaya. They are the equivalent of what the Malayan Chinese would have been if there had been no tin-mines. Indonesian Chinese are the traders and moneylenders of the islands and have been so for hundreds of years; as we saw, Dutch policy up till very recently tended to accentuate their distinctiveness from the Indonesians both as a community and an economic factor. The estate labourer in Indonesia, on the other hand, is neither Chinese nor Tamil, but Javanese; the high population of Java during the nineteenth century and since has always meant that Javanese labour was cheap, and the Javanese in the past has been exported, exploited and repatriated in exactly the same way as the Tamil or Chinese.[1] One of the saddest stories of the war to those who are fond of the Javanese (and it is difficult not to be) was that of the Javanese labourers, partly lured by nationalist propaganda, partly forced by the Japanese, who were exported to work for the latter in their Co-prosperity Sphere and left to die in strange lands when the work was no longer needed.

It is perhaps worth mentioning to conclude this section that there is in Java, as in Malaya, a small, old-established, somewhat aristocratic and fairly influential Arab community.

## POLITICAL AND SOCIAL PROBLEMS

The great post-war problem in Indonesia was the change-over from Dutch control to some form of self-government. Far more than in India or Burma, this problem was a product of the war; but it was not a creation of the war. The Japanese occupation acted like a forcing house on the Javanese republican movement, bringing about in three years changes that might well have taken thirty; but the seed had germinated long before the Japanese arrived.

Three things differentiated the Indonesian nationalist movement

[1] Estate labourers in the Outer Islands: Javanese, 203,963; Chinese, 22,806. For an imaginative description, see Vicki Baum's *The Ship and the Shore*.

from similar movements elsewhere: the comparative absence of racial discrimination by the Dutch, the paternal attitude of the Government, with its consequent discouragement of higher education for Indonesians, and the backwardness of the Outer Islands. The third of these factors has led to the movement being almost entirely Javanese, though leaders have been drawn from Sumatra and other islands; it has also enabled the Dutch to make use of the very genuine distrust of Javanese supremacy among other Indonesians when opposing the claims of the Republican Government at Jogjakarta. The other two factors had the effect of making the Republican cause much more of a revolutionary conspiracy and less of a nationalist movement than elsewhere. The average Indonesian, who did not concern himself with political or economic theory, had less to complain of than most Asiatics, since the social behaviour of his European masters was less irksome. The intellectual, on the other hand, had more; he was subjected to a far more rigorous political control and a far stricter censorship than he would have been in India, and he had far less opportunity for education. His chances of peacefully taking over the reins of government seemed far more remote. Hence it is not surprising that the 'troubles' in Indonesia in 1926–7 took the form of Communist, not nationalist outbreaks. To the politically-conscious Indonesian, indeed, the very things about the Dutch method of rule which made it socially less objectionable to the average Asiatic were its most dangerous features. The fact that the Dutch lived *in* the Indies instead of merely living *on* them meant that 'Self-government for the Indies' could be and was interpreted as meaning government by the Dutch who lived in Java (with a few of their Indonesian friends) instead of government by the Dutch who lived in Holland. It was for this reason that the Queen of Holland's manifesto of 1942 fell so flat with the nationalists: they were not interested in Java's self-government *vis-à-vis* Holland, but in which party in Java should form the Government, the Dutch and their supporters or the leaders of the nationalist movement.

From the point of view of the Dutch and of gradual development, the war was disastrous. In the eyes of the Javanese, Dutch prestige was shattered for ever by the early capitulation, as British was by the loss of Singapore; but the Dutch were not able, as the British and Americans were, to reinstate themselves at least to some extent by a successful military 'come-back.' Japanese occupation of any territory meant handing over most of the administration to the local inhabitants, since the Japanese had neither the skilled personnel nor the interest to take it over. In the years of occupation, the Javanese found that they could manage most of the things the Dutch had managed well enough to satisfy their own standards of efficiency, if not European standards; and this did in fact mean reasonably well. At the last moment the Japanese confirmed their position by establishing a nationalist Republican Government in Java, so that the returning Dutch might be faced with the dilemma of either accepting it or overthrowing it.

In addition to all this, every possible misfortune seemed to dog the returning Dutch administration. Indonesia was transferred from General MacArthur's Command to Admiral Mountbatten's within a few weeks of the end of the war, so that those who had to organise the return were taken more or less by surprise; nor had contact with the resistance movements, if indeed there were any, given the government the opportunity to-size up the situation in advance, as the British had in Burma and Malaya. It can well be understood therefore that when, nearly a month after the surrender, the first Dutch officials landed at Batavia to find the trams and public buildings painted with slogans such as 'Death to van Mook' or 'Better to the Hell than to be colonised again,' they were almost as much surprised as horrified. It is amusing incidentally that these slogans were all painted in English, and one of the Republican leaders confessed to me afterwards that they had not heard of the change of command, and had intended them for the Americans.

The position was an exceptionally difficult one, and can best be understood perhaps by trying to imagine the point of view of each of the parties concerned.

The Indonesian Republicans had seen their cherished Indonesian Republic formed and in operation; if they were not to lose it they must win their game against the Dutch, and the cards in their hand were the fact that they were in possession and that the glamour of independence had created a momentary unity among Indonesians of almost all classes and areas. In both these respects, time was against them: every new area in which the Dutch established themselves diminished the value of the first, and every month that passed increased the danger of old separatist feelings reviving. Clearly, if they were determined to resist the return of the Dutch to the end, then their policy should have been to secure either a satisfactory agreement or open war before their two trump cards lost their value. It was for this reason that they complained so bitterly of the

P

British occupation of the main ports while negotiations were still in progress, since they held that it was merely a device for presenting the Dutch with admirably organised bridgeheads, which if it came to war were the one thing they would require. For the British to do this, while maintaining that they were not in any way intervening in internal politics, savoured to them of hypocrisy. There was one further card which a less honourable opponent than those who then led the Javanese Republic might have played: in the interior of Java and under Javanese control were over 100,000 Allied prisoners of war and internees. An unscrupulous revolutionary party might have paralysed all action by either Dutch or British by holding these people to ransom and making their release a political condition. It is greatly to the credit of the Republican leaders that though this possibility always haunted the Dutch and British Commands, and though in a few instances small numbers of internees did suffer at the hands of extremists, the Republican Government as a whole preferred to see this card also slip from their hands, rather than use it in an inhuman way.

On their side, the Dutch had arrived armed with concessions which they had hoped would be accepted as very liberal; they found that they did not go nearly far enough. As a result, there was a split in Dutch opinion; one party wanted to overthrow the Republican régime by force; the other to come to an agreement by increasing the concessions and perhaps by drawing out the negotiations until the natural lack of unity among the Indonesians had undermined the strength of the Republican Government. Both were convinced, probably with some justification, that the Republican Government in Java did not really represent the free opinion of Indonesia as a whole. The first party had really no chance of putting their plans into operation, because the only force available was British, and the British, for reasons which I shall give below, were not prepared to use it to overthrow the Republican régime. The second party, therefore, carried the day, but they were constantly hampered in their negotiations by incursions of first party members, either at home or in Batavia. Also they found that at first the Republicans, though willing to make considerable economic concessions, were adamant about political independence.

The British position was very difficult both morally and practically. On the one hand they were committed to giving their allies, the Dutch, all the help in their power; on the other, they had accepted the view, with respect to their own South-east Asian colonies, that it would be madness to attempt to reimpose colonial rule by force. It is one of the oldest puzzles of the casuists whether you are obliged to keep a promise to a friend when he appears to be suffering from temporary madness. In any case the practical difficulties would have decided British policy. The only troops available with which to impose a policy of force were divisions of the Indian army, and it was clearly impossible to use them, in the middle of the delicate negotiations leading to Indian independence, in order to reimpose Dutch colonial rule in Java. Moreover, it is doubtful whether the Allied prisoners in the centre of the island would have survived the attempt.

The British, therefore, at the cost of very considerable casualties to themselves and abused by both sides, contented themselves with establishing bridgeheads at Jakarta and Sourabaya, from which the subsequent negotiations between Dutch and Indonesians could be carried out. There followed three years of alternate negotiations and attempts at reconquest, which ended with the final concession of independence to the Republic of Indonesia at the end of 1949. There is no doubt that the influence of U.N.O. and of the U.S.A. were strong against the Dutch in this struggle; but it would be unrealistic to attribute the final result to this intervention. The French attempt to retain their position in Indo-China had the initial support of the British and the subsequent sympathy of the U.S.A. It bled France white for nine years and ended in disaster. It would be equally unrealistic not to realise that the Federal constitution linked with Holland, which the Dutch finally proposed, was designed in the true interests of the Indonesian people and would have brought them much more stability and prosperity than the unitary centralised Republic which emerged. Unfortunately, as so often happens in colonial affairs, the offer came too late and was rejected in a spirit of not entirely unjustifiable suspicion.

The new Republic had to deal not only with the usual Communist attempt at a *ccup d'état*, but with separatist risings breaking out almost immediately in the Celebes and in Achin, which had only recently been brought within the control of the East Indies Government by the Dutch. Ostensibly democratic, it was in fact outstripped in the progress towards its first general election by the 'colonial' Federation of Malaya; and within two years of this election, in 1956, was proclaiming that Western Democracy had failed and that some sort of authoritarian state was required. In fact, if Indonesia is to maintain the integrity of its territory, there seems no alternative between some sort of fairly loose federation of free Indonesian peoples, such as the Dutch Government proposed, and a totalitarian régime rigidly controlled by the central government in Java. And it is becoming increasingly doubtful, whatever the political principles involved, whether the central government in Java can hope to command sufficient force to impose such a régime.

## BIBLIOGRAPHY

*Malaysia: A Study in Direct and Indirect Rule.* R. Emerson.
*Post-mortem on Malaya.* V. Thomson.
*Malaya: Outline of a Colony.* V. Purcell.
*The Chinese in Malaya.* V. Purcell.
*Britain and Malaya.* Sir R. Windstet.
*Netherlands India: A Study of Plural Economy.* J. S. Furnival.
*The Dutch East Indies.* A. Vandenbosch.
*The Netherlands Indies and Japan.* H. van Mook.
*Almayer's Folly; Lord Jim; The Rescue; etc.* Joseph Conrad.
*The Ship and the Shore: A Tale from Bali.* Vicki Baum.
*The Jungle is Neutral.* F. Spencer Chapman.
*Transformation in Malaya.* J. B. Perry Robinson.
*The Republic of Indonesia.* D. Woodman.
*The Hostile Sun.* Tom Stacey.

# CHAPTER NINE

## THE PHILIPPINES

### STRUCTURE

GEOGRAPHICALLY and racially, the Philippine Islands are an extension of Malaysia: culturally and economically, they have been so profoundly affected by the long Spanish occupation and the recent American administration that they demand separate treatment.

Like Malaysia, they consist of a maze of islands rising from the sea. There are over 7,000 of these islands, varying from the two great land masses of Luzon and Mindanao (41,000 and 37,000 square miles respectively) to isolated rocks; less than half of them have areas greater than one square mile. The total land area of the archipelago is 114,400 square miles, and 95 per cent. of this lies in the eleven largest islands. Some of the islands are coral, but most of them, as in Malaysia, are volcanic and represent the tops of submerged volcanoes: it is due to this that so many of the tiny islets consist of fantastic single rocks, often of great beauty, towering straight from the sea. For the same reason, the ocean bed has been shattered in this area as nowhere else, and the Mindanao Deep (35,412 feet) is the deepest part of the sea.

The shape of this archipelago is roughly that of an equilateral triangle, with the largest island, Luzon, forming the apex in the north. The whole outline is not unlike what that of Great Britain would be if the Bristol Channel were widened northwards and most of Wales consisted of sea. The sea which plays this part in the Philippines is bounded on three sides by the islands, counting clockwise from the north, of Palawan, Panay, Negros, part of Mindanao and the Sulu Archipelago; it is called the Sulu Sea and is closed on the fourth or south-west side by the north-east coast of Borneo. For many years it was one of the last haunts of pirates. With this sea taking the place of most of Wales and the Bristol Channel, one can imagine the Sulu Archipelago as Cornwall, Palawan as North Wales, Mindanao as England south of the Thames, Luzon as Scotland and the mass of intervening islands (of which Negros, Panay and Cebu are the most important) as the intervening Midlands and north England. The southernmost tip of Mindanao, closely connected by island chains with the Celebes and New

Guinea, is on approximately the same latitude as northern Malaya; the northernmost tip of Luzon, 200 miles due south of Formosa, is on approximately the same latitude as Bombay.

The Philippine Islands thus lie at the intersection of many ways: from the south, they are the last northern extremity of the great island world of Malaysia—what Multatuli in *Max Havelaar* called 'the girdle of emerald that lies across the Equator'; from the north they are linked through Formosa and Okinawa with the great island barrier of Japan; from the west they are within easy reach of south China; and from the east they were the first considerable stretch of Asiatic mainland to greet the adventurers from across the Pacific. All this has had its effect on their history, and Manila, the capital, must have belonged to almost as many different empires as any city in the world, having been controlled at different times from Java, Sumatra, Indo-China, Borneo, Pekin, Madrid, Washington, Tokyo and, oddly enough, from 1762 to 1764 from London. It is in fact another of those key-points which the 'imperialist' British acquired in war and handed back to their owners on the conclusion of peace. Being volcanic, most of the larger islands are fairly mountainous, but have, like Java, fertile plains and uplands running down to the sea. The sides of the mountains, of which the highest, Mount Apo, reaches 9,600 feet, are very well forested, so that the many rivers running down them maintain their water all the year round, and are admirably suited either for irrigation or hydro-electric power. It is not surprising, therefore, that the soil on the whole is very fertile, though the remarkable number of geological faults throughout the islands mean that fertile and barren land are often surprisingly close together. This may account for the fact that the 'city slicker' trick of confusing a peasant cultivator, so that he acquires title deeds to a different plot of land from the one he intends and breaks in land which turns out not to be his, is unusually common in the Philippines.

The position as to mineral wealth is unusual; until very recently, the Philippines were not considered particularly rich in this direction, though a little gold and copper had always been mined. All this is now changed. The production of gold, which had not reached 5,000 fine ounces per year in 1907, was over 100,000 in 1929 and over 1 million in 1939; it is still increasing, and, in spite of all the tales of the Yukon, the Philippines now produce more gold than Alaska. Deposits of some of the base metals, notably chrome and manganese, have supplied another export, rising even more rapidly,

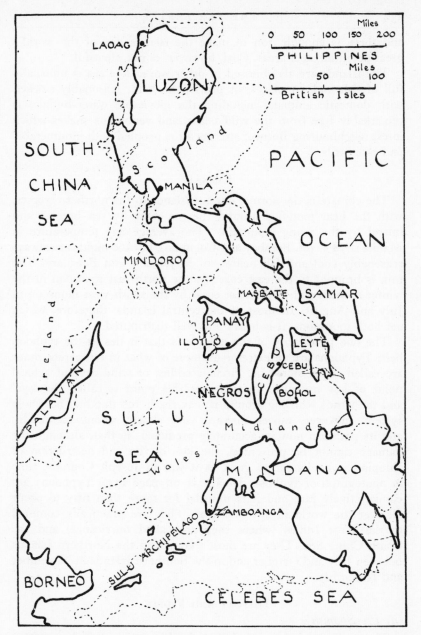

XVII. The *shape* of the Philippine Islands compared with that of the
British Isles. The *extent* of the Philippines is roughly double that of
the British Isles, while the land area of the British Isles is about 5,000
square miles greater than that of the Philippines.

and there is enough iron to make the islands one of the world's great potential steel areas. Coal, however, is not plentiful.

The islands are also blessed in other ways. The sea is unusually full of fish and, in places, of pearls; the land, reasonably stocked with domestic animals, including the inevitable water-buffalo, is remarkably free from the wild beasts and venomous snakes which infest neighbouring Borneo; and the air is peopled with innumerable and rare birds.

## CLIMATE

The climate is the normal one for islands in the northern tropics, with the heat modified around the sea-coast by sea breezes and inland by the rising mountains. The average day temperature in Manila is 79·5° (cf. Bombay and Colombo), but the nights are always reasonably cool and fall below 60° in January and February. The rain is brought to the east coast by the north-east monsoon in the winter months and to the west coast by the south-west monsoon in July and August. In most of the central islands, therefore, which get both monsoons, it is heavy and well-distributed.

The one peculiarity of the climate is that it lies in the typhoon belt. Typhoons are an extreme example of what in temperate zones are called depressions, i.e. circular eddies of wind around a local point of low pressure. In typhoons this point is called the 'eye' and the winds whirling around it may reach 100 m.p.h. The whole system, however, moves forward very slowly, about 10 m.p.h., and its path can now be accurately predicted, so that, although the damage cannot be prevented, the loss of life and destruction of shipping is no longer so great as it was in Joseph Conrad's time (a photograph of typhoon damage is on page 134). Typhoons are comparatively rare and it is unusual for more than fifty to occur all over the world in any one year. They are practically confined to the West Indies (where they are called hurricanes) and the South China Sea. They are most frequent in the Northern Islands between July and October and in the Southern Islands in November and December.

## HISTORY AND PEOPLE

### (a) Pre-Spanish

The earliest inhabitants of the islands were, as usual, negritoes of whom little is known and who survive, as in Malaysia, in a few scattered jungle tribes. About 8000 B.C. came the first Stone Age

people, who arrived by canoe and whose strain is still visible among
the present-day Filipinos.

It was probably not until between 1000 B.C. and A.D. 500 that
the main stock from which the present Filipinos are descended
began to arrive. These were the genuine Malays, the racial stock
which also spread over the whole of Malaysia. From about A.D. 500
onwards it is fairly certain that settlers from Sri-Vijaya, the great
Hindu-Malay civilisation in Sumatra, colonised the Philippines as

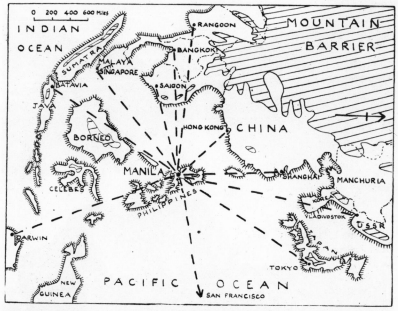

XVIII. Manila, the central outpost: almost equidistant from Darwin and
    Vladivostok.

well as founding their empire in Cambodia. Like the Norsemen in
England, they came a boatload at a time. These boatloads settled
down, under the rule of their leader, at the river mouths and began
that isolated, river-based society which persisted until the days of
Raja Brooke and Conrad's novels.

Very little is known of this period in the history of the islands;
Chinese sources make it clear that trade was carried on with China
at least from the ninth century A.D., and it is almost certain that
this trade extended to India also; but Philippine sources simply do
not exist. There are said to have been Philippine documents in

existence at the time when the Spaniards arrived, but none of any importance survives, and none at all of which the authenticity has been established without doubt.

32. The Rajang River, Sarawak. The scene of many of Conrad's novels must have looked very like this.

The most important event for the Philippines in this pre-Spanish period is one which took place far to the south—the fall of the Javanese Hindu Empire of Madjapahit before the Moslems in 1478. It is a historical curiosity that this extension of Moslem power in the East should have happened almost at the same time as the fall of the Moslem Empire of Granada in the West in 1491. The conquest of Madjapahit gave the Moslems nearly a century in which to spread their faith and culture in the Philippine Islands, and this was mostly undertaken from Borneo, where the Sultan of Brunei was acknowledged as overlord of some parts at least of the Southern Islands. Since the Japanese had just begun to establish themselves in the north, the Filipinos, as a separate nation, were in some danger of extinction when the Spanish explorer Magellan landed in Cebu in 1521.

### (b) *The Spanish Occupation*, 1521–1898

The arrival of the Spaniards decided the future of the Philippines as well as giving them their name—taken from Philip II, who despatched the Armada and was painted by Velasquez. From that time onwards they have, until 1946, been governed and approached from across the Pacific, and have been the meeting place in Asia, first of the two streams of European expansion, and then of the New World and the Old.

Magellan himself died in the islands, and their Cortes or Pissarro was really Miguel Legaspi, one of the greatest of the Spanish conquistadors. He had made his reputation in Mexico, largely because he had discovered the secret that the way to manage backward people was to gain their confidence. He landed in the Philippines in 1565 and founded Manila in 1571. So well did he choose his subordinates and successors that within twenty-five years of his landing the Spanish power was firmly established throughout the greater part of the archipelago.

The Spaniards, as we have seen, found two rivals for control of the Philippines, the Moslems and the Japanese. The Moslem faith had spread to just north of Manila by the time they arrived, but was not yet firmly entrenched, except in the extreme south. We have already noticed the difference between the Spanish or Portuguese and the British or Dutch in their treatment of Asiatic dependencies: the British and Dutch came primarily for trade, though an occasional missionary might follow; the Spanish and Portuguese came primarily to spread the Faith and civilisation, though there was no objection to gathering a certain amount of wealth or political power in the process. There is no greater tribute to the Spanish method than the Philippines to-day; the way in which the friars went out and won over the people to Christianity, until

the Moslems were driven back to the Moro districts of the extreme
south and the Sulu Sea, is one of the epics of missionary work.
It was clinched by a naval expedition to Brunei, which served to
warn the sultans that further expansion northwards was barred;
but for the most part it was the peaceful conversion of a people
who had never known any religion higher than animism, or who
had been exposed to Islam for a comparatively short time. The
Moros, in whom the Moslem faith had taken stronger root, remain
Moslems to this day, and it was not until the Spaniards introduced
steamships that their independent political power, like that of the
Achinese in Sumatra, was doomed. The great success of this Spanish
conversion of the Philippines may be compared in some ways with
the unusual success of Christian missions in Korea to-day, where
again they are directed to a people who have not previously been
attached to any of the great world religions.

Politically, the Japanese were at first a more serious menace
than the Moslems, and in 1592 the Spaniards were reduced to
paying tribute to the great Shogun, Hideyoshi, who, fresh from his
triumph over Korea, claimed the Philippines also for Japan. The
time which the Spaniards bought, however, was enough to enable
them some years later to renounce their dependence, and by the
beginning of the seventeenth century Japan had retired to that
complete isolation from which she was not to be stirred until 1853.

The most remarkable thing about the Philippines as the Spaniards
found them was the smallness of the population. The Spanish estimate was about a half to three-quarters of a million; we have seen
that the Malay type of civilisation is not conducive to high populations, but even Malaya, with less than half the area of infinitely
less fertile land, had a greater population than this. To parallel
less than 1 million in an area capable under modern cultivation of
supporting nearly 100 million, we shall have to refer to the scattered
tribes who formed the native population of North America.

Under the Spaniards, the population grew swiftly, and the
Filipinos soon began to display their unusual ability to absorb
Western culture. The foundations of the Spanish social organisation
were the Church and the feudal relationship between landlord and
tenant. Both these were readily accepted, the Church because it
provided a faith which satisfied the religious appetite of the people,
while fully exercising their love of festivals and pageants; the
feudalism because it merely prolonged and developed that loyalty
to the chief which has always been one of the main characteristics

of the Malay. The descendant of the raja whose boatload had colonised the river mouth became, under the Spaniards, the *cacique*.

The Spaniards, because they wanted first and foremost to win the Filipinos for Christendom, produced the only genuinely fused Euro-Asiatic society in the Far East. Intentionally, they taught the Filipinos to read and write Roman letters, they made them Christians, they intermarried with them; in 1611 they set up the University of San Tomas in Manila (cf. Malaya and Java, where in 1939 there were still no universities). Their object seems to have been to make the Filipino *caciques* as like as possible to Spanish *hidalgos* and Filipino peasants to Spanish peasants. They never had any idea, however, of raising the social and economic status of the peasant nearer to that of the *cacique*; and if in the nineteenth century the friars and the Church became hated as absentee landlords, that is not so very different from what was happening in Spain. As in Europe, the *cacique* might be a good or a bad landlord, and far too much depended on which he was, but it was a social and not a racial problem and the Filipino revolts against the Spanish Government were in origin social, not racial, revolts.

Whatever the faults of their administration, the Spaniards found the Filipinos a few scattered tribes and left them a Christian and, far more than any other Far Eastern people, a Westernised nation; but they were not democrats themselves, and they did not prepare the Filipinos for democracy. This has been a source of much trouble during the American times, since, as usual, many Americans have tended to argue that the Filipinos were not ready for independence when what they meant was that they were not yet capable of working American democracy.

## (g) *American Rule*, 1898–1946

The American victory in the Spanish-American War of 1898 left them with a very difficult problem in the Philippines. The American people as a whole were certainly not aware of having entered the war with any intention of acquiring 'colonies,' and the very word 'colonial' was anathema to many Americans, educated on histories in which they themselves figured as the successfully rebellious colony. The position was further complicated by the fact that the Filipinos had started their war of independence *before* America declared war on Spain; the Filipino, struggling to be free from a feudal Europe, had caught the American imagination, and Filipino guerrillas had been of some assistance, though not as much as they made out, to Admiral Dewey. What is more, although they had not helped much in Manila itself, they would probably have driven the Spaniards out altogether without American help

33. An old church in Cebu. It might be 'Spanish colonial' anywhere.

if left to themselves. Altogether it was a situation curiously parallel in many ways to the state of the liberated Far Eastern territories in 1945, except that in 1945 the resistance movements could never have expelled the Japanese.

Ultimately, the Americans decided to accept control of the Philippines, even though it meant suppressing the nationalist rising; but they did so with a very strongly expressed proviso that their overriding object was to prepare the islands for self-government as soon as possible. On these terms, many of the leaders of the rising agreed to co-operate, but not all. A curious result of this decision was that almost all the American fighting during the Philippine War, in which such men as General Pershing made their reputations, was conducted against the Filipinos and not the Spaniards. The Spaniards, who had practically lost control of the islands before the Americans arrived, assisted them in every way to take over the rebellious colony. The job took the Americans three years and their success was due at least as much to their genuine enthusiasm for the well-being of the people as it was to their overwhelming military superiority.

Having dealt with the extreme nationalist Filipinos, they proceeded to bring under control the bandits and pirates among the Moro tribes; this period coincides with the Dutch expansion north under Van Heutz, and it is to it that Conrad's romantic world of the Raja Laut, Almayer and Babalatchi belongs.

Under the new driving force of the Americans, trade, education and communications were rapidly improved, and in the course of this development it became clear that they fully intended to train Filipinos for every type of post in the new Westernised administration. In trade the crucial decision was the inclusion of the Philippines within the U.S. tariff system in 1909. This exclusive free trade with the U.S.A. produced an enormous increase in the total volume of trade and a complete change in its direction. Sugar production, for instance, rose 1,200 per cent. between 1909 and 1930 (a period when Javanese sugar production was falling); but, whereas in 1900 only 13 per cent. of Philippine exports went to the U.S.A., in 1933 the figure had risen to 86 per cent.—with a similar rise in the proportion of Philippine imports supplied by the U.S.A.

This startling development had, of course, its disadvantages: it made the Philippines, like Malaya, much too dependent on a single crop (in 1932 sugar formed 63 per cent. by value of the total exports), and also, which is worse, much too dependent on a single market. One of the difficulties in the way of Philippine independence was always that the islands were so exclusively dependent on the American market that to find themselves outside the American tariff wall would spell ruin. This was in fact foreseen by some of the Filipino leaders, who opposed the tariff policy from the start on the grounds that, whatever its commercial advantages, it would tie the Philippines irretrievably to the American economy.

In education, the Americans brought about great and rapid advances, particularly in the secondary education of girls. In 1908 the island Legislature passed a Bill setting up the University of the Philippines, which absorbed certain already existing faculty schools, as the new University of Malaya has recently done. This University provided a secular counterpart to San Tomas, founded nearly 300 years earlier. Perhaps more important than these improvements in higher education was the great drive for primary schools throughout the islands; the Spanish had in fact tried to establish universal primary education, and through the village priests had at least done a good deal towards spreading literacy; but a real system of primary schools on the American model was a new and costly conception.

If self-governing democracy on the American model was to be introduced, however, they were clearly necessary; and here arose a controversy which illustrates clearly the difference in viewpoint between the Asiatic and the European. Throughout the period of American transference of power, they found themselves in constant conflict with the Filipino legislative bodies, who wanted to spend a far higher proportion on secondary than on primary education. The reason was that whereas the Americans were interested in educating voters as an essential preliminary to 'democracy,' the Filipino was interested in educating leaders in order to be capable of securing and maintaining independence as soon as possible, democratic or not.

In communications the roads and steamer services of the island were revolutionised to the great advantage of the majority, though it is true that some of the few black spots in the American record are connected with the forced labour required for road-building.

Although the pace at which independence was to be achieved was a matter of dispute between the American political parties, independence was never questioned as an ultimate goal; and this produced a situation very close to that which developed in British India, where idealism and concern for investments, liberalism and imperialism formed an inextricable mixture of motives among the rulers and inspired among the ruled the usual accusations of hypocrisy.

The main commercial interests, whose sinister machinations were detected behind every move of the liberals, were the American sugar industry and dairy interests. It was clearly to their interest to keep Philippine sugar and coconut oil outside the American tariff wall, and for this reason they at first opposed the Free Trade policy. Forbes also suggests that they may have been behind the legislation limiting Filipino settlements on Government lands to 40 acres for individuals and 2,500 for corporations. The ostensible aim of this legislation was to help the small freeholder and prevent the growth of large estates, but it is true that it also operated against the establishment of efficient sugar plantations in the islands. It is the same problem that we have seen wherever Europeans have tried to establish a land system which will really benefit a Malay people, whether in Malaya, Java or the Philippines: if you try to preserve the land for the peasant, he will not get the maximum economic return out of it, because he is not interested; if you want the maximum economic return and throw the land open, the peasant will be squeezed out by the Chinese or European. You cannot have it both ways. Apart from this, it is certain that much of the support for immediate independence in America was organised by the 'Sugar Lobby,' who were anxious to exclude Filipino sugar from the American market and neither knew nor cared anything about imperial problems.

Politically, the progress of the Philippines to independence was comparatively quick, though, as usual, not as quick as the Filipino leaders would have liked. The comparison with British India is interesting, if one allows for the vastly greater problems involved in India. Both countries started about the same time, the liberation from the Spaniards in 1899 comparing as a starting point with the foundation of the Indian National Congress in 1885. From 1901 to 1907 the islands were governed by the Philippine Commission, an autocratic and paternal body, not unlike the Viceroy's Council, which contained from 1901 onwards three Filipino as well as five American members. From 1907 to 1916 a Philippine Assembly, elected for two-year terms, was added; but the executive power remained in the hands of the Governor-General and the Commission. The first great step forward was the Jones Act of 1916, which placed the government fairly in the hands of an elective Filipino Legislature of two houses, but with the proviso that all laws must be approved by the Governor-General and ultimately by the U.S. Senate. The parallel in time with the Montagu-Chelmsford Reforms is clear, though things in the Philippines were in fact moving considerably quicker. Finally, the Tydings-McDuffie Act of 1934

Q

set up a genuinely self-governing Philippines Commonwealth, still subject to American 'intervention,' it is true, but pledged to independence in 1944. The Japanese occupation prevented the fulfilment of this pledge till 1946, but in that year the islands became independent. Again we can see a parallel with the Government of India Act of 1935 and the final achievement of independence in 1947.

### PRESENT SOCIAL STRUCTURE

The modern Filipino, like the 'true-born Englishman,' is the descendant of all the many races that have mingled in his history. Dr. H. Otley Beyer, of the University of the Philippines, estimates that in a mythical 'average' Filipino the racial stocks would be distributed as follows:

|  | per cent. |
| --- | --- |
| Negrito and proto-Malay . . . | 10 |
| Indonesian . . . . . | 30[1] |
| Malay . . . . . . | 40 |
| Chinese . . . . . . | 10 |
| Hindu . . . . . . | 5 |
| European and American . . . | 3 |
| Arab . . . . . . | 2 |

This mixture of stocks seems, as so often, to have proved very successful and it is remarkable how many of the leading men of the islands are of mixed Filipino and Spanish or mixed Filipino and Chinese blood. The typical Filipino is described by Forbes as having 'straight black hair, dark brown eyes, light to dark brown skin, and being not more than five feet four in height.' Although of such mixed descent, the Filipinos are undoubtedly as much a single race as anyone, the only important minority, the Moros, being due to a religious, not a racial, difference.

Within this single race, however, there are strongly marked communities separated by language. The most important of the languages spoken in the islands are Ilocano, spoken in north-west Luzon, Tagalog, spoken round Manila, and various Visayan dialects spoken in the south. These languages, though of common origin and closely related, are not mutually comprehensible. An attempt is therefore being made to develop a national language based on

[1] This is presumably the race sometimes known as 'Nesiot' and connected with the present-day Polynesians. It should not be confused with the modern Indonesians, who are almost entirely Malays and comparatively recent arrivals in Indonesia.

Tagalog, as the Siamese national tongue is based on the Siamese of Bangkok. For international use, business and scientific communication, English, which gradually replaced Spanish during the American occupation as the educated language, will probably persist.

The total population of the Philippines, estimated at half a million when the Spanish arrived, had risen by the time they left to over six millions and at the end of forty years of American rule to 16 millions—about equal to the population of Siam or Hyderabad. This growth of population, as we have seen elsewhere, is a very common feature of the twentieth century in the Far East; but the Philippines are remarkable in that there is still ample land available to justify a much greater increase.

That does not mean that there is no land hunger at all in the islands; the population is in fact very ill-distributed. The reasons for this are the usual ones: the average Filipino is very averse to leaving home; the Ilocanos, it is true, have emigrated fairly easily and won the nickname of the 'Yankees' or 'Scotsmen' of the Philippines, and a few Visayans are found further afield; but in general leaving home is not popular. Moreover, it is always exactly the landless man, the man who ought to move, who lacks the capital to do so. Consequently, Mindanao is almost empty (the Bureau of Forestry calculates that about a third of the area is cultivable, but undeveloped), while parts of Luzon are overcrowded. As usual, there has been a drift, though not a very marked one in the Philippines, to the towns.

Women lead a free and responsible life among the Filipinos (cf. the Burmese); the 'joint family' feeling is strong and almost always it is the wife who is the manager and to whom the husband pays over his whole weekly pay packet. This is slightly modified among the richer classes by imitation of Spanish customs; but among the middle-class Filipinos women outnumber men as managers of small retail businesses. The Westerner should remember in gauging the significance of this that such activities are in general despised by the Malay.

In religion the Filipinos are the only Christian people of the Far East, unless one counts such minorities as the Karens of Burma. The figures are:

| | | | | |
|---|---|---|---|---|
| Christians | . | . | . | 12,981,726 |
| Moslems | . | . | . | 677,903 |
| Buddhists | . | . | . | 47,852 |
| Pagans | . | . | . | 626,008 |

With regard to those last eight pagans, one should remember the warning on the unreality of all Far Eastern statistics given in Chapter IV.

Under the Americans complete religious freedom was established, and this produced a number of somewhat fantastic Christian cults, rather reminiscent of the West Indies or the Southern States of the U.S.A. Many bandit leaders have called themselves 'Popes' and at one time no less than three 'Jesus Christs' were in gaol simultaneously. One sect, however, is of real importance, the Filipino Independent Church. This was founded in 1902 and is sometimes called the Aglipayan Church, after its first chief Bishop, an ex-Roman Catholic priest named Aglipay, who only died in 1940. It retains the Roman ritual combined with a very modernist disbelief in miracles and reverence for 'Science.' Its present numbers are difficult to calculate, but the claim to 'nearly half the Christian population' quoted in Professor Stamp's *Asia* seems probably an exaggeration. The pre-war census figures were only just over a million and a half.

The main influence of the Church has certainly been a civilising and a stabilising one. The Filipino social unit has always been the village, or *barrio*, and at the centre of every *barrio* stands the Church. In Spanish times the priest was probably too much the 'Father-mother-priest-governor-policeman-landlord-doctor-teacher' of his flock, and it is just as well that there should now be another inevitable building in the *barrio*—the American primary school. Nevertheless, the Church, with its common faith, its cycle of festivals and its code of conduct, however often abused, has done what no other Western institution could have done.

The *barrio*, as we have seen, is the social unit. Manila, which, like Rangoon, has actually grown since the war, is a great city and in many ways was before the war a model of municipal development; but, like Bangkok, it was the only great city in the country. Seventy-two per cent. of all Filipinos still live by agriculture and go no further afield than their village. There is the same sharp division between a small educated minority and the vast mass of unchanging peasants as elsewhere in the Far East; wealth per head is lower even than in Japan. But though the gap between rich and poor is fantastically wide by European standards, it is perhaps not quite as wide as elsewhere in the Far East; and if the *cacique* can be a cruel landlord and a rapacious moneylender, he still retains something of the personal connection and sense of responsibility that belonged to the chief. It may not be much, but it is something, and among former 'colonial' peoples the Filipinos have already shown an exceptional capacity to develop stable, modern and democratic institutions.

## MODERN ECONOMIC STRUCTURE

As everywhere else in the Far East, the basis of the country's economic structure is still the debt-burdened peasantry, living at a bare subsistence standard. Less than half of them own the land they work or the ground their huts are built on. The trade economy superimposed on this basis is in a state of transition.

Both under the Spaniards and the Americans the Philippines were treated as producers of certain primary products: hemp, which grows better there than anywhere else in the world, sugar, copra, tobacco, timber, embroideries—and, more recently, buttons, if they can be called a primary product.

We have seen that the American 'Free Trade' policy gave them an assured market in the U.S.A. for these products in return for a virtual American monopoly of Philippine imports. It seemed clear that if the Philippines were to become independent this exclusive relationship must be brought to an end. But trade channels cannot be changed overnight. A period of ten years was therefore allowed under the Tydings-McDuffie Act, which provided for Philippine independence, and during this period two things were supposed to be done: the great Philippine export trades were to be 'hardened off' by paying a gradually increasing proportion of the import duties which they would ultimately have to face if they found themselves outside the American tariff wall; and every attempt was to be made to diversify the domestic economy of the islands so that they should not be too exclusively dependent on their main crop exports to the U.S.A.

The first part of this seems an unrealistic policy. No amount of hardening off could disguise the fact that if they had to compete from outside the tariff wall the Philippine exporters could not sell their sugar and tobacco at a profit in the U.S.A.; and the sugar they could certainly sell nowhere else.

The plan to diversify their economy was undoubtedly a sound one; but the country is poor and such things take many years. Even on the low rate of taxation imposed there were continual complaints that the islanders were being overtaxed on a 'European scale,' and Government ventures in cement, footwear, canning, textiles, etc., were all as likely to prove a liability as an asset to the Treasury. The best hope for diversification seems to lie in the development of the islands' forest and mineral resources. We have already noticed the remarkable increase in mineral output and a similar increase in timber would not be impossible since some experts believe the Philippine 'stand' of hard timber to be now the most extensive in the world.

Seeing that such a complete change in the country's economy within ten years was clearly out of the question, it is not surprising that even before the war there were strong moves from the Philippine side to preserve a little longer some degree of tariff preference with the U.S.A. The war made a decision on these lines inevitable, for the country, in its devastated state, was in no position to meet new troubles; moreover, the concept of 'regional security' had modified to a considerable extent the extremity of people's views about independence. It is not surprising, therefore, that the independence proclaimed in 1946 has left America with the right to maintain bases in the islands and has retained also a good deal of the old economic interdependence. To those who are familiar with the oriental left wing, it is even less surprising that this is still a cause of contention between the Philippines and the U.S.A., even after the military agreements of 1951 and the Manila pact of 1954.

The internal trade of the country is, as usual, mainly in the hands of the Chinese. They control 80 per cent. of the retail trade and about as much of the banking; they finance, store and process most of the rice crop (cf. Siam and Indo-China); and they did, before the war, 40 per cent. of the lumber trade. Since the war there has been a good deal of discriminatory legislation against small-scale Chinese traders, e.g. 'barrow boys,' in Manila.


## Post-war Problems

The great post-war problems centre around population, the usual agrarian discontent, and the trade and security difficulties of independence. Of these population is probably the most fundamental.

The islands could undoubtedly support more than three times their present population and land-hungry Chinese are clamouring for entry to develop them. Before the war the immigration laws, passed no doubt with an eye mainly on the Japanese, limited immigration to 500 a year. Can or should these or similar laws be

34. Philippine troops returning from the Korean war march through the shopping centre of Manila.

maintained? The Filipino sees the stranglehold which the Chinese have developed on his internal economy; he sees that their numbers have risen from roughly 40,000 under the Spaniards, and indeed up to 1918, to over 300,000 in 1956. It is not, of course, yet a problem comparable with Malaya's or Siam's, but the commercial influence of the Chinese Chamber of Commerce in Manila was already very great before the war, and nothing is more certain than that, with free immigration, the Chinese population, and their commercial control, would grow by leaps and bounds. Who knows even whether the Japanese also, who before the war had nearly 30,000 nationals in the islands and practically controlled the fishing industry, might not in time renew their demand to enter? As an American dependency, it was difficult, but no doubt possible, for the Philippines to pursue a policy of exclusion; as an absolutely independent nation, it is hard to see how they could keep it up for long.

The agrarian discontent has developed on the usual lines—that is, the Japanese disrupted the agricultural economy of the country, the Allies took advantage of this to arm those who were hardest hit as guerrillas, and these peasant rebels from central Luzon, the one area where there is real over-population, continued to oppose the first independent Philippine Government. The Hukbalahaps, as they were called, followed the usual course of legitimate left-wing opposition until 1948, followed by violent rebellion. In 1953, however, their leader, Luis Taruc, abandoned the Communist line and accepted the terms offered by President Magsaysay.

The trading position of the islands was also profoundly affected by the Japanese occupation and the anomalies of the reconstruction period. The Japanese had no use for Philippine sugar and many of the mills were either destroyed or allowed to go out of production. Consequently, the problem of dealing with the country's sugar surplus has vanished in the post-war period. Where in 1940 the export of sugar was nearly 1 million metric tons and accounted for 40 per cent. of total exports, in 1946 *output* was less than 12,000 metric tons and no surplus for export at all was expected before the 1947–8 season.[1] This is possibly not a bad thing, since sugar was the export which came most into competition with other American sources of supply, and copra, which has taken its place as the leading export, does not suffer from this disadvantage.

The importance of copra in the island's immediate post-war economy is amazing. The Philippines had, since 1920, produced

[1] Production figures in metric tons for 1947 are: Sugar 70,650, Copra 998,140, Corn 472,190, Hemp 82,000.

between a quarter and a third of the world's copra (dried coconut and the source of coconut oil). The plantations are developed on a more industrial scale than in Ceylon and had not suffered from the ravages of war. The post-war shortage of fats produced an insatiable demand for Philippine copra, with very high prices, and after the war coconut and hemp products, which were only 31 per cent. of exports in 1940, rose to 93 per cent. (Copra 45 per cent. of world output 1956.)

Under the Philippine Trade Act, concluded on the acquisition of independence, the 'hardening off' policy of the Tydings-McDuffie Act has been revived, but the time allowed for the process lengthened. The preferential advantages for Philippine products entering the U.S.A. are to be removed at the rate of 5 per cent. per annum, so that the process will not be complete till 1974. The first result of the generous, and somewhat conscience-stricken, attitude of the U.S.A., was a galloping inflation. Vast sums of American money were poured into the Philippines, both for reconstruction and in the form of local expenditure by troops and missions. There was no possibility of financing an expansion of local industry and production by this sudden influx of wealth nearly quickly enough to absorb it productively: it became, therefore, a source of corruption and luxury. The Government of President Roxas made some hasty attempts, largely on paper, to develop Philippine industry, but in common with other successor states of Asia found that the industrialisation of a peasant society is something which simply cannot be improvised. The boom was not entirely without its good results, and Professor Toynbee notes that in Manila no less than ten universities with a total of at least 68,000 students have risen from the ruins.

Most important also, for South-east Asia as a whole, was the election in 1953 of President Magsaysay, largely on an 'anti-corruption ticket,' and the subsequent collapse of the Communist-Hukbalahap insurrection. The significance of this type of 'second generation' government in the successor states is discussed in the last chapter.

BIBLIOGRAPHY

*The Philippines: A Nation in the Making.* F. M. Kersing.
*The Philippine Islands.* W. C. Forbes.
*The Philippine Problem.* W. Anderson.
*The Philippines: A Study in National Development.* J. R. Haydon.
*The Philippine Answer to Communism.* A. H. Scaff.
*Land and People in the Philippines.* J. E. Spencer.

# CHAPTER TEN

## JAPAN

### STRUCTURE AND CLIMATE

JAPAN consists of four large islands, lying about 500 miles from the China coast and 100 miles from the tip of Korea. Their position is very similar to that of Great Britain in relation to Europe, and the total area not very different. This parallel is so obvious and has been so much borne out in history that it is being constantly overlooked by those who distrust, above all, accepted notions. There are, of course, differences in position—Japan is, for instance, very much further from Asia than Britain from Europe—and the historical parallels are naturally not exact; nevertheless, the comparison is a fruitful one to those who are starting without any accurate picture of Japan, and who are prepared to take it for the rough-and-ready thing that it is.

The islands run in a chain from north-east to south-west and are, starting from the north, Hokkaido (area 30,115 square miles), Honshu (87,805), Shikoku (7,246) and Kyushu (16,174). Hokkaido, in the north, is the last refuge of the aboriginal inhabitants, the Ainu, and was not in historical times considered strictly a part of Japan; it is still considerably less developed than the rest of the country.

This island chain is extremely mountainous, the ranges running mainly in two folded series along the east and west coasts with a deep valley between; in the south-west this valley is filled with the Inland Sea, an almost entirely land-locked stretch of sea that must have given the ancient Japanese the same inducement and the same opportunity to embark on the waves as the Ægean gave to the ancient Greeks. In the main island of Honshu this central valley has been almost entirely filled up by a great knot of volcanic peaks, rising to over 8,000 feet, of which the most famous is Fujiyama. Fujiyama, as innumerable pictures have shown, is an exquisitely regular snow-covered cone which has become an object of semi-religious devotion to the Japanese.

It will be seen therefore that the rarest thing in Japan is a plain, and Professor Dudley Stamp has calculated that three-quarters of its whole surface slopes at a degree of more than one in seven. Another estimate, that of Dr. Reischauer, is that only 20 per cent.

of the land surface is level enough for cultivation. The only extensive plain is the Kwanto Plain, around Tokyo.

Not unnaturally, with its mountainous and indented coastline and landlocked waters, Japan is rich in excellent harbours; the rivers, on the other hand, are short and swift, useful for hydro-electric power, but not for communications.

This physical configuration makes Japan a country of great beauty, and of a beauty unusually attractive and understandable to Western-ers; it may also have led to the fact that there is no race in the world so sensitive to natural beauty as the Japanese (see illustration on page 278).

The climate of Japan is, of course, part of the general climatic system of the continent to which it lies so close. Nevertheless, it is profoundly modified by the sea. Japan is washed by two great ocean currents, the warm Kuro Shio Current flowing northwards and the cold Okhotsk Current flowing southwards; both currents flow mainly along the east coast. It is the meeting of these two just north of Japan that produces conditions similar to those off Labrador, famous for fogs and fish. The Kuro Shio is the more important of these two and is the great North Equatorial Current from the Java Sea, the equivalent in the Pacific of the North Atlantic Drift. The surface temperature keeps as high as 82° all the way from Singapore to south Japan, but falls rapidly along the Japanese coast. The Kuro Shio does not do as much to warm Japan as the North Atlantic Drift does for England, since it flows mainly along the east coast of the islands and the prevailing winter winds come from the west. On the other hand, its course is followed by atmospheric depressions, starting with the typhoons of the South China Sea, and it therefore brings rain.

It is partly for this reason that, although the heaviest rains are, of course, in the south-east during the summer monsoon, the whole of Japan gets some winter rain. In one area on the north-west coast, where the winter winds crossing the sea strike a mountainous coastline, the winter snow is very heavy indeed, and this and the south-east both have average yearly rainfalls of over 100 inches.

It should be remembered that the Japanese islands stretch over a very wide range of latitude, the north being about level with Bordeaux and the south with Delhi. Apart from this, the altitude of the land varies a great deal and the Japanese people are therefore accustomed to wide variations of temperature and climate.

## HISTORY AND PEOPLE

Some Japanese historians hold that the break in Japan's history occasioned by the great feudal wars, which ended with the establishment in power of the Tokugawa family in 1600, was so fundamental that no study of Japan's history before this date is necessary to those who wish to understand modern Japan.

This view is almost certainly exaggerated, but it is true that we need not consider more than the barest outline of historical events before this date. On the other hand, the Japanese are perhaps the most difficult people in the world to understand, and trends and characteristics are often illustrated in this period which could no doubt be paralleled in the Tokugawa period, but not so vividly. We cannot, therefore, leave this period out, but its interest for us lies not in historical events, but in the origins of permanent features in the Japanese character and social organisation.

### (a) Origins and First Contacts with China

The origin of the Japanese people is a mystery which is not solved by supposing them to be descended from the gods. Certainly they are a highly individual race. The earliest known inhabitants of the islands, the Ainu (sometimes known as the 'Hairy Ainu'; see illustration on facing page), were not a Mongol but probably a proto-Caucasian people; hence the position of the Japanese in Hitler's hierarchy as honorary Aryans. It seems likely that there was more assimilation and less massacre of these people than was at one time believed, and it is possible that they had considerable effect on forming the Japanese race, the bulk of whose ancestors were certainly Mongol. Most of these Mongol ancestors reached Japan from northern Asia through Korea, but it is virtually certain that there is also a southern strain in the Japanese, and this probably derives from south China, where, as in the Indo-Chinese peninsula, it may well have mingled with proto-Malay.

The racial history of Japan therefore, as well as its position, is like that of Britain. Both were islands lying off the coast of a more civilised mainland and both seem to have acted as a 'melting pot' where different racial elements, unable to wander further, were compelled to fuse. The history of the two countries has also its striking similarities, which do no harm provided that the parallel is not pressed too far. It is impossible, for instance, to read of the repulse of Kubla Khan's Armada by the Japanese in 1281 without

thinking of the Spaniards; and when we smile at the Japanese legend
of the *Kamikaze*, or 'Divine Wind' which scattered the Mongol

35. An Ainu family group (Hokkaido).

ships, we should remember Queen Elizabeth's medals, struck nearly
300 years later, with their legend: 'God blew with his wind and they
were scattered.'

It would, of course, be absurd to suppose that Japan's history was more like that of a European than an oriental people simply because of coincidences like this or because Japan, alone of Asiatic peoples, developed feudalism. Nevertheless, one can go too far and be so eager to avoid facile comparisons that one overlooks genuine similarities. It has always seemed to me that one of the difficulties in understanding the Japanese is that they are, in fact, more like western Europeans than any other Orientals are; and so Westerners either make the mistake of thinking that, because they are more like us, the differences do not matter, or that, because they are different, the likeness is a delusion. We have seen that one of the differences between the geographical positions of Britain and Japan is that Japan is much more isolated—500 miles by sea from China and 100 from Korea. For primitive ships, this was a very serious distance, and consequently Japan was compelled to rely more than any other highly civilised nation on her own efforts. The only other peoples equally cut off from the centres of ancient culture were the North and South Americans, the Bantu and the aborigines of Australia. Of these only the Japanese contrived to build up and to preserve a highly developed culture of their own.

In such a position, it is not surprising that whenever communication was opened up with China in early times, the Japanese found themselves in the position of pupils. It is significant that on such occasions they were always exceedingly anxious to learn from China, but that what they learnt they rapidly made their own. Unlike the Annamites, Koreans and other neighbouring races, they lived too far off ever to be completely sinified. In fact, a rhythm can be traced in Japan's cultural relations with China, in which periods of enthusiastic absorption seem to alternate with periods of isolation and digestion, in which the newly acquired Chinese culture is transformed into something Japanese.

The old conception of the Japanese as mere imitators, incapable of creation, is in fact hopelessly wrong; no people's culture is more truly their own. The illusion which gave birth to this view was created by the fact that, whereas all other great nations have built up their cultures by constant interchange with each other, the influence of other civilisations on Japan has come in one or two great waves; and at these times the Japanese have packed into a few years the borrowings that other people have spread over centuries.

The resulting self-reliance of the Japanese and confidence in their own destiny may account just as much for their extreme friendliness and readiness to learn from strangers in this early period as for their injured arrogance later on. There is no sign of any animosity against foreigners—except invading Mongols—before 1600. To those who have suffered from the arrogant xenophobia of Japanese officials in recent times, it is difficult to realise that the historical attitude of the Japanese to foreigners is at least as well illustrated by the following edict of Hideyoshi (1582–98), quoted from Sir George Sansom's *Japan*:

'When a quarrel occurs at Nagasaki between a foreigner and a Japanese, and one wounds the other, the officials shall enquire into the circumstances, and if it is five each out of ten (i.e. if both parties are equally at fault) the Japanese shall be punished.'

The first great absorption of Chinese culture dates from A.D. 645 and included an attempt, imposed from above, to apply the whole mechanism of the T'ang state to Japan. It failed, as it was bound to, because the economy of the country could not possibly support a machinery of government which in fact proved too heavy a burden even for China. Its breakdown led to the beginning of a feudalism not at all unlike that of medieval Europe. Indeed, we can trace from this point another rhythm in Japanese history which is not unfamiliar —a constant series of attempts to establish a central government of the whole country, each of which fails from lack of economic support and is supplanted by the practical rule of feudal barons, until a sufficiently powerful baron arises to make another attempt at central government.

With the T'ang imperial system, Japan took over in this wave of imitation two other things of supreme importance, Buddhism and the written language, but before going on to consider the religion and literature of Japan, some points about the failure of this first attempt at a centralised government on Chinese lines are worth noting. In spite of the immense prestige of the Chinese system, the Japanese refused to modify their own conception of hereditary right. What they did was to adopt the Chinese classless bureaucracy in appearance, but confine the appointments to members of the chief families, thereby preserving the typically rigid Japanese class organisation. The parallel between this and the apparent adoption of Western parliamentary government in the nineteenth century has been often noted.

## (b) Religion

Buddhism first reached Japan towards the end of the sixth century A.D. Before that the religion of the Japanese had been a naturalistic pantheism which saw God, or the gods, in every tree and stream, and therefore more particularly in the trees and streams of Japan. This belief, which in the minds of Japanese poets and artists long antedated such Westerners as Wordsworth, persisted throughout Japanese history at two levels: with the peasant it remained what it is to-day, a thing of household gods and village shrines, not unlike the beliefs of the ancient Romans; with the rulers it survived as a more or less awed recognition that, whatever religion you followed, the fate of the Japanese people was somehow bound up with the gods, whose ancient shrines at Ise and Idzumo still demanded their due reverence. From the seventh century to the nineteenth, this ancient 'Way of the Gods' was indeed far in the background of Japanese religious life, but it was never wholly abandoned. Its name, Shinto, was first given to it to distinguish it from the imported religion, Buddhism, in the sixth century.

Buddhism at first was a foreign cult imposed from above by the admirers of all things Chinese. It was not until the mid-thirteenth century that genuinely Japanese sects were developed and Buddhism acquired a real following among the people as a whole. Of these sects the 'True Pure Land' gained the greatest following, the Nichiren was the most exclusively Japanese and the Zen the most important.

'True Pure Land' Buddhism is a development of Amida Buddhism (see Chapter IV 'History and People' (e)). It reached its logical conclusion under Shinran (1173–1262), who taught that a single invocation of Amida Buddha was sufficient to ensure salvation, and that the ordinary man, having performed that one religious act with truth faith, might just as well devote the rest of his time to behaving as a good citizen in the station of life to which he had been called.

Nichiren, the founder of the sect which takes his name, was even more typically Japanese in his modification of Buddhism. He was fanatically intolerant of all other sects, significantly enough on the grounds, not that they were wrong, but that they were undermining Japanese spirit. 'Japanese' Buddhism, he was convinced, was the only possible religion for his countrymen, and in his own ultra-Japanese sect lay the only possible hope of salvation. In his relations with the Government of his day he seems to have behaved not unlike the prophet Elijah. Doctrinally, the difference between Nichiren and 'True Pure Land' Buddhism seems only to have amounted to ensuring salvation through the pronunciation of a different set of syllables; but behind this apparent simplification there lay, of course, a background of abstruse theological justification. It is worth noting that some at least of the patriotic assassins of modern Japan were members of this sect (see Hugh Byas' *Government by Assassination*).

Zen Buddhism had a profound effect on Japan. It is, however, a mystic cult and therefore by definition unexplainable. One can only say that the Zen Buddhists seek by arduous meditation a direct mystic illumination which they cannot, of course, transmit to others. Zen Buddhism has therefore no scriptures, no doctrines and no ritual. All that can be said to be passed on from Zen master to pupil is a technique of meditation, and it seems that this is largely concerned with stimulating the mind to transcend itself by means of paradoxes and incongruities. Zen is strongly puritan and ascetic, and appealed to the spirit of self-sacrifice and self-discipline which were strong in Japanese feudalism and later in Japanese militarism. Its effect on Japanese art has been profound, and combined with the Shintoist sense of the immanence of God in nature to produce, at its best, an amazing purity and intensity of vision. Of course, like all other mystic sects, it has probably had its charlatans, and these were suspected from the first; also, like all other puritan movements, it has included those who disguised a lack of spirit and content as restraint and simplicity. Nevertheless, it is probable that much of the best in Japanese life, thought and art has been developed under the influence of Zen Buddhism.

The history of Christianity in Japan is unusual and dramatic. It dates from the arrival in 1549 of St. Francis Xavier. A year or two earlier the first Portuguese merchants had landed, and it is clear that the favourable welcome given to the missionaries by the Japanese feudal barons was partly due to their eagerness to secure foreign trade. For they saw that the traders paid great deference to the missionaries.

Converts were made fast, at first only among the poor folk, but later also among the upper classes, and it is clear that, whatever the original attraction, many became devout and sincere Christians even to the point of martyrdom. At the time of their greatest number, they may well have amounted to several hundred thousand.

Martyrdom came to them, not from the opposition of the Buddhist clergy, but because Hideyoshi and the first Tokugawa Shoguns saw clearly that in other parts of the world the missionaries had been the forerunners of the conquistadors; and they wanted no conquistadors in Japan. Unfortunately, this impression was only

R

confirmed by the tales which members of the various Christian sects told against each other in order to discredit their trade or religious rivals. Liberally at first, but with increasing severity, edicts against the Christians were enforced and their numbers reduced, though many of them persevered in their faith in spite of hideous tortures. All Spaniards were expelled in 1624; in 1638 the Christian peasants of Shimabara were the leaders in one of the many agrarian risings which marked the misery of the countryside during the Tokugawa period; 37,000 of them were slaughtered almost to a man and the Portuguese, who were suspected of complicity in the rising, were also expelled. From this time on, all contact with the West was banned and Christianity was a capital offence. Even so a few Christian families contrived to practise their faith in secret until the restoration of religious freedom under the Meiji Emperor.

Since then over 3,000 Christian churches have been licensed in Japan and the new Christian missions have won a small (less than 1 per cent. of the population) but influential following. As in China and elsewhere in the Far East it is not the quantity but the quality of the Japanese who have turned to Christianity which is encouraging.

## (c) Art and Language

There is no doubt that the Japanese are, like the Chinese, an extremely artistic people. It seems doubtful whether there is any other race to-day so large a proportion of which derives genuine and intense pleasure from beauty of form. To many people the most attractive feature of Japanese life is the wide and spontaneous appreciation of the pleasure to be derived from a simple almost ascetic life surrounded by objects of beauty, either natural or man-made.

Three factors seem to have contributed to this: the natural beauty of the Japanese landscape, the Nature worship inherent in Shinto and the simplicity and asceticism of Zen Buddhism. The degree of trouble to which the Japanese will go to improve the shape of a landscape or even of a single tree is often a surprise to Westerners, who, on the whole care very much less for beautiful surroundings. This artistic feeling is particularly noticeable in reference to the conditions of everyday life. G. C. Allen, in his *Short Economic History of Modern Japan*, notes that 'the Japanese, though their life has always been simple, demand a high standard of artistic merit in articles of everyday use. So not merely their furniture and

36. A late nineteenth-century print, by Miyagawa Shuntei, showing hair styles and flowered *kimonos* of Japanese girls as they are still to be seen in Japan today. Note the wooden shoes (*geta*) with two transverse bars under the sole, ideal for muddy weather.

ornaments, but even some of their common domestic utensils have
to be made by craftsmen.' The famous gift of cherry trees to the
American capital was, in fact, typical of the Japanese outlook.

The main defects in Japanese artistic production have been due
to that process of absorbing Chinese culture, not gradually, but in
sudden gulps, which we have already noticed. It has meant at first
an uncritical imitation of Chinese models, as if they were static
examples of perfection instead of phases in a developing culture;
when, however, a genuinely Japanese painter, such as Sesshiu,
for instance, makes the Chinese manner truly his own, the result
is a style as perfect and as poetical as anything the Chinese
produced.

In certain directions—most of them incidentally refinements of
the simple man's everyday life—the Japanese have either surpassed
their masters or created art-forms of their own. Among these are
landscape gardening, flower arrangement and that strange ritual
of everyday life æstheticism, the 'tea ceremony.' This last was a
Zen development, and originated in a highly formal social meeting
of a few friends for the appreciation of a beautiful work of art or
arrangement of flowers. It is typical of the Japanese tendency to
bring all the actions of daily life into a formal artistic or hieratic
pattern; and it has all the merits and all the dangers of such a
process, including the danger of relapsing into an empty formalism.
There is a tendency among the 'tough' young Japanese of to-day
to regard all this, however, as 'women's work.'

The most important respect in which the Japanese swallowed
Chinese culture whole was in adopting the Chinese method of
writing. We have already seen what a handicap this method of
writing has been to modern China; to modern Japan it has been a
disaster. Spoken Japanese was already a formed language by the
sixth century A.D., when the first great wave of Chinese influence
was felt. Its origins are uncertain: possibly a mixture of the Ural-
Altaic, which one finds, for instance, in Turkish or Finnish, and a
southern type akin to Polynesian. Wherever it came from, it could
hardly have been more different from Chinese, being polysyllabic
and having a syntax and word order like that of the Aryan tongues.
Unfortunately, it was a purely spoken language and had no script
or alphabet. The Japanese therefore adopted the Chinese characters.
This meant at first adopting the Chinese written language entire,
and until about the tenth century the Japanese may have spoken
their own language, but they wrote Chinese.

When the absorption period gave place to digestion at the end of the ninth century, the Japanese turned to the difficult problem of writing Japanese in Chinese characters. It was excessively difficult because the Chinese characters stood for a thing, not a sound, and represented each a monosyllabic word, whereas what Japanese required was an alphabet like ours. Two devices seemed possible: either to use the Chinese character to represent the whole object desired and pronounce it in the Japanese way, or else to use the Chinese character to represent its sound without any reference to its meaning, and then use these sounds to build up Japanese words; this last method would at least have provided a syllabary, if not an alphabet. Unfortunately, the Japanese did both. What was worse, they invented at least two separate syllabaries, picking on different Chinese characters with similar sounds to represent the same sound in Japanese.

In course of time this produced a written language of such appalling complication that even to-day it has not been reduced to order. Even now a symbol may often have one of several meanings, and some psychologists have traced the Japanese tendency to equivocation to the fact that in their language words do not mean exactly what they say, even as much as they do in ours. From a practical point of view, the results have been catastrophic. It has been estimated that a well-educated Japanese has to learn by heart 5,000 characters, and that the difficulty of the language adds four years on to the time that it takes him to acquire a higher education; in the primary schools they have time to learn little else. The Japanese typewriter is one of the most fantastically ingenious machines in the world and to acquire a good speed on it takes two to three years' steady practice.

For modern newspaper cables, telegrams, etc., an attempt has been made to write Japanese in Roman letters (Romaji). This would have been perfectly easy at first, but it has come too late. By now a great number of modern words have been added to Japanese by adopting Chinese characters which have different meanings but, unfortunately, the same syllabic sound. Dr. Reischauer points out that there are, even in an ordinary dictionary, twenty different words which look different in the Chinese characters, but which would all be written in Romaji 'koko.' A good example of the way confusion is caused is the famous 'Black Dragon Society,' which sounds to us so like something out of a film. It is in fact the Amur River Society and 'Black Dragon' is simply an alternative meaning of the

Chinese characters used to write 'Amur River.' The Annamites were lucky in getting the Quoc Ngu in the seventeenth century.

It has sometimes been suggested that the Japanese purposely refrained from simplifying the language, since it increased their military security if practically no foreigners could learn it. Those who know the Japanese passion for military secrets will find this not so fantastically improbable as it sounds.

On Japanese literature the results were wholly bad, since it has meant that with few and notable exceptions her writers have either imitated the Chinese or actually written in Chinese. To painting and drawing, however, it has probably been useful, since the extreme importance attached to well-drawn characters must have had something to do with that exquisite sureness of line which distinguishes early Japanese art from any contemporary production of the West.

When one considers, however, what the Japanese have done in the arts and sciences in spite of this handicap, the case for some desperate and radical reform of the language becomes even stronger.

## (d) Feudalism

The breakdown of the central government (in so far as it had ever existed) in the twelfth century led to a feudal period in Japan, during which the real power lay with the local barons, who came to be known as Daimyo, or 'Great Ones.' Sometimes these Daimyo acted in concert; at other times they indulged in violent civil wars, the greatest of which led up to the establishment of the Tokugawa family as supreme overlords in 1600.

The title under which the Tokugawa exercised this power was that of 'shogun' (supreme general), which they held nominally from the Emperor, and this technique of reducing the nominal ruler to the status of a puppet is the most distinctive feature of Japanese feudalism. The first stage was the relegation of the Emperor and the Imperial House to their purely religious and symbolic functions by the Fujiwara family in the middle of the ninth century A.D. Like the Merovingian mayors of the palace or the Nguyen family in Annam, the Fujiwara kept the reins of government in their own hands. It was on the collapse of their administration in the twelfth century that the new feudal leader, Yoritomo, leaving the Emperor's formal position untouched, took for himself for the first time the title of shogun. When in 1219 his family were in turn eliminated, the new ruling family, instead of assuming the shogunate themselves, preferred to keep the power but not the name in their own hands and governed through a puppet shogun, now usually chosen for ceremonial reasons from the Fujiwara family.

Meanwhile, a tradition of early abdication had grown up in the imperial line, since the Emperor's position seemed to entail far more duties than either rights or powers. In many cases, however, the abdicated Emperor kept the few remaining strings of imperial patronage in his own hands, leaving a young child as titular emperor. Thus it comes about, to quote Sir George Sansom, that 'We have in Japan of the thirteenth century, the astonishing spectacle of a state at the head of which stands a titular emperor whose vestigial functions are usurped by an abdicated emperor, and whose real power is nominally delegated to an hereditary military dictator but actually wielded by an hereditary adviser of that dictator.'

Knowledge of this tradition, that real power in Japan is almost always wielded not by the ostensible holder of it, but by the man behind the scenes, is most important in interpreting modern Japanese society. The elimination of the great financial families (the Zaibatsu), for instance, is likely to have little or no real effect if it consists simply of eliminating figureheads. In fact, the difficulty of tracing who really wields power makes any attempt to 'de-Nazify' or 'de-militarise' Japan from outside almost worthless.

Apart from the love of preserving outward forms, which showed itself in this system of puppets within puppets, the main characteristics of Japanese feudalism which affect modern Japan were:

(a) Loyalty to the feudal lord took precedence over loyalty to the family. This conflict of loyalties is in fact a favourite theme of Japanese drama, and the Japanese view is unique in the Far East. It alone would almost account for the fact that the Japanese are the only oriental people to have built up a disciplined and even chauvinistically patriotic modern State.

(b) The soldier (i.e. the mounted knight) was the ideal, and the peasantry were reduced almost to the state of serfs.

(c) The Buddhist Church played a part very similar to that played by the Christian Church in Europe. Fighting abbots, over-wealthy monasteries and puritan reformations among the under-privileged classes were all features of Japanese feudalism.

(d) Whenever the elaborate pretence of central government failed completely to be effective the streak of practicality in the Japanese character showed itself. The 'house-codes' of the great Daimyo were applied in a rough-and-ready way, but reasonably fairly as a legal system; bureaux like the Kebiishi (the forerunners of the political police) or the Archivists developed, apparently on their own initiative, systems of summary jurisdiction and legislation, which provided a practical and realistic substitute for the empty formalities of the court. It is perhaps worth noting that in occupied territories in 1942 the Japanese Army developed a similar sort of summary justice; and that, in spite of its comparatively greater savagery, it was often more popular with the inhabitants than the complicated, long-winded and unintelligible process of the European-ised courts.

## (e) The Tokugawa Shogunate 1600–1868

In 1600, as we have seen, the period of feudal wars was brought to an end: but not the period of feudalism. The object of the Tokugawa shoguns was to preserve stability at all costs. This they attempted to do by one of the most remarkable social 'freezing' operations in history. We have seen that they stamped out Christianity for fear it should lead to Western intervention, and in 1636 they passed the amazing edict that no Japanese was to leave Japan, no Japanese who had left was to return and no foreigner was to be allowed to land. What is perhaps even more amazing is that for over 200 years the edict was rigorously and successfully enforced.

Having thus ensured that no outside influence could upset their plans, they proceeded to the task of preventing either social or political change. To prevent social change, society was divided legally into rigid classes, Daimyo, Samurai (warrior), farmer, artisan and merchant, in that order; no one might leave his class, and the two upper ones, in the absence of war of any kind, were parasitic on the three lower, producing nothing, but living on their rents. The theoretical superiority of the farmer to the merchant was good Confucianism; the superiority of the Samurai to either was Japanese feudalism. The prevention of political change meant seeing that no other of the great Daimyo families was able to oust the Tokugawa. This was done by an elaborate system of spies and hostages: the other great Daimyo were compelled to spend half of each year at the Tokugawa court (cf. Versailles) and when they were not there their wives or families had to stay there in their place. Roads between the great fiefs and the capital were kept under control by limiting the number of bridges and erecting barriers, at which the guards were instructed to watch for weapons coming into the central Tokugawa territory or women going out, since either of these might indicate that one of the outer Daimyo was contemplating a revolt.

Unfortunately for the Tokugawa, no satisfactory method of 'social freezing' has yet been discovered, and this apparently foolproof system held in it from the first the seeds of its ultimate decay. In the first place, it was established on a rice economy, just at the moment when a money economy was taking its place. Consequently, the despised merchant soon had the Samurai, who was legally entitled to 'cut him down' without penalty for insolence, hopelessly in debt; for the Samurai's income was a gratuity from his Daimyo, and his Daimyo's income consisted of rice. By the middle of the nineteenth century, the Samurai as a class had lost their position of power entirely to the merchants. It is important for the understanding of modern Japan's class structure to realise that the movement which overthrew the Tokugawa was led by Samurai, largely in the hope of freeing themselves from this position.

Secondly, the establishment of the Tokugawa régime almost coincided with a revival of Confucianism, which completely ousted Buddhism among the ruling class. Since loyalty was a primary virtue of the Confucian system, the Tokugawa shoguns gave this movement all their support. Unfortunately for them, however, it led almost inevitably to a revival also of Shinto, and the realisation that on Confucian principles loyalty was owed, not to the shogun, but to the emperor.

Finally, it was impossible for Japan to close her doors indefinitely on the rest of the world, and every year that the isolation went on rendered her ultimate position weaker.

These three factors combined between 1853 and 1868 to bring about the opening of Japan to foreign trade, the collapse of the Tokugawa Shogunate and the return of the Imperial House to a place in public life after an absence of 1,000 years.

### MODERN SOCIAL STRUCTURE

#### (a) The Meiji Restoration and the Policy of the New Ruling Class

To start a description of the social structure of any country with the ruling class may seem to be putting the cart before the horse. Japan, however, is a country where social change has always been imposed from the top. In fact, the main difference between the Westernising of Japan and that of China is that in Japan it has been carried out primarily as a conscious operation, planned and controlled by the ruling oligarchy—another great 'gulp,' in fact, of foreign influence. In China it has been a natural assimilation, often spreading against the will of the government and certainly in accordance with no preconceived plan.

When in 1854 the Tokugawa shoguns were compelled to admit the foreigners to Japan, they realised clearly that their policy of exclusion had exposed Japan to a very serious danger of absorption or at least 'protection' by some Western power. They started at once, therefore, a policy of Westernisation and modernisation of the country. Two very significant facts should be remembered about the movement which led to their voluntary surrender of power: firstly, it was the shoguns and not the Samurai from the outlying fiefs who were in favour of modernisation; the battle-cry of the anti-shogun party was at first 'Honour the Emperor. Expel the barbarians'; secondly, the signal for collapse was the assassination by a 'patriot' of the Prime Minister who had concluded the treaty admitting the foreigners.

What in fact happened was that a group of extremely able young Samurai from the outlying southern fiefs of Satsuma and Choshu took advantage of the internal collapse of the Tokugawa régime and the growing Confucian feeling in favour of direct loyalty to the Emperor to stage a traditional feudal revolt. The 'weakness' of the Tokugawa in giving way to the foreigners made it possible to base their appeal, not only on loyalty to the Emperor, but on Japanese patriotism. As the rise of new clans is the last example of a feudal pattern of violence, so the assassination of a 'weak' Premier and the tame acquiescence of the Tokugawa leaders is the first example of a procedure only too common in modern Japan. Once the group of young Samurai gained power, which they held, of course, in the name of the fifteen-year-old Emperor, the more intelligent of them realised that the Tokugawa policy of modernisation and admitting the foreigners had been right and therefore adopted it for themselves. Before they were secure, they had to deal with a revolt of those of their own followers who felt that the 'restoration had been betrayed,' and it is significant that the great Saigo, the leader of the Satsuma rebellion, is one of Japan's national heroes; for the purpose of the Satsuma rebellion was to bring the restoration back to its original feudal and reactionary principles. The effect of the Meiji restoration was to place a new oligarchy of ruling families in the seats of the Tokugawa and to establish their right to that position by a theory of direct loyalty to the Emperor. Modern Japan cannot be understood if the great change which took place in the mid-nineteenth century is regarded as having been inspired by either Western, liberal or democratic motives.

In its simplest elements, the new ruling oligarchy consisted of the following groups:

(a) The young Samurai from the southern fiefs of Choshu and Satsuma, who assumed control respectively of the Army and of the Navy.

(b) A number of princely families around the Emperor's court, such as the Fujiwara and Tokugawa themselves.

(c) A few extremely powerful merchant banking families, drawn from the class who had already gained economic control. These last, under the name of Zaibatsu (financial cliques), played an extremely important part in Japan's economic development. The most important of them were Mitsui, who financed the new government at the critical stage when it could not even command the insufficient revenues of the Tokugawa régime, and Mitsubishi, who provided the shipping for the new Government's first expeditions to Formosa and Korea.

The policy of the new Government was to learn as quickly as possible those technical achievements of the Westerners which would equip Japan to meet them on even terms. The idea of equipping Japan to carry out her 'manifest destiny' of hegemony in Asia may already have been in their minds. For whichever purpose, the first essentials were a strong Army and Navy. As a foundation for these, Japan's leaders were clever enough to realise that she would require a Westernised industrial economy.

The policy of the new Government therefore included the formation of a national conscript Army on the German model, and this alone would have necessitated the abolition of the old feudal system under which Samurai alone bore arms. In fact, the feudal system had become so far divorced from economic reality that its abolition released a great fund of hitherto unemployed energy, and many of the most successful of the new merchants and industrialists of the new Japan were the Samurai or sons of Samurai, who thus re-entered normal society.

In theory, the new Constitution which was granted by the Meiji Emperor appeared like a cautious imitation of the British, although in one important respect it was more like the American, for the Cabinet were responsible not to the Diet (Parliament), but directly to the Emperor. In fact, however, it was as much Japanese as the Japanese version of T'ang China had been, and one of the most typically Japanese features was that the real rulers had no specific constitutional position at all, but were the three groups mentioned above, who controlled everything from behind the scenes.

This means that most political developments in modern Japan can best be interpreted as a struggle for power behind the scenes. Thus the emergence of political parties on the Western model at the beginning of the twentieth century probably represents an attempt on the part of those clans who resented the Choshu-Satsuma monopoly to get their share of political power. Their bid, in fact, failed, and the political parties soon became the tools of the Zaibatsu.

For some time it looked as if 'big business' in the form of the Zaibatsu was to become the next power behind the throne, but those who counted on this had reckoned without a new force, the Army.

### (b) The Independence of the Army

For a generation at least the leaders of the Army were still the ex-Samurai of Choshu who had created it, and the Army might therefore be regarded as an instrument in a feudal balance of power. As a professional Army drawn from all parts of Japan was built up, however, and as young officers of this Army advanced to high rank, a new loyalty directed towards the Army itself was developed. The Army was intentionally drawn from the peasantry, who were less affected than any other class by 'modern' or 'Western' ideas, and its core, the professional officers, came mostly from yeoman families in agricultural districts. This officer corps inherited the Samurai traditions of the warrior's loyalty, coloured with that exaggerated romanticism which Japan, alone of all oriental peoples, developed.

When in the 1920s it appeared as if the Zaibatsu, by manipulation of the political parties, might succeed to the power position of the 'elder statesmen,' it was the Army who in fact ousted them. Their feelings can well be understood: it was intensely galling to the average Army officer to see a new class of 'un-Japanese' business-men with no reverence for the past, no respect for the Emperor or the warrior, no sense of Japan's manifest destiny, too much money and a regrettable taste for spending it on Western frivolities controlling the destinies of the nation. They felt that in loyalty to the Emperor it must be stopped and, because of the romantic Japanese view of loyalty which elevates it above all other considerations, they felt justified in stopping it by any means whatever. They chose assassination and political sabotage.

We have seen that the tradition of assassination had been set at the outset of the Meiji restoration. From 1930 onwards it was carried on with a gusto which can best be brought out by a list of the victims:

1930.  Prime Minister.
1932.  Head of Mitsui, Prime Minister and former Finance Minister.
1935.  Director of the Military Affairs Bureau.
1936.  Finance Minister, Inspector-General of Military Training and Admiral Saito (ex-Prime Minister).

Those victims within the Army itself were singled out because of their attempts to restore discipline and bring the Army under the control, if not of the central government, at least of its own heads. In carrying out this programme, the young Army officers were, of course, assisted by the 'patriotic' societies, many of whom carried on a general criminal business as a side-line, secure in the knowledge that to 'sincerity' and 'patriotism' almost anything would be forgiven. Behind this outburst of resentment by the young Army officer there was a deep-seated and understandable feeling that the peasantry, with whom, as we saw, the Army was particularly linked, were being exploited for the benefit of the commercial classes, but what is so difficult for the Westerner to understand is the psychology of the assassins. It would be a grave mistake to suppose, however, that they were abnormal; the nature of modern Japanese society cannot be appreciated unless it is realised that these men enjoyed, not only the tacit consent and approval of their superior officers, but the enthusiastic hero-worship of large sections of the people. The full analysis of this phenomenon would take too long here, and is well set out in Hugh Byas' *Government by Assassination*; one quotation from that book will indicate what we are up against in the matter of understanding. It is the reply of a naïve conspirator when asked why he plotted to assassinate the Prime Minister: 'I had no concrete idea. I merely thought it would be better to get rid of the Premier, believing his murder was necessary for the permanent development of the nation.'

For political sabotage, the Army was in a particularly powerful position. Traditionally, in Japan the War Minister was a serving soldier and not a politician; as soon as the Army saw the slightest danger of a civilian attempting to hold this post in a 'politicians'' government, they got the Cabinet and the Emperor to sanction new regulations, which gave legal form to the tradition. The same applied to the Navy Minister, and it meant that the Army or Navy could cause the immediate fall of any government by ordering their minister to resign and, if he refused, striking him off the active list, so that he became legally incapacitated to hold his post. It is an interesting sidelight on the doctrine of direct loyalty to the Emperor that the Army were always quite ready to paralyse the Emperor's administration in this way. The classic example came in 1937, when the Emperor sent for General Ugaki to form a Ministry and his car was intercepted *en route* to the palace by a War Office General, who 'advised' him that the Army wished him to refuse. General Ugaki preferred to obey the Emperor, so the Army, by forbidding any serving officer to join his Cabinet, made it impossible for him to form a government. There was a great deal of talk, particularly among popular assassins, at this time about direct rule of the Emperor and removing those who 'stood between the Emperor and his people,' but all it really meant was replacing them by someone else whom the assassins considered more sincere.

It may seem that the Army has got rather more space than it deserved or than it would get in any other country, but its position in pre-war Japan is in fact the clue to all that happened. The Navy, though technically in an equally strong position, exercised no such power, partly perhaps because, having been formed on the English rather than the German model, it had a different tradition, but mostly because its standard of education was higher and its connection with the discontented peasantry not so intimate. But the Navy could act independently of the central government too, as it showed at Shanghai. There were in fact two separate societies in pre-war Japan: a strongly traditional peasant military society still feudal in its refusal to accept the control of the central government, and a rapidly Westernising industrial and commercial society. Whatever the Diet or even the Cabinet might say, it was the peasant military society that held the reins of power behind the scenes.

## (c) Growth of Population

The most fundamental social change brought about by the Meiji restoration was a leap upwards in the population, which had remained stationary or even declined towards the end of the Tokugawa period. Thirty-five millions in 1873, it had risen to 45 millions in 1903 and was over 78 millions in 1948. Unlike all other oriental countries, Japan was able to combine this rise in population with a rise in

the standard of living. Up to about 1880–90, the real income per
head was about the same as in China, and under the Tokugawa the
Japanese peasant had been even worse off than some of his oriental

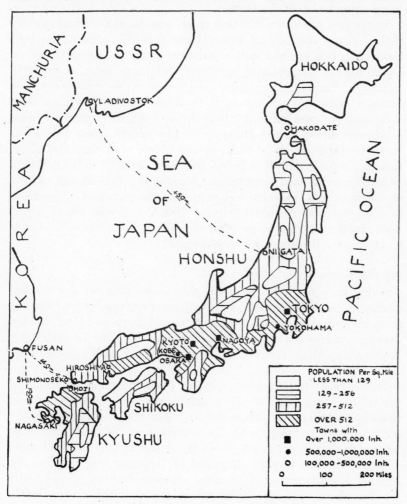

XIX. Japan: distribution of population.

brethren. From then, at least until the 'Guns or butter' period from
1931 onwards, the standard rose steadily. Real incomes had trebled
or quadrupled and even the peasant standard was higher than
anywhere in the Far East and as high as that of eastern Europe.

Political writers have often suggested that this rising population meant that Japan had to find an outlet for emigrants, and that this was a cause of her expansionist policy. This view will not stand up to an examination of the facts.

In the first place, the fact that Japan was the one oriental country with a rising standard of living shows that the pressure on land was not in fact as great as, for instance, in Korea. Secondly, when Japan did in fact expand, very few emigrants went to the new territories; only 7,000 genuine settlers went to Manchuria, for instance, between 1932 and 1937. By 1936 there were still less than 1 million Japanese all told living abroad, and most of these were in Hawaii, Brazil or the Philippines. The reason is not difficult to find; the Japanese are a home-loving people, and they also knew that they were better off in Japan than they would be in the colonies. What Japan did need economically was assured markets and sources of raw materials. Japanese indignation at the exclusion of Japanese immigrants from Australia and the U.S.A. was due not to a real desire on the part of any great number to go there, but to the insult to Japanese self-respect which was implied.

## (d) The Japanese Peasantry

Along with the increase in the total population went a marked change in its composition. In 1872, the first year for which any accurate estimate is possible, approximately 77 per cent. of the people were engaged in agriculture; at the present time the percentage is about 43. There is no other oriental country with a record anything like this.

It is a relief to turn for a moment from the romantic mania of the young Army officer to the peasant as he is in his village. It is a remarkable tribute to village life in Japan that there is scarcely a writer, however violent in his condemnation of political Japan, who has anything but praise for the villager; just as you will find those who are harshest in their judgment of Japanese men speak in the highest possible terms of Japanese women. Perhaps it was partly for this reason that during the war it was practically impossible to find a 'Japanese expert,' i.e. someone who had lived a reasonable time in the country, who did not shock the fire-eaters by continually finding something to approve of in the Japanese, and who did not intend to go back if possible after the war.

The peasant family is little altered from traditional times. The father is very much the head, and all money earned goes to him;

it is for him to dole out pocket-money to other members if they need it, but in general village life does not depend on money, since local products are exchanged direct for rice. The family is an economic unit, with everyone playing a part on a holding which is rarely bigger than 2½ acres. The house is a simple structure with sliding screens which can be moved about to partition off different 'rooms,' and mats and cushions on the floor instead of furniture. One special feature is the bath-house at the rear, separated from the main house, and a hot bath after the day's work is one of the Japanese peasant's greatest pleasures. Houses are usually built in little groups, and in order to save fuel one house in each group will stoke up its bath each day and all share; it makes for a very neighbourly feeling. This neighbourliness is also promoted by the fact that a lot of jobs in the village are done by communal labour—rice transplanting, road and bridge building—and by the fact that every one as a child has gone to the village school. The little groups of houses within the village are called *buraku*, and manage their own affairs to a considerable extent, and here also it is the family and not the individual that is the unit.

This traditional village life has been affected, of course, by the coming of the motor bus and railway and by electric light and power, but it is still the basis of Japan's agriculture and three-fifths of the peasant farmers own their farms; rent, for those who do pay rent, is about half the rice crop. The central government has also had its effect in the villages through the schools, which are universal and became in pre-war years centres of militaristic indoctrination, a function which they shared with the reservists and women's patriotic organisations. It seems, indeed, to be a characteristic of the Japanese peasant, possibly due to a long history of contempt and oppression, that he is exceptionally docile to authority. Unfortunate though this may have been in the past, it may have its advantages in the future.

## (e) The Townsfolk

The capital of Japan has usually been one of the world's larger cities, but the industrialisation policy of modern Japan has meant not only the expansion of Tokyo, but the rise of a number of other great cities also, and the creation of an urban population which has no parallel in the Far East. The population of Tokyo is now approximately 6¾ million, that of Osaka over 3 million and there are four

S

other cities, Nagoya, Kyoto, Yokohama and Kobe with normal populations around the million mark.

Whereas in 1893 only 6 per cent. of the population lived in towns of 100,000 population and upwards, that proportion has now risen to 25 per cent. It has been these great cities which have absorbed

37. The centre of Tokyo: just like any Western city in winter.

the growing urban population, and there has been much less expansion in the proportion living in medium-sized towns with populations between 10,000 and 100,000.

In each of the great towns there is a modern district of tall ferro-concrete office blocks, which are supposed to be earthquake-proof and many of which can be seen in the photographs of Hiroshima after the bomb, still standing amid the waste of flat devastation. The townsfolk's homes, however, are mostly traditional Japanese wooden houses spread out over a large area, many of them with little gardens, and more and more with one 'Western' room. For the townsfolk, although they did not abandon traditional Japanese customs, took eagerly to many of the social habits of the West, and it was fashionable to have one room in the house furnished in Western style; even the Emperor, the centre of Japanese traditionalism, had adopted before the war the habit of one 'Western style' meal in the day. The Western culture which spread so fast in the towns, particularly in the 1920s, was, of course, American. For a few years everything American was the rage, and the 'modern boy' and 'modern girl' of the big cities did their best to imitate what they saw on the films. Part of this social change has stuck, and the Japanese of the great cities are still enthusiastic supporters of baseball. Part of it deeply shocked the traditionalists, and was suppressed firmly and sometimes savagely from the late 1920s onwards. The Japanese, it is true, have no very good record of public morality themselves, but they have a great sense of public decorum, and it is easy to sympathise with those who objected strongly to the rage for Western jazz, Western 'girl shows' and Western bars. Unfortunately, the militarists used this conservative feeling to gain support for their suppression of everything Western, and this included all forms of liberal thought. It was not merely the superficialities of Hollywood or Forty-second Street that Japanese youth was absorbing from America; Western symphony orchestras were as popular as Western revues; but all foreign influences came under the ban together. The most serious loss in this general holocaust was probably the infant trade union and labour movement, which died— or, rather, committed suicide—at the call of reactionary Nationalism.

The extent to which American cultural influence on the townsfolk will revive will depend very largely on the behaviour of the occupying troops, and is discussed in a later section.

## MODERN ECONOMIC STRUCTURE

### (a) Natural Resources

The most important factor in Japan's future as a great industrial power is the poverty of her natural resources. We have seen that her soil is not such as to allow her to become a great producer of food or fibre crops. In minerals she is equally badly off. She is the fifth or sixth world producer of copper, but apart from that is an importer of every mineral required for modern industry, and is particularly short of iron ores, of which in peacetime she could provide only 4 per cent. of her requirements from home production. Coal production had by 1936 just topped 40 million tons, but there are no great reserves and no possibility of great expansion; the great bulk of her coal had therefore to be imported from Manchuria or north China.

The only respect in which Japan is well placed from a raw material

point of view is that the continental shelf around the islands is one
of the world's great fishing grounds, and fish plays in the Japanese
diet the part that meat plays in ours.

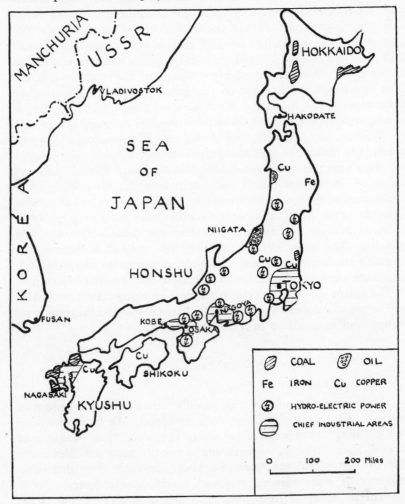

XX. Japan: industrial resources.

There are very small native sources of petroleum, but production
never much exceeded 100 million gallons and supplied less than a
quarter of the country's requirements. Here again there are neither
reserves nor means of expansion.

## (b) Agriculture, Forests and Fisheries

We have seen that the staple diet of Japan is rice and that this is grown in the usual oriental fashion by peasant farmers on small-holdings. Rice production in Japan has risen steadily since the time of the Meiji restoration, mainly as a result of improved methods and fertilisers introduced on the initiative of the government. The productivity of the Japanese farmer is now considerably higher than that of the Chinese, though both are well below the European. In spite of this, the Japanese rice-producer has not been able to keep up with the growth in consumption. Since 1890, when for the last time there was a net export of rice, Japanese imports have risen steadily, and in the years 1935–7 reached 62 million bushels, nearly 20 per cent. of consumption. The cause of this has, of course, been mainly the growth in population, but it is worth noting that an increase in the standard of living is also indicated by a rise in consumption per head, which was steady until 1929 and then fell back to about the level of 1915.

Secondary grain crops are wheat, barley and oats, which are grown in rotation on part of the rice-land when the paddy has been cut. Far more important than any of these, however, is the raising of silkworms. Raw silk not only provided, and still provides, the Japanese peasant family with their cash income, but provided Japan as a whole with her one acceptable export at a time when foreign currency was essential for the initial equipment of the country. Professor Allen has pointed out what a stroke of luck it was for Japan that just at the time when she required to trade with Europe, an outbreak of silkworm disease there should have given her an almost unlimited market for what was then almost her only possible export. Nowadays we are so accustomed to thinking of Japan as an exporter of cheap manufactured goods that we tend to forget that until the slump of 1929 hit her American market, her main export was raw silk produced on Japanese farms; the collapse of this situation had a good deal to do with the peasant distress mentioned in the last section. The method of silk production is basically the same as that described in the chapter on China, with the exception that in Japan standardisation of eggs, mechanical reeling and controlled marketing have gone much further. It has in fact ceased to be an industry carried on by the farmer beyond the stage of raising cocoons—except that his daughter very possibly goes to work in the nearest reeling factory.

Japan is relatively a well-forested country, having approximately

50 million acres of forest which are well managed, as the forests of Korea have been under Japanese management. Nevertheless, Japan is a net importer of timber, as of so many other raw materials.

Japanese fisheries may be divided into three rough classes: peasant fisherman operating all round the coasts and combining this with a crofter's life; larger-scale fishing syndicates, mostly now operating oil-driven trawlers; and the few large-scale companies which own the whaling fleets and the floating canneries.

38. The tree and the wave. A Japanese painting in real life.

Most of Japan's million and a half fishermen belong, of course, to the first class, and it is their catch which is hawked round the village and makes the 'fish-man' such a familiar figure. It is indeed misleading to compare British and Japanese pressure on land by calculating a 'man-acre' ration if British pasture is taken into account, for the equivalent of pasture as a food source to the Japanese country family is the sea. The second type of Japanese fisherman was well known all over the southern seas and often suspected, no doubt rightly, of being a spy; he too, may bring back his catch to the Japanese larder. The third type is an industrialist, producing either oil for industry or canned fish for export. Taking all three types

together, Japan's annual catch of fish, even at two-thirds of the
pre-war average, is still more important than Britain's is to her.

### (c) Commerce and Industry

Japanese commerce and industry, like the Japanese social system,
was planned and organised from above. The whole idea of industrialisation at the time of the Meiji restoration was a Government plan,
and since there were no industrialists and very few capitalists in
Japan at the time, the Government was compelled to undertake
industrial enterprises itself. This was particularly true in regard to
industries such as iron and steel which were required for strategic
reasons, but which were not particularly attractive commercially.

In this State development of industry the new masters of Japan
were, of course, assisted by the Zaibatsu. Two, at least, of the great
Zaibatsu families, Mitsui and Mitsubishi, dated from before the
Meiji era and were bankers as well as traders. The Japanese public
had at first no funds to invest, and when capital did accumulate,
individual investors never learnt to invest directly themselves in
industry to anything like the extent that this happens in the West.
Consequently, the Zaibatsu never lost that financial control of
industry with which they had started, since they controlled the
banks through which individual investment was later directed.
When later still public trust in banks was to some extent diminished,
the private investor turned to investment trusts and here too he
was in reality handing his money to the Zaibatsu to invest for him,
since they controlled the trusts. In the immediately pre-war period,
they were even gaining control of the village industries by entering
the loan market in competition with the individual small 'brokers'
who had previously financed them.

The division of Japan into two separate societies, which we have
noticed in the social structure, was, however, repeated in the
economic sphere. Although the organisation of large-scale industry
was thus concentrated in exceptionally few hands, a great part of
the economy of the country remained untouched by these changes.
It is much more difficult to calculate what proportion of the nation's
wealth and manpower was concentrated in the small industries
providing mainly housing and household utensils, but it is certain
that it was very considerable, and that as far as the life of the countryside went it remained and remains just as important as the large-scale
Westernised industry.

The year 1929 marks a radical change in the development of

Japanese large-scale industry and commerce; up to that time Europeans were still doubtful on the whole whether Japan could develop into an industrial nation capable of competing with the West. After that one heard more of panic questions as to whether the West could compete with Japan and whether it was fair that she should be asked to do so.

The first Japanese industry to be developed on a large scale was textiles. This was not surprising in view of the fact that cheap labour rather than ample capital is the foundation of a cotton-spinning industry. By 1913 textiles already formed more than half the total of Japanese exports, and by 1929 the figure had risen to 65 per cent. It should be remembered that 29 per cent. and 37 per cent. of these figures respectively represented raw silk and that in 1929 43 per cent. of all Japanese exports went to the U.S.A. She was in fact primarily a source of raw materials and not a competitor with the Western exporters of manufactured goods. Two things should perhaps have been noticed by those who were later surprised by the development of Japanese trade: first, that the proportion of manufactured products to raw materials rose steadily, and, second, that Japan's trade with her colonial Empire rose from 12 per cent. of her total overseas trade in 1919 to 20 per cent. in 1929; this trade was a normal colonial trade—that is, Japan exported finished products and received from the colonies raw materials. What she was capable of doing with her own colonies she might clearly attempt with other people's.

In 1929 came the great slump. Japan's new economy was even more severely hit than the established systems of Britain and America; moreover, she lost almost overnight her great raw silk market in the U.S.A. The result was, first, the revolt of the peasant-military half of Japanese society, which now saw in military expansion the only hope of prosperity, and, second, the necessity, even apart from this, to find new markets to replace the old. The changes that came over Japanese industry and commerce can be traced to one or other of these two causes.

First of all there was a great increase in the iron and steel industry; steel production, which had been $2\frac{1}{4}$ million tons in 1929 rose to $5\frac{1}{2}$ million tons in 1936 and was nearly 8 million tons in 1942. This increase was mainly due to such technical improvements as doubling the average capacity of blast furnaces, but these industries also absorbed an increased proportion of the country's manpower. Based on an expanding iron and steel industry was a greatly expanded shipbuilding programme, which resulted in the Japanese merchant fleet being the third largest in the world by 1937, with a gross tonnage of 4½ million tons.

Much of Japan's output of steel went, of course, in this ship-building programme and in armaments, but there was also a continuous increase in the production of machine tools for Japanese industry, which fed the change in the nature of her exports. Textile production increased, though its *relative* position in the nation's economy declined, and here also there was a continual progression from the original export of raw silk and cotton yarn, first to cotton fabrics and then to higher and higher grades of these. This change was necessary if Japan was to find markets for her cotton goods, since other Far Eastern countries, notably India, were now exploiting even cheaper labour to invade the lower-grade market, as Japan had done herself twenty years earlier; it meant direct competition with Lancashire, however, and was the first indication to the Westerners that Japan might drive them out of the Far Eastern market altogether.

Two other developments in textiles are important: the expansion of the woollen industry to cover the whole weaving process, so that Japan became independent of imports other than the raw wool, and the establishment of the rayon industry. The woollen industry had always been backed by the military as an essential for clothing the Army in any potential war with Russia, but it is a mistake to regard the establishment of the world's greatest rayon industry as having been designed simply to free Japan from the necessity of relying on imported cotton and wool. The rayon industry was a great foreign exchange earner, but it, too, was dependent on imported Canadian wood pulp—though wood pulp was perhaps more easily available near at hand than either cotton or wool.

Finally, Japan astonished the world by producing and marketing in the Far East those semi-luxury products of light industries which had previously been a European monopoly, and marketing them at a price which the Oriental could afford. It has already been pointed out that the popularity of cheap Japanese bicycles, vacuum flasks, rubber-soled shoes, fountain pens, etc., was more use to them at the beginning of their conquest of south-east Asia than any amount of talk about a Greater East Asia Co-prosperity sphere.

In spite of this great industrial expansion, it is easy to get an entirely false notion of the extent to which Japan actually had 'captured the world market.' Her share of the world's total foreign trade in 1936 was less than 4 per cent., and actually declined from

1935 to 1936; moreover, fully a quarter of it by now was within her own Empire. The cause of the panic among some Western business circles was not that Japan was cornering the world market, but that she was now competing for the first time in commodities which had previously been a Western monopoly, and making it clear every time that she could undersell the West.

## WAR AND POST-WAR

The war was undoubtedly the most important event in the whole of Japanese history. Japan had never before been defeated, and what the psychological effect of defeat will be it is still too early to judge. It is only possible to hazard a few guesses.

Morally, the Japanese seem to have taken the defeat very easily and rather well; there was no sense of individual guilt, since the Emperor ordered the cease fire and individuals simply obeyed, which was very different from surrendering in battle. One got the impression immediately after the surrender that, having received the Emperor's orders, they were determined to show that they could carry out a capitulation better than any other army in the world. Moreover, if there is one thing the Japanese understand and appreciate in practical affairs it is authority, and the surrender made it clear where, for the moment, authority lay.

The post-war control of Japan was taken firmly in hand by General MacArthur and was from the first an American commitment. It was carried out with a generosity, an idealism and an optimism characteristic of the great social engineers. Three objectives stood out at first: the ending of Japanese militarism, land reform and the dissolution of the great trusts, the Zaibatsu. All three were intended to contribute to the transformation of Japan into a genuine democracy and were at first accepted willingly enough by the Japanese, partly from respect for the authority of a conqueror and partly because such changes suited the Japanese tradition. The democracies had won the war, and it seemed reasonable to try out democracy, just as it had seemed reasonable to try out other technical devices from abroad when they were found to work efficiently.

Land reform was in any case a popular measure, as it is throughout Asia, and a necessary forestalling of what might otherwise have become a Communist propaganda cry. By 1949 S.C.A.P. had bought compulsorily just over 5 million acres from landlords and distributed them roughly at the rate of an acre a head, to former tenants, so that the proportion of land worked by landless tenants fell from

46 per cent. of all cultivated land in 1944 to 12 per cent., an unusually low figure, in 1949. It is true that individual holdings are still too small and scattered for maximum efficiency, and the peasant as usual finds that the place of rent has been taken by taxes; but rice production per acre in Japan is still a model to the rest of Asia, and the country contrived, in the bleak years immediately following defeat, to feed itself without any rice imports at all. It seems surely probable also that this great operation of land reform, for all its disappointments, has more genuinely met the needs and wishes of the peasants than the confiscation followed by collectivisation which is practised in China.

The elimination of the Zaibatsu was a much more difficult business, as any government which has ever tried to enforce anti-trust laws knows only too well. Ostensibly General MacArthur expressed himself satisfied that the hold of the great families was broken and the way open for genuine democracy. But the realisation, reached within the first two years after surrender, that Japan must rebuild her industry and her export trade if she was not to be a permanent drain on the American exchequer, was an incentive to overlook the inevitable subterfuges and at least to pretend not to recognise the faces behind the masks.

The recovery of Japanese industrial production from 1948 onwards was indeed remarkable. The figures given by S.C.A.P. are as follows, taking the average production from 1932 to 1936 as 100: 1946, 34·3; 1947, 40·8; 1948, 49·4; December 1949, 100; March 1951, 112·8. Against these remarkable figures must be set the fact that the population had increased by over 10 million and a considerable change had taken place in the pattern of trade. Although Japan's productive capacity in cotton, the major pre-war industry, has climbed back to the pre-war average of spindles actually employed, the rayon industry has not fully recovered from the war-time devastation, and foreign trade in 1951 was still less than half-way to the pre-war level. Her merchant fleet too, although now the seventh in the world, carries only half the Japanese foreign trade, where before the war it carried 70 per cent.

The outbreak of the Korean war in June 1950 naturally changed the whole position of Japan. From being a defeated enemy, against whose resurgence America and her Allies had to take long-term precautions, she became a bulwark, a base and a potential arsenal in the new struggle against militant Communism. The Koreans, whose memories of the Japanese occupation were too bitter, would not allow a single Japanese to land with the U.N.O. forces, but the re-establishment of Japanese industry and even of sufficient Japanese military power to defend herself against Communist aggression became avowed American policy. The first step was the negotiation of a Japanese peace treaty with the former allies in 1951—except of course Russia. Through the links of ANZUS and the U.S.A.-Philippine security pact, Japan found herself joined in a strategic association with her former victims. Throughout 1952 she received small supplies of American defensive equipment under a sort of Lend-Lease agreement, and the conclusion in 1954 of the U.S.A.-Japanese Mutual Defence Agreement saw the final rebirth of the Japanese armed forces and the end of the demilitarisation policy.

It was of course inevitable that Japan should sooner or later become once more a great power in this strategically vital north-eastern corner of Asia. Already it is clear that she is modifying 'democrasie', some of whose features were very un-Japanese, to suit her own deeply persisting national character. But there is no need to assume that this means a return to the rather uncharacteristic Chauvinism of the 1930s.

## THE JAPANESE CHARACTER

So much has been written, mostly contradictory, about the Japanese character that it would be absurd in a sketch of this length to attempt a personal summing up. I hope that this chapter will have given some hints, and for those who are seriously interested there is a fascinating literature on the subject. Here I want merely to elaborate one personal view, which is that a clue at least to the understanding of the Japanese is to think of them as romantics and sentimentalists—which other Orientals are not, but so many Europeans are. The romantic attitude I take to be that which exalts the abnormal above the normal and the individual judgment above abstract reason; this, I believe, is a help in understanding the Japanese cult of 'sincerity.' It is also an essential of the romantic attitude to take one relationship in human life and so exalt its value that it transcends all other considerations and ultimately life itself; it is thus that the romantic is said to be 'in love with death.' I believe that where the West has romanticised love, the Japanese have romanticised loyalty; where the great Western romantic story is Tristan and Iseult or Antony and Cleopatra, in which every consideration of honour or policy is sacrificed for love, the great Japanese romantic drama is the *Forty-seven Ronin*, where every consideration of love or policy is sacrificed to loyalty; and both these dramas end in death. I think that if we can realise that a romantic Japanese feels about loyalty as a romantic Westerner feels about love, we shall get a footing for a moment inside the Japanese mind. As to sentimentality, I think all who know the Japanese would admit it, but I mention it because it might not occur to those who do not, and it explains a lot of self-deception and emotionalism, which might otherwise appear most 'un-Oriental.'

### BIBLIOGRAPHY

*A Short Cultural History of Japan.* Sir George Sansom.
*A Short Economic History of Modern Japan.* G. C. Allen.
*A Japanese Village.* J. F. Embree.
*Things Japanese.* B. H. Chamberlain.
*Government by Assassination.* H. Byas.
*Japan, Past and Present.* E. O. Reischauer.
*A Case History of Japan.* F. Horner.
*The Chrysanthemum and the Sword.* Ruth Benedict.
*Glimpses of Unfamiliar Japan.* Lafcadio Hearn.
*The Three Bamboos.* Robert Standish.
*The Allied Occupation of Japan.* E. M. Martin.
*The Occupation of Japan: Second Phase.* R. A. Feasey.
*The New Japan, Government and Politics.* H. S. Quigley and J. E. Turner.

# CHAPTER ELEVEN

## KOREA, MANCHURIA AND FAR EASTERN RUSSIA

## KOREA

FOR thirty-four years, from 1911 until the Japanese surrender in 1945, Korea was annexed to Japan, but its right to be considered a separate country is unquestionable.

### STRUCTURE AND CLIMATE

Geographically, Korea consists of a peninsula, slightly larger than England and Scotland, projecting almost due south from the north China coast; the area is 85,228 square miles. For eleven miles in the extreme north-eastern corner of this peninsula, the Korean border marches with that of the Russian maritime provinces.

This northern border is a natural one, following the line of the Yalu River from its mouth on the west coast until it reaches the mountainous region around the volcano, Paektu-San, the 'white-headed mountain,' so-called from the pumice on its crest. From there it runs down the valley of the Tuman River to the east coast. It was recognised as an international boundary somewhere between A.D. 500 and 1000, although even to the present day it has never been accurately delimited in the wilds of the Paektu-San Mountain.

Not only is it an ancient boundary, but on the western or Yalu River side it has been unusually effective in separating the peoples. The whole river area was left for many years as a sort of 'no-man's-land' both by Chinese and Koreans, who preferred to see it infested by bandits than a cause of 'frontier incidents' between the two peoples. On the shorter eastern end of the boundary, where the Tuman River runs down to the Sea of Japan, there has been much more movement of population. The comparatively sparsely populated Manchurian province of Chientao has attracted settlers from across the river until now more than 700,000 out of its million inhabitants are of Korean origin; in the same way, the even emptier provinces of the Russian Far East are said to have a Korean population of 180,000.

Shannon McCune has pointed out that the Yalu border is a noticeable one for the traveller to cross: north of it the peasants wear dark blue clothes and grow wheat; south of it they wear white (or did until very recently) and grow millets or rice. On all other sides but the north, Korea is encircled by the sea: on the west by the shallow Yellow Sea, with its great tidal range and few currents; on the south and east by the deep Sea of Japan, with a tidal range of only a few feet. The west coast has several good harbours, the east very few. To the south, only 100 miles away across the Chosen Straits, lie the islands of Japan.

Korea is a mountainous country all over, and even the south-west corner, the granary of the country, is what we should call hilly. The main range runs southward along the east coast from Paektu-San, with spurs running out to the west. As you might expect, the slopes on the western side are comparatively gentle, while on the east the mountains fall very steeply to the sea. Ingenious tunnels have been built through them to divert water from the gradual slopes of the west to these more precipitous eastern ones, in order to provide hydro-electric power.

The rivers of Korea are short and swift, often flowing through deep gorges and over rapids so that they are of little use for irrigation. The Yalu, the longest, is only 491 miles long, but can be used for floating timber in its upper reaches and for navigation lower down; the Koreans use what must be a rather terrifying sort of raft, propelled by airscrews, to get over the trouble caused by rapids.

The climate, of great importance, as usual, to a country still 75 per cent. agricultural, is of the monsoon type, with a moderate rainfall, varying from just over 50 to just under 40 inches and almost entirely concentrated in the summer months. In normal circumstances, it is a climate at least as favourable as that of Japan, very slightly hotter in summer and considerably colder in winter. Unfortunately, Korea is cursed with a very erratic rainfall. Not only, as in all monsoon countries, is there the danger of a year when the rains fail, but only too frequently, even if the yearly rainfall is up to average, far too much of it falls in a sudden deluge that washes away the standing crops in devastating floods. On one second day of August in Seoul 14 inches of rain, more than a quarter of the average rainfall for the whole year, fell on a single day. The swift, deep rivers accentuate the flood danger from these abnormal falls and make Korea exceptionally susceptible to crop failures.

## HISTORY AND PEOPLE

The Koreans are a Mongoloid race, on the whole taller and fairer than the Chinese or Japanese and often powerfully built. The Japanese made considerable use of Korean 'toughs' as 'strong-arm men,' and during the occupation of Korea most of the manual labour was done by Koreans.

The history of the Korean people is long and in places distinguished. The name Korea itself is drawn from an imperial dynasty, the Koryo, which was established as early as A.D. 918. The greatest period of the country's history, however, lies in the 200 years between the accession of the first Emperor of the Yi Dynasty in 1392 and the invasion of the country by the Japanese conqueror Hideyoshi, in 1592. During this period, Korea, as part of the great, embracing Chinese culture, was undoubtedly one of the leading countries of the whole world in the arts of civilisation. They had invented a phonetic alphabet in the fifteenth century and introduced printing with movable metal type in 1403, a full fifty years before it was introduced in Europe. In navigation they were using the compass in 1525 and in their attempts to repel Hideyoshi they experimented with cannon, shells and even a primitive and highly successful ironclad warship. Almost all that the Japanese learnt in this period from the Chinese—that is, Buddhism, painting, the making of porcelain, architecture and the cultivation of silk—seems to have reached them through the Koreans.

Hideyoshi's invasion and six years' ravaging of the country was the end of Korea's golden age. When at last he was compelled to retire, his invasion thwarted because he could not maintain regular command of the sea, he took with him an immense quantity of loot and all the best artists and artisans in the country. These were compelled to turn their skill to training the Japanese. Korea, like Japan later, closed her frontiers to the whole world, with the exception of her titular suzerain, China; and even the border with China, as we have seen above, was intentionally made as difficult as possible to cross.

Korea's self-chosen isolation was broken into by the Japanese in 1876, and the country forcibly opened up to the world, in much the same way as Japan herself had been by the Americans. When the curtain is lifted on Korea again we find the country subject to a typical oriental despotism in its last stages of decadence and inefficiency. There is an obvious parallel with Oudh at the time of the British annexation, and the majority of Western opinion sympathised at the time with the plan of absorbing Korea which Japan set gradually and deliberately in motion. What subsequently alienated this sympathy was the treatment of the country after annexation and the duplicity with which the plan was carried out.

First, in 1895, Chinese influence was eliminated, after a short war which the Japanese Army began, as they have begun all their modern wars, with a surprise attack before the declaration of war. Unfortunately, however, the Korean Emperor refused to act as a puppet and fled to the Russian Embassy, from whence he carried on the government. The necessity to eliminate Russia also from the Korean scene was one of the causes of the Russo-Japanese War, which broke out in 1904. Korea, still a sovereign state on the outbreak of this war, immediately proclaimed her neutrality, but Japan paid no attention to this, invaded and occupied the country, guaranteed it its independence, forced it in 1906 to accept a protectorate, and in 1911 annexed it.

To this process of absorption the Koreans offered no organised resistance, for their government was much too inefficient to raise or control an army capable of taking the field against the Japanese. It is wrong to assume, however, that the Korean people willingly accepted the Japanese domination. Japan was anxious from the first to suggest that this was the case, and that the Koreans really welcomed the guidance of their 'elder brethren'; yet even their statistics show that in the eighteen months ending December, 1908, while 14,566 'insurgents' were killed, only 8,728 surrendered. Nor does the savage suppression of every Korean organisation that could possibly have an even faintly political flavour really indicate a mood of quiet confidence. This Korean resistance reached its head on January 20th, 1919, in one of the most remarkable events of recent world history and one which the advocates of passive resistance would do well to study. The intellectual and moral leaders of Korea had been much impressed by the principle of self-determination, publicly pronounced by the victorious allies at the end of the war, and particularly by the idealism of President Wilson's apparent concern for the rights of small nations. They hoped that if they could organise an overwhelming but completely non-violent demonstration of the Korean people's desire for independence, the conscience of the world would compel the Japanese to grant it; and, at worst, that its peaceful and law-abiding character would protect them from reprisals. On both counts they were hopelessly wrong. The demonstration

T

was secretly organised—an amazing feat in view of the Japanese secret police system—and on January 20th half a million Koreans (according to Japanese figures) came out into the streets and shouted, 'Twenty million years for independence.' The Japanese authorities were completely thrown off their balance for the moment, but finally reacted by savage repression of the movement, which, somewhat belatedly, they ascribed to the machinations of German agents! The conscience of the world took no notice whatever.

## MODERN SOCIAL AND ECONOMIC STRUCTURE

Modern Korea is the product of the country's geographic structure and history violently distorted by the thirty-four years of Japanese imperial occupation. The population figures are, as usual, pure guess-work before the twentieth century, but there seems for most of the second millennium A.D. to have been a population of between 5 millions and 8 millions, slowly increasing up to the end of the seventeenth century and then slowly decreasing up to the last quarter of the nineteenth. The end of the nineteenth and first half of the twentieth centuries has seen a very rapid rise in population in Korea, as everywhere else in the Far East. The census figures are roughly 15 millions in 1913, 20 millions in 1925 and 24 millions in 1940. Allowing for the wave of emigration which has led to 10 per cent. of the present Korean population living outside the country, this means an annual rise of about 2 per cent. and a pressure on the land at least as great as in rural Japan. Korea is in fact suffering from the almost universal problem of a growing and land-hungry population; and those apologists for Japan who justified her expansion on the grounds that she had to find somewhere for her surplus population to go cannot fairly claim that there was any room for them in Korea.

Korea is still overwhelmingly an agricultural country of the monsoon type. The typical Korean is the self-sufficient peasant living, or failing to live, on the narrow margin of an ancestral plot. Over four-fifths of the population were engaged in agriculture in 1920, and the proportion is still probably about three-quarters. It is predominantly a rice agriculture, with livestock and silkworms playing a very small part. Irrigation is mainly on a small scale and controlled within the village. In addition to agriculture there have always been many fishing villages along the east coast.

This sort of traditional society changes very slowly, as we have seen elsewhere, and the Japanese occupation has probably not much affected the lives of individual peasants. It seems doubtful whether even the fact that the Japanese gradually acquired the ownership of nearly half the land in the country made much difference to a people already living on or about bare subsistence level. The fisheries were certainly greatly modernised and expanded, but as the increased production of fish all went to Japan the Korean fisherman was left in much the same position as before, with diminished liberty. Similarly, Korea's rice output increased by 30 per cent. between 1910 and 1929; but the additional supply was almost all exported to Japan.

The great change brought about by the Japanese was the introduction of modern industry and the temporary destruction of educated Korean society within Korea. Japan's ostensible policy for the Koreans was that they were to be treated as 'younger brothers' and therefore, presumably, to be given opportunities as great as those enjoyed by Japanese nationals. It is quite clear, however, that the real policy of the Japanese expansionists was to use the Koreans to produce whatever Japanese policy at the time required for the use of Japan, from brutalised toughs for the Kempei Tai to armaments for the Kwangtung Army. The Japanese industrialisation policy found a country fairly well equipped in the essential supplies of power and raw materials; the estimated reserves of coal are enough for hundreds of years at the present rate of consumption and the hydro-electric potential at least as great as that of Italy or France. In recent years hydro-electric plants have far outstripped coal as a source of electric power. The country is also rich in forests, which the Japanese have preserved fairly well by replanting almost as fast as they have felled. Apart from coal, the most important mineral deposit is the iron ore of Mosan, on the Manchurian border and only 100 miles from the Russian frontier. The importance of the field is, of course, increased by the extreme shortage of iron ore in Japan.

The Japanese industrial policy for Korea was fairly simple: large-scale industry was kept closely in Japanese hands and fostered by every administrative device in competition with the native cottage industries of the Koreans. Also it was made very hard for anyone, even a Japanese, to start up any industry without Government support. In spite of this, the Korean village industries (silk, pottery, agricultural instruments, medicine, furniture, liquor, etc.) held their own pretty well at first and still accounted for 40 per cent.

of the country's output in the 1930s. That this percentage had fallen
to 25 by 1940 is mainly due to a change in the policy of Japanese
large-scale industry after the beginning of the Manchurian and
Chinese campaigns in 1931. Up to that moment they had not
encouraged the establishment of heavy industries in Korea, but had
confined Korean output to light consumer goods for the Japanese
market. From 1931 onwards they saw that Korea could be made
the arsenal for their armies in China and Manchuria, and many
first-rate modern factories were erected. The plant of the Korean
Nitrogen Fertiliser Corporation at Konan (manufacturing explosives,
naturally) claimed to be the second largest of its kind in the world.

The erection of these plants, and the building of the roads and
railways required to feed them, gave the impression of great economic
progress in Korea under the Japanese. It is difficult to see, however,
what the actual Korean inhabitant gained from it—except the
privilege of working, as a labourer, a ten-hour day for men and
an eleven-hour day for women and children. Exact figures of ownership are unusually hard to establish, but it is fairly safe to say that
75 per cent. of Korean industry as a whole, and all large-scale
industry, was Japanese-owned. A Tata Ltd. or Birla Bros. in Korea
would have been an impossibility. The illustration of 'younger
sisters' in a factory school, though, of course, a 'propaganda picture,'
shows indirectly the part the Korean was expected to play in
industry.

On the classes above the level of the peasantry, the social effect
of the Japanese occupation was disastrous. It is true that the court
of the last Korean Emperor was a wild phantasmagoria of corruption
and superstition comparable only with that of King Thibaw in
Burma; but it was the very elements from whom reform might and
probably would have come that were suppressed by the Japanese
administration. Every association of Koreans that was not definitely
under control of the Government was frowned upon, and many were
ruthlessly destroyed. Even the Christian Churches were taught
their lesson when, in 1911, 135 of the most eminent Korean
Christians were arrested on a charge of having plotted the assassination of the Governor-General. Of this group, all warranted by the
Christian missionaries as men of the highest character and integrity,
three died of their sufferings in prison, nine were banished without
trial, and 106 were sentenced to prison terms of five to ten years.

The Japanese made every effort to keep the young Koreans
from seeking higher education, with the result that schools were so

few that one-quarter of all high-school students and one-half of all college students were educated at missionary or other foreign schools. There were, of course, a small number of Koreans who decided to collaborate with the Japanese and seek service with them by becoming more Japanese than the Japanese themselves, just as

39. A Korean girl carries her little brother out of the battle area. In the foreground a dead South Korean soldier.

the tough Korean peasants who were taken into the gendarmerie acquired a brutality which gave many Europeans a poor opinion of Koreans as a whole. Such things were inevitable in a long occupation. The impasse in which the young Korean student found himself did accentuate, however, the general Far Eastern problem of the 'unemployed graduate' and provided more and more recruits for the various Korean revolutionary organisations which flourished in China, Russia and the U.S.A. On the outbreak of the Sino-Japanese War these revolutionary organisations largely amalgamated (apart from those in Russia), and though they suffered from the dissensions usual among *émigrés*, some of them gave useful help to the Allies, supplying, for instance, a small group of Japanese-speaking officers for our forward propaganda units in Burma.

The Far Eastern war was Korea's chance to reassert her independence. This was accepted by all the Allied Powers as a war aim, but, as part of the Potsdam bargains, the surrender of the Japanese was made to the Russians north of the 38th Parallel, and to the Americans south of it. The country was thus divided into two spheres of influence. In the north the Russians, using their habitual technique of puppets, were able to set up a Communist North Korean Republic as early as August 1948, which claimed sovereignty over the whole country. The Americans, not far behind, declared in December of the same year that the South Korean Government was the only legitimate government of the whole country. Both were, in the terminology of their sponsors, the only 'democratic' governments, but neither, in the troubled state of the country and beneath the threat of civil war, could afford to allow the civil liberties normally associated with democracy. One consequence of the partition was a steady stream of refugees from the north to the south. This mass exodus from the Communist to the non-Communist half of divided states, whether in Germany, Viet Nam or Korea, seems to be the one certainly predictable effect of partition on ideological grounds, and to have no reference to the natural wealth of the two areas.

Between two such governments no permanent peace was likely, and as early as 1949 the Communists in the north were building up a formidable force of veteran 'volunteers' from among Koreans trained to arms in China or the Russian Far East. In June 1950 this force was launched against the south, probably under the impression that American ground forces would not be committed to oppose it. Its initial complete success was checked and reversed as soon as United Nations troops arrived in strength. These were overwhelmingly American, but contained strong contingents from the British Commonwealth and Turkey and smaller contingents from many Asian countries.

The arrival of the United Nations troops near the Yalu river frontier precipitated massive Chinese intervention in the war. Whether this was an aggressive movement designed to expel American influence from the Asian mainland, or was genuinely prompted by fear that the United Nations forces would cross the frontier and proceed to overthrow the Communist régime in China, must be left to history to decide—if it can. The result was fierce fighting ending in a stalemate. During this time the Americans equipped and trained the South Korean Army, who took an increasing share in the defence of their own country. The casualties in the armed forces of the U.N., a reasonably good guide to the level of sacrifice, were, by the end of the war, 64 per cent. South Koreans, 32 per cent. Americans and 4 per cent. other nations. A truce was finally agreed, much to the fury of the South Koreans, on a line roughly equivalent to the 38th Parallel.

The results of the war have been bankrupt states on both sides of the line, supported only by massive economic aid from East or West; and a vehement determination on the part of other small Asian countries not to let their countries become a battle-ground.

## MANCHURIA

### STRUCTURE AND CLIMATE

Manchuria consists of a wide plain stretching down southwards to the Yellow Sea and almost entirely enclosed by mountains. Its area is just over 500,000 square miles. On the west and north-west the Great Khingan Range marks it off from the high inhospitable plateaux of Mongolia;[1] on the east a chain of mountains acts as a prolongation northwards of the Korean Paektu-San feature and, apart from the gap formed by the Ussuri valley at Vladivostok, links up with the Sikhota-Alin Range in the Russian maritime provinces. There is thus a natural barrier between Manchuria and the Sea of Japan. Politically, as we have seen, the Russian and Korean borders meet for a short stretch so that this barrier is reflected in the political boundaries, and to the east Manchuria has no outlet whatever to the sea.

This mountain range ends in the Liaotung Peninsula, which, projecting southwards into the almost landlocked Yellow Sea, provides Manchuria with its two important harbours of Port Arthur and Dairen. To the south-west there is a very narrow gap at Shanhaikuan between the mountains and the sea, giving access to Pekin; in the north-east there is a much wider gap where the Ussuri

[1] There is a small strip of Manchurian territory to the west of the Great Khingan.

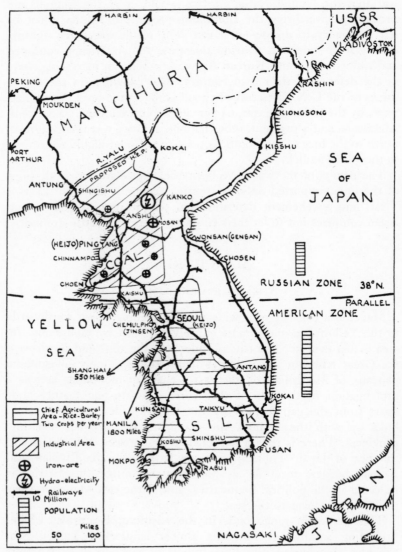

XXI. Korea divided by the 38th parallel, showing communications and resources.

and Amur rivers meet at Khabarovsk. The nortnern trontier is
the Amur River and not the mountains to the south of it.

Manchuria is still affected to some extent by the monsoon climate
and gets its rain in the summer months, but it is at the extreme
northern end of this system, and the rainfall, which is 26 inches at
Mukden, decreases rapidly as you go north. Similarly, the average
winter temperature is decreasing till in Harbin it is already below
zero, and the growing season for crops is short, but, except in the
extreme north-west, long enough for wheat to ripen. Any great

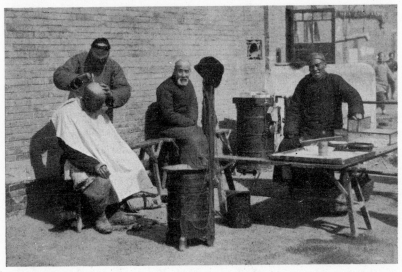

40. The cold and sunny winters of Manchuria make an outdoor hair-cut
a pleasure.

increase in the food production of this part of the world seems more
likely to come from further development of Manchuria than from
the scientific breeding of wneat strains for growth in the Arctic.
On the whole, Manchuria has a climate not unlike that of Canada
and its possible importance as a granary is very great.

### HISTORY AND PEOPLE

The original Manchus were a people of Tungus stock whose
importance in history lasts from the beginning of the seventeenth
to the end of the nineteenth centuries.

Before that they were only one of the barbarian races whom the
Chinese fenced off by the Great Wall, and it might almost as easily
have been the Mongols again as they who supplanted the Ming

Dynasty in China. Since then they have intermingled with the Chinese to such an extent that they no longer exist as a separate race. Even in Manchuria itself the population was already 90 per cent. Chinese by 1900.

The Manchus first established a settled and civilised society around Mukden, the present capital, about the end of the sixteenth century. In 1644, as we have seen, they took advantage of dissensions in China to seize the throne for a Manchu dynasty. For just over 100 years they preserved the existence if not the purity of the Manchu stock by forbidding Chinese immigration into Manchuria, although many Chinese were already settled there and more came illicitly. About half their invading armies had in fact consisted of Chinese, enrolled as 'banner men,' and the various restrictions against Chinese did not apply to them. As soon as the ban was removed the Chinese began to flood in to Manchuria and have now completely swamped the original Manchu population.

In recent history Manchuria has been a storm centre, as the meeting place of Russian and Japanese expansion at the expense of China, while China's control over it has been nominal and intermittent. The Russians were the first in the field. By 1860 they had pushed their southern border as far south as the Amur River, and as the weakness of Imperial China became more and more apparent, the advantages—and the possibility—of including Manchuria in their 'sphere of influence' grew more obvious. In 1894, just after the beginning of the Trans-Siberian Railway, it looked for a moment as if they were going to be forestalled by the Japanese, who, as a result of the Sino-Japanese War, acquired Korea and a lease of the strategic Liaotung Peninsula. The 'Great Powers' intervened, however, and informed Japan that they could not approve such a threat to China's sovereignty and the 'Open Door' policy, and Japan therefore accepted an indemnity instead of the lease. It is not surprising that the Japanese were furious when, in 1898, the peninsula was leased to the Russians and a naval base started at Port Arthur. By 1903 Russian troops, sent to assist in suppressing the Boxer Rebellion of 1900, had still not withdrawn from southern Manchuria and war seemed the inevitable result of the tension. This came in 1904–5 and the victory of the Oriental over the European state had an electrical effect on Asiatic nationalism throughout the Far East.

Soon after the war the Russians and Japanese reached an agreement that north Manchuria should be a Russian 'sphere of influence' and south Manchuria a Japanese. This was an unreal compact, aimed at China, and the rivalry persisted underneath. After the Russian Revolution the rivalry became more acute, since the Japanese feared not only Russia, but Communism. It is important to realise that in this period of strife the Japanese always regarded Russia as a more dangerous foe than China, and one of their most constant demands on China was that she should accept Japanese aid in stamping out Communism.

From 1911 to 1931 Manchuria was governed by Chinese war-lords, of whom the most important was the pro-Japanese and anti-Russian Chang Tso-Lin (1922–8). In 1931, after the assassination of Chang Tso-Lin, the Japanese decided to assume complete control of the country and set up, as their 'puppet,' a Manchu Emperor to rule over an ostensibly independent Manchu state called Manchu-kuo (proclaimed, 1932). The Japanese organisation of Manchukuo is probably the best example of the 'puppet state' method of annexa-tion which has yet been seen. It is not surprising that this should be so, since, as we have seen, government through puppets is almost the oldest and most universal Japanese political tradition.

On the surface, the Manchukuo Government enjoyed complete freedom; the Japanese troops in Manchuria, for instance, were only there on its invitation. In fact, the Japanese controlled completely the Manchukuo Government and through it the whole country. A good example of this technique is found in the treatment of foreign business-men. At first they enjoyed in Manchuria all the freedom and privileges that they had enjoyed in China; then, in 1936, the Japanese 'voluntarily' renounced all special rights for their business-men, and the Manchukuo Government promptly announced that all other nations would be treated on a footing of equality with the Japanese. Thus no one had any rights any more, and if the Govern-ment chose to grant licences, visas and permits to Japanese only, that had no international significance and was clearly within its power; in any case, it was no use an aggrieved power taking the matter up with Japan, which would never dream of interfering with Manchukuo's sovereignty.

The acquisition of Manchuria gave Japan a land frontier 2,000 miles long with the U.S.S.R., and the naturally increasing tension was manifested in innumerable frontier incidents, particularly since, in many places, the boundary had never been accurately delimited. The most serious of these, at Changkufeng near the Korean border, developed in 1938 into a full-scale, if limited and undeclared, war. Both parties probably regarded it as a trial of strength, and it seems probable that only the intervention of the European War and what seemed a golden opportunity for Japan to acquire south-east Asia, forestalled a second Russo-Japanese war in the early 1940s.

At the end of the Japanese War, the Russians were quick to recover the position in Manchuria which they had lost in 1904. The Sino-Soviet Treaty of 1945 included:

(a) The restoration of a naval base at Port Arthur to Russia. Theoretically it is a joint Russian-Chinese naval base, but as port defence is entrusted to Russia by the terms of the agreement, the strategic position is pretty clear.

(b) The restoration of joint Sino-Russian control of the Chinese Eastern Railway and South Manchurian Railway main lines (now renamed Chinese Changchun Railway). As in 1896, the President of the Company is Chinese, but the Manager Russian.

(c) The restoration of Dairen (Dalny) as a free port with a Russian port chief. This was its status under the Sino-Russian Convention of 1898.

As soon as it became clear, however, that the Communists were in power as the *de facto* government of China, the Russians embarked upon a policy of close alliance rather than attempted control. In Sinkiang and Outer Mongolia, the old areas of contact, they deferred to Chinese interests or agreed to joint operations; they abandoned all concern for Tibet; and in 1952 they resigned to China all those legal rights in Dairen, Port Arthur and the railway which they had re-established in 1945.

## MODERN SOCIAL AND ECONOMIC STRUCTURE

### (a) *Natural resources*

The social and economic structure of Manchuria is partly the cause and partly the result of its strategic importance. There is no doubt that its value as a source of raw materials and food was one of the main reasons why both countries, and particularly the Japanese, were anxious to gain control of it. On the other hand, the way in which these resources have been developed, and particularly the communications system, has been dictated by strategic considerations. We have already noticed that potentially Manchuria is a great food-producer, a fact which becomes of greater importance every year.

It was not wheat, however, which, before the war, Manchuria produced. The three great crops, each averaging something in the neighbourhood of 4 million metric tons per year, were soya beans, millets and kaoliang.

Soya beans are a valuable food and a source of oil for soap and all those products which usually go with it, including explosives. Their development on a large scale has been largely due to Japanese enterprise, and the oil is extracted locally, both oil and bean cake being exported from Dairen. This product, together with the iron and steel of which we shall speak next, made Manchuria invaluable as an arsenal. The virtual monopoly of Manchuria in the production of soya beans has been broken by the preparation of soils for their cultivation elsewhere, notably in the U.S.A.; but the Manchurian production dropped only from just over to just under 4 million metric tons, and there seems no reason to suppose that they will cease to be a major crop. Kaoliang and millets are grains grown mainly for local consumption. Kaoliang is an 'all-purpose' crop locally, like coconuts and bamboo elsewhere, providing clothes and shelter from its straw as well as food and drink from the grain. Manchuria is admirably suited for extensive farming on the American model and the history of its development has favoured this method. The Chinese Press reported in 1946 that one Japanese rice-farm in Manchuria had occupied 50,000 acres. For the same reasons, collective farms would probably prove economic units, but it must be remembered that neither of these types of farming are popular with the Chinese peasants, who have already settled there. About 27 per cent. of Manchuria is forested and the potential wealth in timber is very great and much more accessible than that in Siberia.

The mineral wealth of Manchuria is extensive, the most important feature being the bituminous coalfield round Fushun, south-east of Mukden. This field enjoys vast reserves, seams of exceptional thickness and proximity to the iron ore deposits of Anshan and Penhsiu. It is not surprising, therefore, that the Japanese early saw in Manchuria, not only a potential granary, but a source of iron and steel; and it was they who built the great iron and steel works at Anshan. In 1936, before they became a military secret, iron ore production had reached nearly 2 million tons and coal 12½ millions yearly. In fact, by the middle 1930s Manchuria was capable of meeting almost the whole of Japan's demand for pig iron, but not for steel.

Gold and shale oil are also found in smaller quantities, but it is as a potential steel-producer and granary that Manchuria's import-ance lies; how great this is in an area woefully short of both food and steel can be imagined. The Japanese claim to Manchuria never had any legal justification, but if one considers its economic value to them and the Japanese blood and treasure which had been expended on it, it is not difficult to see why they were determined that it should not slip from their grasp.

## (b) Distribution of People and Occupations

Until the last decade of the nineteenth century, Manchuria was one of the great empty regions of the world. Since then it has received a great influx of Chinese settlers and smaller quantities of Russians, Koreans and Japanese, but there is still plenty of undeveloped land. We have seen that even in the seventeenth century the Manchus were largely sinified, and that they enrolled as their 'banner men' the Chinese settlers along the fringe of territory just north of the Great Wall. There was no period when Chinese migration to Manchuria did not go on, particularly annual migration from Shantung to the Liaotung Peninsula to work during the short Manchurian harvest season. Until the relaxation of the Manchu land laws at the end of the nineteenth century, however, this migration was on a comparatively small scale. The great filling up of Manchuria from China belongs to the twentieth century, and reached its climax during the régime of Chang Tso-Lin, when, during the years 1926-8, over a million Chinese a year entered Manchuria.

To understand the present social structure of the country, therefore, one must consider at least in outline the conditions under which these immigrants arrived. They were predominantly refugees from a China torn by famine, civil war and financial chaos, moving, not from any pioneering spirit, but because they could no longer live at home. It is not normally the northern Chinese who emigrate. Owen Lattimore (*Manchuria, Cradle of Conflict*) has pointed out that it was a movement against the traditional stream of Chinese expansion, which has always been an advance southwards and which finds its outlet to-day in the spread of the 'overseas Chinese' in south-east Asia. The same author suggests that the Chinese attitude to emigration north of the Great Wall is not really expansionist at all, but looks back to China; those Chinese, for instance, who had settled beyond the Wall during the Ming Dynasty automatically sided with the Manchu invaders of China and flowed back with them as the 'banner men,' instead of warding them off or even pressing further into Manchuria. Any Chinese who settles in this area is likely to identify himself with the historical role of its inhabitants as the 'reservoir' from which successive invasions of China have drawn their strength, rather than to press forward as fringes of Chinese expansion. This interpretation, if true, is obviously of great importance to-day, in view of the conversion of Manchuria to 'Communism.'

The great majority of these refugee settlers came as tenants, recruited in China by relief organisers to settle and develop the vast Manchurian estates which had already been acquired by the 'big interests.' They were provided by their backers with land and equipment and expected thereafter to pay anything from 40 per cent. to 60 per cent. of their crop as rent. As their crop would also be handled entirely by the transport companies, grain companies and distilleries owned by the 'big interests,' they had little hope in the normal course of events of developing into peasant proprietors. Only in the extreme frontier areas, where it paid the 'big interests' to get their land developed at any cost and where takers were few, were sufficiently favourable terms offered to allow the settler to acquire his own land. It is not surprising, therefore, that a number abandoned their controlled settlements and either squatted else-where or joined the many ex-soldiers as bandits in the mountains and forests.

The Japanese control of Manchukuo made little difference to the position of the peasant except to increase the possibilities of employ-ment in industry for those who left their farms, and in many cases to change the identity of the 'big interests.' Since the land was developed in this way, the attraction of a Communist Party which proposed to give the land to the peasants must have been well nigh irresistible.

The peasant population of Manchuria, then, consists mainly of Chinese tenants, likely for both economic and historical reasons to join in a Communist invasion of north China. The main peculiarity about its urban population is that two of the greatest towns after Mukden, Harbin and Dairen, are respectively Russian and Japanese in character.

The importance of Harbin dates, of course, from the period of Russian influence, but it received a great influx of White Russian population immediately after the Revolution. It was at that time probably the largest Russian city in the whole of the Far East. It retains its predominantly Russian character to-day, but the distinction between 'Red' and 'White' is fast fading.

Dairen, on the Liaotung Peninsula, was developed by the Japanese as the great exporting port through which Manchuria's products, mainly soya beans, were shipped abroad. Although only just under 200,000 Japanese lived in the Dairen area before the war, the whole character and control of the town was Japanese.

The remaining alien group in Manchuria is the Koreans, whom we mentioned earlier in this chapter. Part of Manchuria is suitable for rice cultivation, and since the northern Chinese are not accustomed to rice-farming and the Koreans are, it was not unnatural that this area should be settled by Koreans, often financed by the Japanese. The total population of Manchuria in 1940 was 43 millions. It is therefore roughly six times as strong in manpower, food and industrial production as the whole of the Soviet territories in the Far East.

### (c) Communications

Compared with neighbouring areas, Manchuria is exceptionally well supplied with communications. Road traffic is practically confined to the winter months, when the roads are frozen to a good hard surface and there is no alternative use for draught animals. This is, however, the time of year when much of the crop transporting would have to be done, and road transport is usually the first stage in getting the crops to the markets or ports.

The rivers also are fitted to play an important part in Manchuria's life. Since she is mainly an exporter of bulky crops, the rivers flowing outwards from the centre of the country to the ports are well adapted to the traffic. The most important are those which flow to the north, the Sungari and Ussuri, which both flow into the Amur and are navigable far into the interior of the country. The obvious outlet for the produce of northern Manchuria is therefore by river to Khabarovsk and the towns and ports of the Soviet Far East. It was only political tension between Russia and Japan which prevented the growth of a far larger river trade on the Sungari, Ussuri and Amur before the war. To the south the Liao River will take wooden junks, but is too shallow for steamships.

It is in its railway system, however, that Manchuria is far in advance of the rest of China. This system reflects both the twisted course of the country's frontiers and its recent political history. The first line to be built was the Chinese Eastern Railway, completed by the Russians in 1903 at the height of the first Russian period of influence. This connects Chita on the Trans-Siberian with Vladivostok, cutting across northern Manchuria and shortening by almost half its length the all-Russian route from Chita to Vladivostok via Khabarovsk. The shares in the promoting company were jointly held by Russians and Chinese, but the administration was Russian—an arrangement which illustrates well the Chinese habit of taking up Western industrialisation for the money profit to be got out of it without any interest in the actual engineering or manufacturing operation.

After the war of 1905, the southernmost section of this line, from Changchun to Port Arthur, was ceded to the Japanese and formed the nucleus of the Japanese-controlled South Manchurian Railway. In 1920, the Russians being temporarily powerless, the Chinese assumed full control of the Chinese Eastern Railway, but when diplomatic relations were resumed between Russia and China in 1924 a new 'commercial' régime was set up. Under this scheme it was agreed that the Manager and one Assistant Manager must be Russians, thus again giving the Russians technical control, but the scheme did not last very long, since as soon as Manchuria came completely under Japanese control in 1931 the railway lost its strategic value to Russia. During the first period of appeasing Japan, therefore, they sold it to Manchukuo (i.e. the Japanese) in 1935.

The South Manchurian Railway, as we have seen, was constituted in 1906 out of the southern portions of the C.E.R. It is linked with the Korean system and with the Chinese Pekin-Mukden Railway at Mukden. The S.M.R. was much more than a railway company and was in fact the main channel for Japanese investment in Manchuria, owning docks, mines, factories and every kind of industrial enterprise.

The first railways of Manchuria were therefore either Russian- or Japanese-controlled, and the Chinese Government signed a secret clause, attached to the agreement of 1906, transferring the southern section of the C.E.R. to Japan, by which they agreed not to build any railway parallel to and in the neighbourhood of the new S.M.R. In typical Chinese fashion, it was never defined what 'in the neighbourhood of' meant, so that the agreement was in fact subject to constant reinterpretation in the light of developing circumstances. This is how the Chinese understand all agreements—a fact which not infrequently shocks and worries Western lawyers.

When the Manchurian war-lord Chang Tso-Lin found in 1926 that he could not even move his own troops over the C.E.R. without

U

paying cash for their tickets, it brought it home to him and to the
Chinese that they could not hope to exercise any real control over
Manchuria unless they owned some at least of the railway system.
Largely with the help of British capital, they undertook a good deal
of railway building themselves, some of which might certainly be
said to have been 'parallel' to the S.M.R., though whether it was
'in the neighbourhood' was anybody's guess. This and the subsequent Chinese attempts to divert traffic from the S.M.R. to their
own lines were additional factors leading to the Japanese invasion
of Manchuria in 1931. Under the Manchukuo régime the total
railway mileage was 7,380 miles. The diagram facing page 306
illustrates the main lines and their connections with Chinese,
Korean and Soviet systems.

## SOVIET TERRITORIES IN THE FAR EAST

It is usual to include in the Far Eastern section of the U.S.S.R.
those territories lying between Lake Baikal in the west and the
Pacific or Sea of Japan in the east; and between the Manchurian
and Mongolian frontiers in the south and the Arctic Sea in the north.
    This is an extremely difficult area about which to acquire any
accurate up-to-date knowledge. Very few independent travellers
have visited it in recent times and, whatever else has happened, it
is certain that the changes in the last thirty years have been so
remarkable that any old account is hopelessly out of date. On the
other hand, all Russian governments, whether Tsarist or Communist,
have tried to attract settlers to this area and therefore painted a
rosy picture of it in official publications. All recently published
accounts have inevitably been based almost entirely on official
Soviet sources, and one is uncertain often, in reading them, whether
one is reading a slightly rosy account of what has actually happened,
or an optimistic panegyric by someone in the propaganda bureau
on what he hopes will happen in the remote future.
    Statistics are a particular snare in this respect. Statistics are
regularly manipulated by official writers for propaganda purposes,
and are indeed one of their favourite devices. In this area some
Westerners seem to have been misled by extremely optimistic
accounts of the estimated *potential* wealth of the Soviet Far East
into writing as if it were here and now an exceedingly rich country.
I suspect that if they were able to go there they would find, like

Baudelaire's voyager to Cythera, that *'après tout c'est une pauvre terre.'*

A good example of the reliability of statistics in this area is pointed out by E. S. Bates in his book, *Soviet Asia* (1942):

'When the U.S.S.R. were negotiating for the sale of the Chinese Eastern Railway to Japan in 1933, two totally different official versions of the traffic on the railway were printed; one set of figures showed up half the profit that the other set showed up. But both showed up good commercial results, in spite of a record (printed in the paper that showed up the higher ratio of profit) of 38 armed attacks on trains, 10 acts of incendiarism, 197 attacks on officials, 60 murders, 97 wounded, 400 imprisoned.' One can understand why in the circumstances the Russians wanted to sell the railway to the Japanese: it is harder to believe that it was really making a profit.

The reader of official documents on this area must therefore treat all statistics with the utmost scepticism and be prepared to read between the lines of the communiqués. When he reads, for instance, in the middle of an enthusiastic account of educational reform, that a news despatch from Irkutsk to *Isvestia* ended with the words: 'The first day of the school year augurs well for the future. Attendance of students, professors and instructors was complete and all classes operated on schedule,' he should remind himself that, since there are over 5,000 registered students in Irkutsk, the claim of 100 per cent. attendance is palpably untrue; and from that he might go on to wonder how many other percentage claims are serious and in what other part of the globe it would be a news item at all that the high school classes operated on schedule. In this account, therefore, I shall try to give an unbiased but necessarily personal estimate of what I think actually goes on, and avoid as far as possible apparently accurate but actually misleading figures.

## STRUCTURE AND CLIMATE

The Soviet Far East is physically not unlike an Eastern counterpart of Canada without Canada's populous Eastern States—and even these are to a certain extent represented by the newly developed industrial areas of the Urals and Western Siberia. It is a vast area of over a million square miles with a tiny population smaller than that of London, even at the highest estimate.

The great cold plateau of Central Asia slopes slowly away towards

the Arctic Sea, and the Soviet Far East begins where this slope
is cut by the Amur River, flowing from west to east and 2,800 miles
long. Within 100 miles north of this river the land rises again to
impenetrable mountain country, followed by vast tracts of swampy,
coniferous forest and frozen tundra, neither of them inhabited by
man.

Between these mountain ranges, which average 6,000 to 8,000
feet, run three great northward flowing rivers, each over 2,700
miles long, the Yenisei, the Ob and the Lena. It is a peculiarity of
these rivers that, since they flow into the frozen Arctic Sea, the
upper or southern waters thaw, for the short moment that they do
thaw, before the water at the mouths. Consequently the water,
which cannot escape down the river, spreads out over the whole
valley and turns it into a morass. This is accentuated by the fact
that throughout the whole of this region the subsoil is permanently
frozen. The flood water therefore stands stagnant over the valley
floor until it can be reabsorbed in the river, while dense clouds of
stinging flies render the woods and marshes intolerable to man.

It may be taken therefore that, as far as human habitation is
concerned, the country from 100 miles north of the Amur River
until the mouths of the great northward flowing rivers are reached
is a blank, with the exception of parts of the eastern sea-coast or
where, in the Lena and Kolyma valleys, the goldfields have attracted
small settlements reminiscent of the Klondyke. On the lower waters
of the Lena is the territory of Yakutia, with an area about as big as
the whole of European Russia and a population about equal to that
of Leeds; but the northern part even of this area is cut off entirely
from the south, and is reached only by air or through the Arctic
Sea from Archangel.

Apart from such northern outposts, the Soviet Far East consists
of a number of very sparsely populated territories, strung out
along the north bank of the Amur River from Lake Baikal to the
junction of the Amur and Ussuri rivers at Khabarovsk. Here the
Amur, which has so far flowed from west to east, turns northward
at right angles to flow out into the Sea of Okhotsk, and is joined by
the Ussuri, which rises just north of Vladivostok and flows northward
to its junction with the Amur. Between them and the sea lies a
strip of territory the shape of a hammerhead which forms the
Russian maritime provinces. It is divided by the Sikhota Alin
mountain range, a low spine running north and south and dividing
the territory climatically.

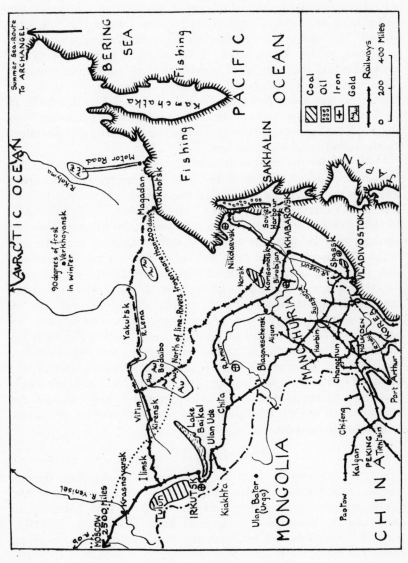

XXII. Railway systems of Manchuria and the Far Eastern Russia.

Travelling westwards from Lake Baikal and the Irkutsk region of central Siberia the first of this string of territories to which you would come would be the Chita region, a plateau given up to cattle and mining and said to produce 65 per cent. of the U.S.S.R.'s tin output. Eastwards again of this and including all territory north and west of the Amur, is the Khabarovsk region, while to the seaward side of the Amur and Ussuri lie the two 'maritime provinces.' The frontier with Manchuria runs along the line of the Amur and Ussuri, so that these provinces form the tongue of land, which, as we have noticed, projects southward and cuts off Manchuria from the sea. This right-angle turn of the frontier has had a decisive effect on the railway system of the area.

Undoubtedly the most important natural factor in deciding the human structure of the Soviet Far East has been the climate. Apart from the tiny maritime region and the Ussuri valley, the whole of this area experiences an intense winter cold. The Khabarovsk January average of 6° below zero (20° *lower* than Moscow's winter average) may be taken as typical of the *least* severe areas in this region. Frosts of 50° and even 60° below zero are not uncommon, and most geographers are agreed that the area north-east of Lake Baikal and inland from the Okhotsk Sea is the coldest on earth. Summer temperatures, during the few months of summer, are, of course, relatively high, and recent Soviet experiments seem to have shown the possibility of growing special sub-Arctic varieties of several crops in this short growing season. Nothing, however, can alter the fact that the subsoil, down to a considerable depth, has been frozen since the Ice Age; and drainage and drinking water must be a continual problem. The running of railways through an area where all water is frozen hard for many months of the year must be wearisome business.

## History and People

Yet this inhospitable land has such natural wealth that, though it never supported a large population of native inhabitants, it has always attracted a struggling and for the most part adventurous sprinkling of Russians. The parallel here with North America, particularly Canada and Alaska in the nineteenth century, is again clear. The main difference is that, whereas the colonisation of North America was almost entirely spontaneous, the Russian colonisation of the Far East has always been largely Government-inspired or even Government-compelled.

Russian colonists passed the Urals by the end of the sixteenth century and reached the Pacific by the end of the seventeenth. At first, however, they lived on sufferance of the Chinese, with whom a treaty was signed as early as 1689. The main attractions to the Russian traders were furs and gold, and these took them

41. The new harbour, Kamschatka: no place for colonists.

across the Bering Strait. It was not, in fact, till 1867 that Russia sold Alaska, or 'Russian America' to the U.S.A.

Under the Tsars, although many attempts were made to drive Russians by force or inducements into eastern Siberia, the population grew very slowly; many of those who went failed to survive and others returned to western Russia. Under the Soviets, a great increase was planned. At first things do not seem to have worked out too well and the total immigration between 1925 and 1929 was less than half a million—no higher rate than that of free immigration in the land-hungry years of 1906 to 1913. From 1930 onwards, however, as a result of wages higher by 30 per cent., tax exemptions and controlled mass movements like that of the Komsomols (young Communists), the *urban* population appears to have been roughly trebled by 1939. There was no significant increase in the agricultural population. Outstanding increases in individual towns are:

|              | 1926    | 1939    |
|--------------|---------|---------|
| Khabarovsk   | 50,000  | 200,000 |
| Vladivostok  | 100,000 | 200,000 |
| Komsomolsk   | —       | 70,000  |

Komsomolsk is an entirely new city, founded and built by the young Communists, of whom the first 4,000 went there in 1932. By 1939 its shipyards claimed to have launched their first ocean-going ship and its population was recorded as 70,000. Its whole history is a piece of Soviet epic, and no sources of information about it other than Soviet epic exist.

This population movement is part of a general shift eastwards of the balance of population and industrial production in the U.S.S.R. Just as the new iron and steel axis of Magnitogorsk-Kuznetsk (stretching 1,250 miles east from the Urals) is taking the place of the Donetz Basin, so industrial self-sufficiency on a much smaller scale is being built up in the Far East.

The reasons for this have been mainly strategic. Fear of Japanese aggression led the Russians both to the improvement of their railway connections with the Far East and to the establishment of industries which could supply a Far Eastern army without drawing on the far-away factories of the Urals or European Russia. Since the end of the War, as we have seen, Russia has taken advantage of the defeat of Japan to recover that control of Manchuria which she lost in the Russo-Japanese War. Her strategic position in the Far East to-day appears, therefore, to be stronger than at any time in history.

## MODERN SOCIAL AND ECONOMIC STRUCTURE

### (a) Natural Resources

The natural wealth of the area may be divided into animal, vegetable and mineral.

Of animal products, the fur trade is of declining relative import-ance, though it still claims to have provided 30 per cent. of the world's supply of furs in the 1930s. More important for the future, perhaps, are the fisheries, mainly off the Kamschatka coast. Conditions exist very similar to those of the great Newfoundland banks and also to the salmon fisheries of the northern Pacific seaboard of America. Exploitation of the salmon was largely in Japanese hands before the war, and fishing rights were a source of continual dispute between Russia and Japan throughout the twentieth century; in the last fifteen years, however, the Soviet fishing industry has been largely mechanised and the export of canned fish, particularly canned crab, was over a quarter of a million tons in 1938.

The vegetable wealth of the area at present consists mostly of timber which no one can reach. There are vast resources of timber in the northern regions, of which very little is cut at present owing to the appalling climate and complete lack of communications. What little is cut is at the mouth of the Yenisei and is transported by sea. There are also points to the north of Khabarovsk from which a small quantity of timber is exported through Nikolayevsk.

In considering grain crops, it is important to distinguish between the astronomical figures constantly quoted as the potential grain yield and the amount actually harvested. It does seem probable that, leaving human factors out of account altogether, Siberia (though particularly western Siberia) could grow more grain than Canada and produce an immense export surplus. Against this we must balance the apparent fact that the greatest triumph of grain production in the Soviet Far East so far has been to render this vast area, with its population about equal to that of Tokyo, barely self-sufficient in food. The fact is that, however scientifically capable of agricultural development, the country is so inhospitable to man and so ill-provided with communications that these potential crops are hardly likely to be harvested within the lifetimes of our grandsons.

In the Ussuri valley and around Vladivostok there is, of course, a totally different situation; this small part of the maritime territory enjoys a sea-coast, monsoon type of climate and maize, millets, wheat and even vines flourish in quite tolerable conditions. There is also first-class grazing country in the Amur and Ussuri valleys and valuable forests on the hillsides. The cultivated area of the whole region has been increased, according to the latest available claims, to nearly 3 million acres, almost all of which is divided into collective farms with an average acreage of 11,500 acres each.

The mineral wealth of the country is the hardest factor to gauge. The coal *reserves* of the Irkutsk field have been estimated to be greater than those of the great Donbas field in Southern Russian; on the other hand, the whole Far Eastern area only laid claim to 3·6 per cent. of the U.S.S.R.'s coal production in 1938. There is certainly good coking coal also in the Bureya valley, and this, with the iron from the little Khingan Mountains, presumably supplies the industries of Komsomolsk and Khabarovsk. There are reputed to be iron, graphite, manganese and many other minerals in good workable quantities in the Sikhota Alin Range. In respect of all these, however, it is as well to remember that the highest claim yet put in for their actual production is that they have rendered the area independent of outside sources.

Gold, on the other hand, is a long-established mining industry, and it is largely due to the goldfields of the Lena River and the more recently developed field of Kolyma that Russia is now rated second of the world's gold-producers. Petroleum as well as coal is found on the island of Sakhalin, which was formerly shared between Russia and Japan, but has now been ceded entirely to Russia. This is the only considerable source of petrol in the northern half of the Far East.

## (b) Distribution of People and Occupations

The first point to re-emphasise in this section is the extremely small population of the whole area. The population of the whole of the Soviet Far East between Lake Baikal and the Pacific cannot be much more than 3 million; and if you include the economically important Irkutsk area around Lake Baikal the number only just tops 6 million. Yet even by the Chinese Eastern Railway Irkutsk is about 1,500 miles from Vladivostok.

This population is mixed: there are sparse remains of indigenous tribes, in one area, Buryat Mongolia, a homogeneous group of half a million Mongols, and in another, the Jewish republic of Birobidjan, 100,000 Russian Jews; in the most important Far Eastern regions, however, the Khabarovsk and maritime territories, the population is 80 per cent. Russian, the other 20 per cent. being equally divided between Chinese or Koreans and tribesmen. It is also the most urban population anywhere in the Far East, the proportion of town dwellers over the area as a whole being about half the total. In Birobidjan three-quarters of the total population live in one town. The six towns of Khabarovsk, Vladivostok, Birobidjan, Ulan Ude, Chita and Komsomolsk hold a quarter of the total population living east of Lake Baikal. Whatever else it is, the Soviet Far East is not a reservoir of manpower.

This urbanisation of the country is the result both of Soviet policy and of the climate. In country as unattractive as this there was little incentive for the development of peasant life or small-holdings, and the Soviet planners had therefore an almost empty canvas to work on. They were able to adopt the system of agriculture most suited to the land—that is, the large mechanised farm, producing the maximum crop with the minimum manpower and supporting a very small rural population. The average size of these collective farms in the Far Eastern territories is 11,500 acres, though in the Chita region they go up to 22,000 acres. Wheat, oats and rye are the main crops, and the proportion harvested by combines very high. Where the population were originally nomad, as in Buryat Mongolia, the collectives are cattle ranches instead of arable farms and some of them have herds of as many as 10,000 cattle. More remarkable than the collectivisation of the herds, however, is the report that the whole nature of the Buryat Mongols has been changed, and that of this people who in 1923 were illiterate nomads 130,000 out of half a million live in the single city of Ulan Ude, while illiteracy is unheard of.

Having thus established an agriculture capable of producing far more than the needs of those engaged in it, the planners were able to build up cities which would be fed from the collective farms and in their turn supply the processing plants and essential consumer goods that the region required. Thus at Ulan Ude in the centre of the great grazing area there is a meat-processing and packing factory with an output in 1940 of 25 million tins. In the comparatively new town of Spassk there are beet-sugar factories that will supply the whole area and cement works that render the importation of cement no longer necessary. At Birobidjan are the saw mills and the wagon shops that supply all the railways with rolling stock. At Blagove-schensk are flour mills and agricultural machinery shops. At Khabarovsk oil refineries to treat the Sakhalin oil, at Komsomolsk shipyards and at Vladivostok a power station. It is, taken all in all, a picture of a carefully balanced economy, but on a very small scale and aiming all the time at self-sufficiency, with no appreciable surplus for export except in furs, gold and fish. Outside the small patches of cultivated or urbanised country, there are still vast tracts of mountain forest and swamp, only occasionally traversed by the trapper or the prospector.

It is extremely difficult to make any judgment on the evidence which reaches us in this country, but it does seem probable that

the Russian method of absorbing such peoples as the Buryat Mongols
and other central Asiatics succeeds in some respects where Western
powers fail. This may be because the Russian is himself nearer to
the Asiatic than the Westerner is. Whatever the reason, Russia
seems able to transform the culture of these peoples with a rapidity
which can only be explained on the assumption that the transformation is to some extent at least accepted and indeed embraced
by the people themselves. The nationalist opposition which baulks
the Westerner at every turn does not seem to arise, because the
assimilation to Russia is carried out through a section of the younger
generation who are themselves enthusiastic Communists. It may be
true that the pro-Russian party in these communities is an efficient
and fanatical minority imposing its will on the people as a whole.
It is essential to realise at the same time that it is always likely to
triumph as long as it is opposed by nothing more stimulating than
an apathetic conservatism or an alien and well-meaning efficiency.
Russia in the Far East controls very little manpower and few
resources of her own; there is every possibility, however, that her
influence may be enormously extended by the widespread adoption
of what is universally called 'Communism,' even if this is practised
on Asiatic rather than Russian lines.

## (c) Communications

Communication by land still consists mainly of the Trans-Siberian
Railway with its southern branch through Manchuria. This has
long been the spine of the country and was converted to double
track between 1937 and 1940 under the threat of war with Japan.
As a link between the various inhabited areas, it is of very great
importance, but in considering its importance as a link with European
Russia it is as well to remember that the run from Vladivostok to
Moscow is 5,000 miles.

As a further strategic safeguard and to open up additional territories, a second branch line has been started which is to run north
of Lake Baikal to Vitim on the Lena River and there branch, one
branch going to Okhotsk via Yakutsk and the other to the port of
Soviet Harbour via Komsomolsk. How much of this line has actually
been built by now it is difficult to say. The section between Irkutsk
and Vitim is almost certainly complete and so is that linking
Komsomolsk with Soviet Harbour and Nikolaievsk. It is probable
that by the time these words are printed the central section between
Vitim and Komsomolsk will also be complete, but not likely that

the northern branch to Okhotsk via Yakutsk will be. A hydro-electric power station is at present under construction at Bratsk which is presumably intended for the electrification of the Trans-Siberian.

In addition to the railways, the Amur River is one of the world's great waterways and, when frozen, a highway; it is its position on the railway and at the junction of the Amur and Ussuri which makes Khabarovsk the natural centre for all this part of the world.

Two motor highways of importance have been constructed in the extreme north—one running due north from the Trans-Siberian to Yakutsk and the other from the port of Magadan on the Okhotsk Sea to the Kolyma goldfields.

The maritime provinces have three ports, Nikolaievsk, Soviet Harbour and Vladivostok, but of these Vladivostok is far the most important, being the only one which can be kept open when the others freeze up. Its only disadvantage is its extremely vulnerable strategic position.

Of great importance to the seaborne commerce of the area has been the opening of the Arctic route from Vladivostok to Archangel and Murmansk. The route is only 6,000 miles long, instead of the 14,000 miles via the Suez Canal which the Russian Baltic Fleet sailed before their defeat at Tsushima in 1904. Thanks to the improvement of ice-breakers and the establishment of meteorological stations along the north coast and a modern port and supply depot at Dixon Island, this route is now used every summer by a considerable number of cargo ships. The story of its exploration and opening up is one of the most fascinating episodes in modern Arctic history.

BIBLIOGRAPHY

*The Soviet Far East and Central Asia.* W. Mandel.
*Soviet Asia.* R. A. Davies and A. J. Steiger.
*Soviet Far Eastern Policy.* Edited by H. Moore.
*Modern Korea.* A. J. Grajdanzev.
*Manchuria: Cradle of Conflict.* O. Lattimore.
*One's Company.* Peter Fleming.
*Korea Today.* G. McCune.
*Korea's Heritage.* S. McCune.
*Soviet Policy in the Far East.* M. Beloff.
*The Peoples of the Soviet Far East.* W. Kolarz.

# CHAPTER TWELVE

## FOOD, ORDER, JUSTICE AND PEACE

EVERY author, in a last chapter, should be allowed to relax, to voice his own opinions about the present and even guess about the future.

What the people of the Far East require are food, order, justice and peace. Unless the food is produced, tens of thousands will starve, but unless order is maintained, the food will neither be produced nor distributed. Order is threatened by two forces—conscious destruction and the revolt against injustice. Therefore, if the forces of order are to conquer those of destruction, they must also remedy injustice. Finally, not even a régime of food, order and justice could survive another war.

### FOOD

In the ten years since these words were written a great deal has happened in the Far East, but nothing, I think, which alters their long-term validity. The immediate crisis in the production of rice did not prove as serious as the International Emergency Food Council anticipated, but the ratio between food production and rising populations still holds the greatest threat for Far Eastern peoples as a whole. A recent article in *The Times*, for instance, estimated that in spite of a 14 per cent. increase in agricultural production since 1949, the average Indian is actually worse fed to-day than he was in 1938. The whole advantage of the improvements in agriculture has been swallowed up by a vast increase in population.

This illustrates, from the largest area, what is a desperate situation for the rice-eating part of Asia in general. In their desperation, with a standard of living, measured in money, ten times lower than that of Britain, these peoples very naturally look to America, Europe and Russia for a lead out of their difficulties. In all three areas they see that a higher standard of living has gone with industrialisation, and they are staking their own future on the rapid industrialisation and development of their countries.

It is easy to see an objection, that this type of development will not in fact grow food; and it is true that both in India and China there has been a tendency to devote too much of the country's limited resources to prestige projects. New railway stations, even new steel-works, do not directly help to feed the peasant in his village hut or the unemployed labourer living in the streets. But it is also true that the agricultural revolution, which alone can solve the problem, will require an immense effort of education, organisation and transport; and such an effort can only be undertaken by a country whose revenues are drawn from a widely developed trade and industry. One disquieting feature, particularly in India, is the slow headway which this revolution is making against the forces of peasant and religious conservatism. There is comparatively little additional rice land which can be brought into cultivation without totally disproportionate expenditure on irrigation and flood control. The best hope is therefore from higher yields, deriving from better cultivation methods. Alas, the average Indian yield, which before the war was one-third of the average Japanese, is now one-quarter. For all the Indian efforts to learn from the Japanese, who are the world's expert rice-growers, they are not keeping up in this essential part of the race.

In this race, to save themselves from famine and to raise their terribly low standards of living within their own lifetimes, the leaders of the smaller countries naturally watch with intense interest the efforts of the two giants, India and China. In both they see a new, confident, Asian government trying to speed up history by a conscious national effort in accordance with a conscious national plan. And they are hesitating between the two systems. The Chinese is the classical Communist system, modified to a certain degree by the Chinese national genius for compromise. It involves rigid State control (with occasional winking of the eye); collectivisation of agriculture; heavy investment in communications and industry; reliance on the U.S.S.R. for all material aid; a violent break with the West; an almost Puritan concern for public morality; and a period at least of ruthless, large-scale oppression to force these measures through. Mao Tse-Tung is very fond of reminding us that a revolution is not a garden party.

The Indian system is also described as a road to socialism; but it lies through the progressive extension of State responsibility and ownership in industry, combined with voluntary co-operation in agriculture. It involves a flexible mixture of State planning and private enterprise in industry; a nation-wide campaign of education for co-operation in agriculture; heavy investment in communications and industry; reliance on the West and on private investment to supplement the State's capital development plan; and an international policy of neutralism.

The majority of South-east Asian peoples would probably prefer to follow the Indian plan, if they decide that it works. Co-operation, goodwill, religion come more naturally to both Buddhist and Islamic countries than scientific materialism and ruthlessness. But overwhelmingly their criterion in deciding which way to 'lean' will be success or failure in raising the standard of living and developing the country's trade and industry. In this respect it is particularly hard for them to judge by facts and not propaganda. Plenty is known about the degree of success achieved or being achieved by the two Indian Five Year Plans; for instance, a rise in national income of 16 per cent. over the first five years. Travel in China, on the other hand, is difficult, and with figures, reports and photographs it is hard to distinguish fact from fancy. Such propaganda devices as the permanent agricultural exhibition in Moscow and the vaunted successes of the Chinese co-operatives, compared with the comparative stagnation of Indian agriculture are probably useful cards in the Communist hand. The Puritan morality of official Communist China, when viewed from a distance, may also be an attraction to a younger generation whose first contact with politics close at hand may well be the traditional corruption of their own administration.

One thing seems certain, that a planned economy and a 'national revolution' of one kind or another will be the pattern of development in all the successor states from the Philippines to Ceylon. It is, in all the circumstances, the most hopeful pattern, and if the Western powers are to play their due part in South-east Asia, they can best do so by providing support for the democratic or neutralist camp at least as solid as that which the Communists can expect from the U.S.S.R. and China. Such 'plans' cannot hope to succeed, however, except under conditions of internal order and security.

ORDER

Geographically, and therefore in the long run, the most serious threat to the preservation of internal order and security is to be found among the newly emancipated countries of South-east Asia. These former colonial territories suffer from a weakness common to a great many areas which have passed through a period of western European control. Many of them were not, either from the point of view of physical geography, economy or race, natural units, but the accidental creations of Western colonial policies or economic demands. The same pattern is clear in Africa. The withdrawal of Western control, particularly in an atmosphere of extreme nationalism and passionate demands for the independence of every racial group, has

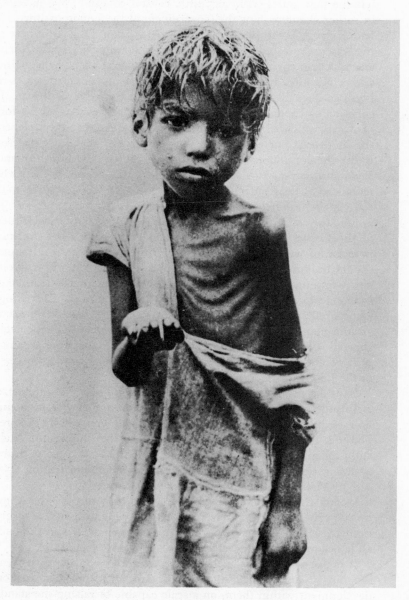

42. Asia's problem: hunger.

left the new states with very little central cohesion. We have seen, in earlier chapters, how the Government of the Union of Burma has had to struggle with separatist movements among the Arakanese and the Karens; and similar threats may easily develop among the Kachins and Shans in the north. The single administration of French Indo-China has already split into four separate independent states and lives, as does Korea, under the perpetual threat of civil war. The cohesion of Indonesia is preserved, if it is preserved at all, by forms of words which correspond to no real facts. Neither the Celebes in the south-east nor Sumatra in the north-west are in any real sense under the continuous administration of the Central Government of Java: and there are islands and areas in Indonesian Borneo where no official of the Central Government has been seen for years, so that the old self-sufficient life, with intermittent piracy, seems just around the corner. It is a striking example of the continuing influence of the former, unnatural and colonial boundaries, that the incorporation of western New Guinea (Irian) in the state of Indonesia should be, for the Government in Java, a major issue. For here is a newly founded state, unable to hold together the racially similar and economically interdependent parts of its own homeland, seeking to incorporate a totally foreign territory of alien race, on no other ground than that both had been at one time part of the same heterogeneous Western colonial empire. It is as if India were seeking to incorporate Penang, on the grounds that it was a former possession of the East India Company.

In India itself the dangers of racial and linguistic separatism are well understood, and for the whole of South Asia the problem of how to preserve unity when it is no longer imposed by a foreign power is crucial. Even those territories like the Philippines, Malaya and Ceylon which are natural geographic units are faced with more or less serious problems of integrating racial minorities or, in the case of Malaya, the fusion of a multi-racial state.

Clearly the fragmentation of the whole area into a patchwork of tiny sovereign states, each passionately defending its God-given right to self-determination, spells economic disaster and the end to all hopes of raising the general standard of living.

It is not merely that such nation states may engage in costly and sanguinary conflict over their new boundaries, but that economic development within them, on a scale capable of raising the standard of living, would be possible only in a few isolated areas. And these would be the areas with rich and easily accessible natural resources.

Brunei or Central Sumatra might, on their own, enjoy the sort of brief, artificial, oil-purchased prosperity of Kuwait; but only at the expense of abandoning all hope of economic progress for Borneo or Indonesia as a whole. There is no long-term future for the Federation of Malaya and Singapore as separate and independent entities. Planning, which either on Indian or Chinese lines seems the only chance of getting sufficiently rapid economic progress, demands a reasonably wide area and command of natural resources to plan over: adopted by a patchwork of under-developed and bellicose princi-palities it could produce nothing but words. It is therefore as vital to these successor states to preserve their unity and ultimately to 'make South-east Asia,' as we are finding it in the West vital to 'make Europe.'

Although the unity which many of them enjoyed in colonial times was an artificial one, the initial upsurge of national enthusiasm, after independence, provided an emotional backing for it at first: and there is talk in Indonesia to-day of 'recapturing the spirit of 1945.' The greatest force acting against it, and in favour of the old separatism, is a sense of injustice, a sense that the 'old gang' of politicians who came into power with independence are bleeding the more outlying parts of the country, the home, very often, of the old minorities, for the benefit of a corrupt clique in the capital. In this respect the feelings of Palembang towards Jakarta are very like those of Kumasi for Accra. If, therefore, the peoples of these countries are to live, and live better than they have done in the past, they must ensure that justice is done and seen to be done. But before we go on to consider some encouraging indications that this in fact may happen, we must deal with the other internal threat to order and stability— Communism.

Communism in South-east Asia was originally directed by the U.S.S.R. and this influence should be distinguished from that of the later but more powerful Chinese Communism. Soviet Communist strategy in South-east Asia should be interpreted in the light of long-term Communist assumptions and aims. These are that the area is 'exploited' by the Western capitalist powers and is of great value to them: to bring it within the Communist sphere would therefore be doubly desirable. Ostensibly, of course, it would liberate the people from Western imperialist exploitation: in fact it would cripple the West economically and at the same time permit the U.S.S.R. to exploit the area herself, in the same way that she has exploited the economy of her European satellites.

It is important to realise that even half of this objective would be, from the Communist point of view, well worth attainment. Lenin said that the route to Paris lay through Peking, and it has long been a Marxist belief that the only reason why the capitalist countries of the West have failed to collapse, as Marx predicted they would, is

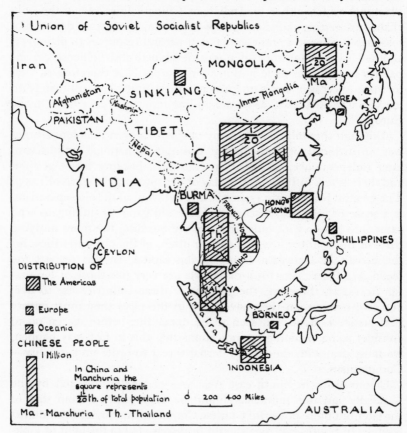

XXIII. Distribution of the Chinese people.

that they have 'exported their misery' to colonial areas. They have, apparently, done this by 'rigging the market' against the colonial primary producer, much as the Soviet State rigs it against the peasant. It is a strange view considering that the most prosperous capitalist country, the U.S.A., is the one least dependent on colonial trade. But be that as it may, it is a permanent Communist assumption;

and for the strategy based upon it, the destruction of the Western trade pattern in the former colonial territories is a worthy objective, even if it is to be replaced, not by a Communist trade pattern, but by chaos.

The tactical objective of Soviet Communism is therefore the simple one of destroying ordered government and the existing trade pattern with the West. We have seen already that, for the people of the region, this can only lead to a catastrophic fall in the standard of living and possibly to starvation.

This tactical objective was pursued immediately after the war by 'legitimate' popular front methods, in the hope that the Communist penetration of the 'resistance' and 'anti-colonial' movements would make possible a peaceful take-over. In Burma Communists were prominent in the first government of the Anti-Fascist People's Freedom League; in Malaya they marched in the Victory Parade; in the Philippines Hukbalahap leaders were elected to the Assembly; in Thailand and Indonesia there were Prime Ministers (Pridi Panomyong and Amir Sjariffudin) who were either secret Communists or fellow travellers.

The tide of events, however, moved against them, beginning with the fall of Pridi in November 1947. It seems almost certain that the decision to reverse the policy line for South-east Asia, and attempt a series of violent risings, was taken at the Calcutta Conference of the World Federation of Democratic Youth and the International Union of Students in February 1948. It was followed almost immediately by the revolt of the White Flag Communists in Burma (March 1948), the outbreak of the 'Emergency' in Malaya (May-June 1948), the Madiun Communist rising in Indonesia (September 1948) and the resumption of the Hukbalahap rebellion in the Philippines with Communist support (October-November 1948). Whether any of these risings were intended or expected to lead to the establishment of Communist states must remain doubtful. Certainly none of them ever looked like doing so. What is surprising is that they fell so very far short even of what were presumably their secondary objectives, the weakening of existing governments and the disruption of trade. Though it would be foolish to discount the danger to South-east Asian countries from this type of purely disruptive Communism, particularly while there remain some 2,000 armed terrorists still at large in the Malayan jungles, it is probably true that, except in Indonesia, the governments of the countries are in a stronger position to meet it to-day than they were ten years ago; and that to most South-east Asians Communism is now a Chinese, and therefore an external, problem.

## JUSTICE

This strengthening of the local government seems to have been partly due to a reaction against the era of corruption and inefficiency which immediately followed the war or the grant of independence. The victory of President Magsaysay in the Philippines, in an election clearly fought on what Americans would call a 'Reform Ticket,' in 1953, seems typical of a pattern that emerges elsewhere. Independence is often won by a colonial country under the leadership of a very mixed band of revolutionaries with little experience of administration. The first government that they form makes many mistakes, contains many corrupt members and is ultimately replaced by a younger and more respectable administration, whose main election platform is an attack on the corruption and inefficiency of the 'old gang.' Certainly the governments of Magsaysay in the Philippines, Ngo Dien Diem in southern Viet Nam and Solomon Bandaranaike in Ceylon appear to be of this type. Even in British administered Malaya the first post-war administration had an unenviable reputation for corruption. It is in the countries in which there has been no such 'second generation' government, Indonesia and South Korea, that the governmental structure still seems weak and, in the former case, a potential victim to disruptive Communism.

## PEACE

Even if all goes as well as we can hope internally, the Far East is no more free of the threat of a major war than is Europe or the Middle East. The results might not be so catastrophic merely because the people are more dispersed, the economy less developed and the standard of living already so much lower: but a major war would mean the end of any hope, for many generations, that the standard of living could be raised.

Fortunately the threat, though undoubtedly there, does not seem to be either imminent or certain. There are only three Eastern powers capable of launching such a war: China, India or Japan. There seems at the moment no danger that either India or Japan will embark upon a career of conquest or that any Western power will re-enter the area for such a purpose. The threat of major war is therefore confined to the possibility that China might do so.

Two objectives might lead China in such a direction—the final liquidation of the rival K.M.T. Government in Formosa and the re-establishment of the Chinese Empire at or beyond its extreme historical limits.

There have been occasions when the tension between China on the one hand and Formosa, backed by the U.S.A. on the other, seemed to endanger the peace of the world. But caution and wisdom have so far prevailed in circumstances which are year by year becoming less, and not more, provocative. As long as there was any chance that the K.M.T. might launch a counter-attack against the mainland, the danger was at its most acute. It seems probable that that period has gradually come to an end with the conclusion of the mass purge period in China (which might have provided a basis of support in China for a K.M.T. return) and the passage of time among the Chinese forces, military and civilian, on Formosa. With that threat removed, the Communist Chinese Government, which has a vast programme on its hands, can afford either to come to a *modus vivendi* with the K.M.T. leaders or to leave Formosa out of its calculations until time has done their work for them. More threatening to the independent territories of South-east Asia is the prospect of gradual Chinese expansionism. Historically China has at one time or another claimed suzerainty as far south as the borders of India and Pakistan and the northern states of Malaya. The forcible absorption of Tibet as a Chinese satellite, the recent agreements with Nepal and the publication of Chinese maps showing parts of Assam as Chinese territory, have alarmed the Indian Government. The 're-drawing' of the Sino-Burman frontier in the north-west led to student demonstrations when Chou En Lai arrived in Rangoon, in which banners were carried with the legend 'Welcome Great Chinaman. Respect our tiny country.' In Thailand, Laos and Cambodia there is considerable alarm about the training and indoctrination of Thai minorities across the Chinese frontiers in Yunnan.

The chief protection which the smaller countries of South-east Asia have against overt attack is of course the Manila Treaty of 1954. The signatories (Britain, U.S.A., France, Pakistan, Thailand, the Philippines, Australia and New Zealand) are pledged to act together against any armed attack either on one of themselves or against certain designated countries in the area. They are also pledged to 'consult' on measures to counter domestic subversion.

This treaty, few though its 'teeth' may be, may well have introduced a sufficient deterrent to prevent any expansionist Chinese government from seeking to absorb its neighbours by direct attack— and therefore to avert the threat of major war.

The threat of 'creeping Communism,' that is, of the subversion of free governments by the gradual infiltration of Communist-

trained minorities across their frontiers and the organisation of
powerful Communist parties within their territories, is one that can
only be met by demonstrating that planning on the Indian or Western
model can be as effective as the Communist brand in bringing about
the Far Eastern Industrial Revolution. If aid from the West and

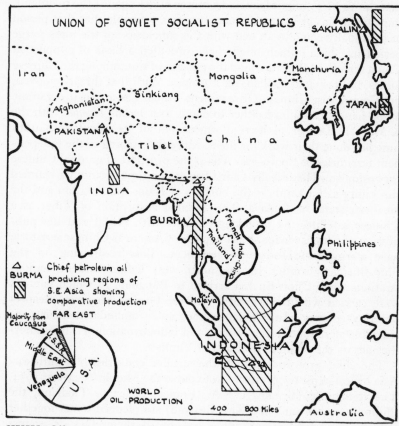

XXIV. Oil resources of the Far East, compared with those of the rest of
    the world.

voluntary investment within the area cannot provide a sufficiently
quick accumulation of capital, then we must fear that even the
purgatory of a generation of forced Communist industrialisation
will be accepted as the only way out.

For the Far East as a whole, and for South-east Asia in particular,
there can be no easy way to the promised land; but for those who

are prepared to practise shrewd statesmanship and to control the excitement of separatist or ideological fanatics, there is a path that

43. Asia's response: a Japanese mother and baby preparing to rebuild their home at Hiroshima.

need not entail too much human suffering; and leaders along this path are still to be found in India, the Philippines, Burma, Ceylon and Malaya.

## BIBLIOGRAPHY

*Atlas of Far Eastern Politics.* Hudson and Rajchman.
*The Future of South-east Asia.* K. M. Pannikar.
*The Approach to Self Government.* Sir Ivor Jennings.
*Collective Defence in South East Asia.* Royal Institute of International Affairs.

# INDEX